RELIGION AND PUBLIC LIFE
IN THE SOUTHERN CROSSROADS:
SHOWDOWN STATES

RELIGION BY REGION

Religion by Region Series
Co-published with the Leonard E. Greenberg Center for the
Study of Religion in Public Life at Trinity College
Mark Silk and Andrew Walsh, Series Editors

The United States is a nation of many distinct regions. But until now, no literature has looked at these regional differences in terms of religion. The Religion by Region Series describes, both quantitatively and qualitatively, the religious character of contemporary America, region by region. Each of the eight regional volumes includes overviews and demographic information to allow comparisons among regions. But at the same time, each volume strives to show what makes its region unique. A concluding volume looks at what these regional variations mean for American religion as a whole.

1. Religion and Public Life in the Pacific Northwest: *The None Zone*
   Edited by Patricia O'Connell Killen (Pacific Lutheran University) and Mark Silk

2. Religion and Public Life in the Mountain West: *Sacred Landscapes in Transition*
   Edited by Jan Shipps (Indiana University–Purdue University, Indianapolis) and Mark Silk

3. Religion and Public Life in New England: *Steady Habits, Changing Slowly*
   Edited by Andrew Walsh and Mark Silk

4. Religion and Public Life in the Midwest: *America's Common Denominator?*
   Edited by Philip Barlow (Hanover College) and Mark Silk

5. Religion and Public Life in the Southern Crossroads: *Showdown States*
   Edited by William Lindsey (Philander Smith College) and Mark Silk

6. Religion and Public Life in the South: *In the Evangelical Mode*
   Edited by Charles Reagan Wilson (University of Mississippi) and Mark Silk

7. Religion and Public Life in the Middle Atlantic: *The Fount of Diversity*
   Edited by Randall Balmer (Columbia University) and Mark Silk

8. Religion and Public Life in the Pacific: *Fluid Identities*
   Edited by Wade Clark Roof (University of California, Santa Barbara) and Mark Silk

9. Religion by Region: *Religion and Public Life in The United States*
   By Mark Silk and Andrew Walsh

RELIGION AND PUBLIC LIFE
IN THE SOUTHERN CROSSROADS:
SHOWDOWN STATES

Edited by
William Lindsey
and
Mark Silk

Published in cooperation with the Leonard E. Greenberg
Center for the Study of Religion in Public Life at
Trinity College, Hartford, Connecticut

ALTAMIRA
PRESS
A Division of
ROWMAN & LITTLEFIELD PUBLISHERS, INC.
Walnut Creek • Lanham • New York • Toronto • Oxford

Published in cooperation with the Leonard E. Greenberg Center for the Study of Religion in Public Life at Trinity College, Hartford, Connecticut

ALTAMIRA PRESS

A division of Rowman & Littlefield Publishers, Inc.
1630 North Main Street, #367
Walnut Creek, CA 94596
www.altamirapress.com

Rowman & Littlefield Publishers, Inc.
A wholly owned subsidiary of The Rowman & Littlefield Publishing Group, Inc.
4501 Forbes Boulevard, Suite 200
Lanham, MD 20706

PO Box 317
Oxford
OX2 9RU, UK

British Library Cataloguing in Publication Information Available

Library of Congress Cataloging-in-Publication Data

Religion and public life in the southern crossroads : showdown states / edited by William Lindsey and Mark Silk.
     p. cm. — (Religion by region ; 5)
     Includes bibliographical references and index.
     ISBN 0-7591-0632-0 (cloth : alk. paper) — ISBN 0-7591-0633-9 (pbk. : alk. paper)
     1. Southern States—Religion. 2. Religion and politics—Southern States. I. Lindsey, William D., 1950– II. Silk, Mark. III. Series.

BL2527.S67R45 2004
200'.976—dc22   2004023434

Printed in the United States of America

♾™ The paper used in this publication meets the minimum requirements of American National Standard for Information Sciences—Permanence of Paper for Printed Library Materials, ANSI/NISO Z39.48–1992.

CONTENTS

CONTENTS	3
PREFACE *Mark Silk*	5
INTRODUCTION—AT THE CROSSROADS *William Lindsey*	9
RELIGIOUS AFFILIATION IN THE SOUTHERN CROSSROADS AND THE NATION— Religious Self-Identification and Adherents Claimed by Religious Groups, National and Regional Comparisons	23
CHAPTER ONE—THE SOUTHERN CROSSROADS: RELIGION AND DEMOGRAPHY *Bill Leonard*	27
CHAPTER TWO—PROTESTANTS: FROM DENOMINATIONAL CONTROVERSIALISTS TO CULTURE WARRIORS *Andrew Manis*	55
CHAPTER THREE—HOLINESS AND PENTECOSTAL TRADITIONS: MAKING THE SPIRIT COUNT *Jane Harris*	79
CHAPTER FOUR—NEGOTIATING CATHOLICISM: RELIGIOUS IDENTITY VS. REGIONAL CITIZENSHIP *Kathlyn Breazeale*	103
CHAPTER FIVE—AFRICAN-AMERICAN AND NATIVE-AMERICAN RELIGIOUS FOLK: DOWN BUT NOT OUT *Cheryl Kirk-Duggan*	127
CONCLUSION—SHOWDOWNS *William Lindsey and Mark Silk*	161
APPENDIX	171
BIBLIOGRAPHY	173
INDEX	175
CONTRIBUTORS	189

Preface

Geographical diversity is the hallmark of religion in the United States. There are Catholic zones and evangelical Bible Belts, a Lutheran domain and a Mormon fastness, metropolitan concentrations of Jews and Muslims, and (in a different dimension) parts of the country where religious affiliation of whatever kind is very high and parts where it is far below the norm. This religious heterogeneity is inextricably linked to the character of American places. From Boston to Birmingham, from Salt Lake City to Santa Barbara, even the casual observer perceives public cultures that are intimately connected to the religious identities and habits of the local population.

Yet when the story of religion in American public life gets told, the country's variegated religious landscape tends to be reduced to a series of monochrome portraits of the spiritual state of the union, of piety along the Potomac, of great events or swings of mood that raise or lower the collective religious temperature. Whatever the virtues of compiling such a unified national narrative—and I believe they are considerable—it obscures a great deal. As the famous red-and-blue map of the 2000 presidential vote makes clear, region has not ceased to matter in national politics. Indeed, in this era of increasing federalism, regions are, state by state, charting ever more distinctive courses.

To understand where each region is headed and why, it is critical to recognize the place of religion in it.

Religion by Region, a project of the Leonard E. Greenberg Center for the Study of Religion in Public Life at Trinity College in Hartford, represents the first comprehensive effort to show how religion shapes, and is being shaped by, regional culture in America. The project has been designed to produce edited volumes (of which this is the fifth) on each of eight regions of the country. A ninth volume will sum up the results in order to draw larger conclusions about the way religion and region combine to affect civic culture and public policy in the United States as a whole.

The purpose of the project is not to decompose a national storyline into eight separate narratives. Rather, it is to bring regional realities to bear, in a systematic way, on how American culture is understood at the beginning of the twenty-first century. In line with the Greenberg Center's commitment to enhance public understanding of religion, these volumes are intended for a general audience, with a particular eye towards helping working journalists make better sense of the part religion plays in the public life—local, statewide, regional, and national—that they cover. At the same time, I am persuaded that the accounts and analyses provided in these volumes will make a significant contribution to the academic study of religion in contemporary America.

The project's division of the country into regions will be generally familiar, with the exception of what we are calling the Southern Crossroads—a region roughly equivalent to what American historians know as the Old Southwest, comprising Louisiana, Texas, Arkansas, Oklahoma, and Missouri. Since we are committed to covering every state in the Union (though not the territories—e.g., Puerto Rico), Hawaii has been included in a Pacific region with California and Nevada, and Alaska in the Pacific Northwest.

Cultural geographers may be surprised to discover a few states out of their customary places. Idaho, which is usually considered part of the Pacific Northwest, has been assigned to the Mountain West. In our view, the fact that the bulk of Idaho's population lives in the heavily Mormon southern part of the state links it more closely to Utah than to Oregon and Washington. To be sure, we might have chosen to parcel out certain states between regions, assigning northern Idaho and western Montana to the Pacific Northwest or, to take another example, creating a Catholic band running from southern Louisiana through south Texas and across the lower tiers of New Mexico and Arizona on into southern California. The purpose of the project, however, is not to map the country religiously but to explore the ways that politics, public policies, and civil society relate—or fail to relate—to the religion that is on the ground. States have had to be kept intact because when American laws are not made in Washington, D.C., they are made in statehouses. To understand what is decided in Baton Rouge, Louisiana's Catholic south and evangelical north must be seen as engaged in a single undertaking.

That is not to say that the details of American religious demography are unimportant to our purpose. That demography has undergone notable shifts in recent years, and these have affected public life in any number of ways. To reckon with them, it has been essential to assemble the best data available on the religious identities of Americans and how they correlate with voting patterns and views on public issues. As students of American religion know, however, this is far from an easy task. The U.S. Census is prohibited by law from asking questions about religion, and membership reports provided by religious bodies to nongovernmental researchers—when they are provided at all—vary greatly in accuracy. Most public opinion polling does not enable us to draw precise correlations between respondents' views on issues and their religious identity and behavior.

In order to secure the best possible empirical grounding, the project has assembled a range of data from three sources, which are described in detail in the Appendix. These have supplied us with, among other things, information from religious bodies on their membership; from individuals on their religious identities; and from voters in specific religious categories on their political preferences and opinions. (For purposes of clarity, people are described as "adherents" or "members" only when reported as such by a religious institution. Otherwise, they are "identifiers.") Putting this information together with 2000 Census and other survey data, the project has been able to create both the best available picture of religion in America today and the most comprehensive account of its political significance.

Religion by Region does not argue that religion plays the same kind of role in each region of the country; nor does it mean to advance the proposition that religion is the master key that unlocks all the secrets of American public life. As the tables of contents of the individual volumes make clear, each region has its distinctive religious layout, based not only on the numerical strength of particular religious bodies but also on how those bodies, or groups of them, function on the public stage. In some regions, religion serves as a shaping force; in others it is a subtler conditioning agent. Our objective is simply to show what the picture looks like from place to place and to provide consistent data and a framework of discussion sufficient to enable useful contrasts and comparisons to be drawn.

A project of such scope and ambition does not come cheap. We are deeply indebted to the Lilly Endowment for making it possible.

Mark Silk
Hartford, Connecticut
August 2004

INTRODUCTION

AT THE CROSSROADS

William Lindsey

Missouri, Arkansas, Louisiana, Texas, and Oklahoma—these make up the region we call the Southern Crossroads. It's the Southeast with a difference. Three of the states joined the Confederacy; two didn't, but had strong roots in the Old South. Yet all partake of other regions, other cultures: the Midwest, the West, Mexico, the Caribbean. Altogether, the Crossroads is a place of borders and boundary lines, beginning with the Mississippi River—the "strong brown god," as T.S. Eliot called it. And where there are borders and boundaries, there are people on either side conscious of them, insisting on them, fighting for them and against them. Historically, this was a region of showdowns, where people fought intimate battles over turf, slavery, family pride, and, always, religion. In the late twentieth and early twenty-first centuries, this has been the region that has provided many of the leaders and much of the style of the culture wars. Remote from both coasts, filled with cultural peculiarities and idiosyncrasies, it has nevertheless provided a model of religion in public life that, for better or worse, is casting its spell over the nation as a whole.

Borders and Boundaries

The Crossroads is a flashpoint region, where the intersection of frontier ideals and Old South realities has historically produced political and religious clashes of pronounced intensity. It is intersected by at least four distinctive cultural boundaries, dividing the Upland South from the Gulf Coastal Lowlands and Acadian Louisiana, and South from West, on a line running through Texas and Oklahoma.[1]

Historically, Louisiana, Arkansas, and Missouri were French territory until the early nineteenth century. Because of their inaccessibility and remoteness,

Louisiana and Missouri, intimately connected by the river boundaries that linked New Orleans and Natchitoches to St. Louis, were the key players in the French territorial occupation of the nation's mid-section. But even in Arkansas the French presence was, for quite some time, culturally formative. The state's name, with its final silent "s," derives from French attempts to transcribe native-American terms for the region. Pine Bluff, a once significant port 40 miles down-river from Little Rock, was initially a French fort that later attracted large numbers of Irish, Italian, and other Catholic European immigrants. The city's oldest street, which runs along the river, is still called Barraque (pronounced by locals as if it rhymes with "barbecue").

Early on, French hegemony in the Crossroads was contested by Spain, on a boundary that reached through Louisiana to the village of Los Adaes, 15 miles west of Natchitoches, where the French were ensconced. The encounter is summed up in the conundrum of the Natchitoches meat pie: Is it an empanada (whose shape, ingredients, and seasoning it closely resembles), or a Southern adaptation of the Québecois tortière, as some locals argue? The significance of the Spanish-French (and later Spanish-American) border separating Texas from the rest of the region cannot be underestimated; it has decisively shaped the Crossroads—Texas above all—and is another important borderland that makes this region distinctively different from the Southeast. It was, among other things, a refuge. The court records of the Southeast in the first half of the nineteenth century are littered with the acronym G.T.T. (gone to Texas) and therefore beyond the reach of the law. Southerners crossed over from the Old South into Spanish territory or the Republic of Texas for any number of reasons besides seeking better land. Some were escaping debt (particularly after the Depression of the 1830s) or failed marriages. Others were eluding prosecution for criminal activity. Still others seemed intent on merely disappearing from "civilization."

The western boundary of Arkansas, which at one time marked the dividing line between Indian Territory (I.T.) and the rest of the Crossroads, was the premier boundary line marking the western extremity of the Old South. It was also, in the mind of the region and of the nation as a whole, the final frontier of law and order before one passed into the no-man's land of the West. It has had a particularly strong psychological significance in Arkansas, where Fort Smith ("the gateway to the West") was established primarily to monitor those coming to or going from I.T., and to keep order in a presumably lawless land. The intensity of the belief in I.T.'s lawlessness is indicated in the novels and historical work of the Arkansas writers Charles Portis and Dee Brown, as well as in the gruesome legacy of Judge Isaac Parker, the notorious hanging judge at Fort Smith, who sentenced over 150 people to death on the gallows, ostensibly to signal that the civilized states of the East would not tolerate western lawlessness. As an historic footnote, however, it is important to note that violence was as endemic to the culture of Arkansas (reflecting deep historical trends of the Southeast) as it was believed to be in I.T. In its early days of statehood, Arkansas experienced brawls on its Senate floor; in perhaps the most spectacular such incident, in 1837 Speaker of the House John Wilson stabbed Representative J. J. Anthony to death in a quarrel over wolf-pelt bounties. Writing in his diary on 18 August 1874, Dr. Wilson Bachelor, who in 1870 moved from Savannah in west Tennessee to the Arkansas River valley about 25 miles east of Fort Smith, notes that in four years and six months on the Arkansas frontier, he had heard of more people dying by violence than in all his years growing up in Tennessee.[2]

Finally there is the North-South boundary that also runs through the Crossroads region, separating the South from the Midwest. The crucial cultural significance of this boundary must not be overlooked in a region where "The War" remains for many the Civil War, and in which the hanging of David O. Dodd, the "boy martyr of the Confederacy," is still commemorated annually in Arkansas' capital city with fulsome editorial commentary by the state's daily newspaper, the *Arkansas Democrat-Gazette*—commentary that is invariably hotly contested both by letters to the editor from citizens pleading with the paper's editors to forget The War and by sarcastic jibes from the statewide independent weekly, the *Arkansas Times*.

State by State

Louisiana is, by any account, Deep South. Harriett Beecher Stowe made the state emblematic of the entire slaveholding South by setting *Uncle Tom's Cabin* in the Cane River country around Natchitoches. In fact, all of Louisiana was deeply invested in the economy of slavery prior to the Civil War, and its grand plantation houses in areas such as the River Road have become archetypes of a culture that looks to the Southeast, particularly Virginia, the mother state of the Old South, for architectural templates—understandable, given that some of the most noteworthy examples of these houses were built by people with Virginia roots. Yet Louisiana also offers premier instances of a Creole-Caribbean plantation architecture that represent a fusion of African, French, and Spanish cultural exemplars found only sporadically in the Southeast. The Cane River country, the first part of the state settled by Europeans, is full of noteworthy examples of such houses, as are south Louisiana and, famously, New Orleans.

As in architecture, so in religion and ethnicity, Louisiana diverges from the cultural pattern of the Old South in its largely Catholic and Latin southern half. The Latin portions of Europe and the Caribbean (with its considerable African ties, which have often been downplayed in discussions of the roots of Creole culture) played a decisive role in establishing the cultural and religious norms to which Louisiana adheres. As the Irish-Greek writer Lafcadio Hearn maintained, even after a near century of American hegemony (the Creoles would say unwelcome intrusion) in New Orleans in 1879, one could sit in a French Quarter patio in 1879 and still imagine oneself in Bordeaux, the West Indies, or Madrid.[3]

Louisiana, and the Crossroads generally, early on adopted the casual approach to violence that characterized the Old South, especially where honor was deemed to be at stake. In his autobiography Marshall Harvey Twitchell, a Vermonter sent to Bienville Parish in northwest Louisiana to enforce Reconstruction, describes going out walking with his fiancée, Adele Coleman, one evening in 1866. Coleman, a native of the parish and music teacher at Sparta Academy, calmly asked for his pistol, whirled around, and shot into the shrubbery along a nearby fence, flushing out a young man who had been vying for her attention. Noting that "a certain kind of pride and honor were of more importance than life to [the inhabitants of the area]," Twitchell concludes that, had Coleman shot the man, the community would have vindicated her. He himself became an unfortunate victim of Southern violence when he lost both his arms after being shot during the infamous 1876 Coushatta riots that effectively ended Reconstruction in northwestern Louisiana.[4]

One hundred years later, violence mixed with sectional antagonism was still alive and well in the Crossroads. In 1980, when President Ronald Reagan is said to have quipped to a group of laid-off autoworkers in Flint, Michigan, that they could always move to Texas, tensions began to run high in the state over issues of driving etiquette. Native Texans, who tended to construe these issues in North-South terms, peppered the state's newspapers with complaints about the "rudeness" of Yankee driving habits. Bumper stickers vilifying drivers from Northern areas began to appear in Houston and elsewhere, and in some instances cars with Michigan license plates were plastered with these. Instances of road-rage violence proliferated, and some long-time Texans appeared to consider cutting in front of a driver without warning a more egregious violation of social propriety than pulling a gun and shooting the offender.

Road manners point to the Deep South cast of its culture, but Texas is undeniably Western as well. A number of ranching families of the Texas borderlands have handed down stories of their pioneer ancestors' opposition to slavery and desire to escape from the slave-holding South. To this day east and west Texans speak as though the inhabitants of the other part of the state occupy a different planet, and sibling quarrels of greater or lesser joviality abound about precisely where the dividing line falls. In many such quarrels, the burden of proof falls on the diverse culinary traditions of the state. As Alison Cook's "The Texas Food Manifesto" notes, east Texas is clearly demarcated from west by the proclivity of its cooks for such Deep-South staples as grits, hushpuppies, chicken, buttermilk, and greens, whereas west Texans lean to beef, beans, and sourdough.[5]

But what really makes Texas distinctive in the Crossroads is its Latino heritage—much older and much more decisive for the state's culture than the state's Anglo or Northern European heritage. Much of this heritage is, of course, Roman Catholic, making Texas the only state of the Confederacy besides Louisiana that has a sizable Catholic population. That hertiage may account for the immigration of significant numbers of other Catholic groups to Texas—Germans in the Hill Country and Rio Grande valley, Czechs in Bell county and elsewhere, and Irish in Corpus Christi. As Cook notes gastronomically, "Nowhere else did the antebellum South collide with Mexico and meet a large mass of Central Europeans and produce a whole breed of chuck-wagon cooks, with a bunch of food-crazy Louisianans and conservative Midwesterners throwing in their two cents' worth on the fringes."[6]

If Louisiana is the Deep South anchor of our region and Texas its Western outpost, then Arkansas may be characterized as its heart, certainly its geographic heart, and, for Clintonphobes, perhaps its Conradian dark heart. The image of Arkansas as a benighted, remote, backwoods region became part of the national literary heritage through classics such as Mark Twain's *Life on the Mississippi*.[7] Prior to the latter part of the nineteenth century, when the annual flooding of the delta that made the state almost inaccessible from the east began to be controlled by irrigation ditches and levies, it was regarded as a remote and primitive frontier, a dark and unknown thicket of "miasmatic jungles," to use H.L. Mencken's typically merciless tag.[8] Through the Clinton presidency, Arkansans (who have historically been exceedingly touchy about their state's image) maintained that the national media appeared to delight in perpetuating fables of Arkansas backwardness, no matter how far-fetched or outlandish. Yet in typical cross-grained fashion, not a few Arkansans actively abetted the media in concocting such fables, carrying on a venerable tradition in which gullible outsiders are fed tall tales for the natives' amusement.

Yet Arkansas is an enigmatic state that, in key respects, enshrines the complexity of the whole region. At a time when other Southern states were flocking to the Republican fold, Arkansans insisted on going their own recalcitrant way, first electing as governor and then supporting as president a man widely regarded by conservatives (along with his wife) as an incomparable threat to the well-being of Western civilization. In their tenacious support for the Clintons, Arkansans were not acting out of character. If the Carolinas' signature politicians of the twentieth century were Jesse Helms and Strom Thurmond; if Georgia's and Alabama's and Mississippi's were named Talmadge and Wallace and Bilbo; Arkansas sent the intellectual J. William Fulbright to represent it in the U.S. Senate, even as it chose the notorious segregationist Orval Faubus as its governor.

The third of the Crossroads states to have joined the Confederacy, Arkansas is divided into lowland and upland portions, the former inextricably linked to the plantation economy, the latter hardly touched by (and antipathetic to) it. Like

North Carolina and Tennessee, which contributed more of the state's first settlers than any other states, Arkansas experienced significant internecine struggle during the Civil War between the rich slaveholders of the southern and eastern half of the state, who sought to make Arkansas a replica of the slaveholding South, and small farmers of the upland areas, who resented the influence the slaveocracy exerted on the state's economy and government. In Arkansas, that struggle was notoriously vicious and long-lasting, giving rise to bitter feuds that continued to trouble the state well into the latter half of the nineteenth century. Indeed, the legacy of these feuds has proven so enduring that their story has yet fully to be told; descendants of participants still living in the state continue to have something invested in keeping the stories quiet.

Oklahoma everyone knows, of course: it's I.T. But as with the other states of our region, focus more closely and a much more intricate picture emerges. Certainly the Native American heritage is central to a state that was formerly a reservation for various tribes hounded westward when their land was seized by the U. S. government. But this demographically small state also comprises other distinctive subcultures that interact (sometimes uneasily) with the Native-American cultural base to make Oklahoma unique. In the words of James K. Zink, the opening of I.T. to white settlement in the "Silent Migration" period after 1865 produced "a kaleidoscope of tribal and ethnic cultures" in what became Oklahoma—a cultural mix abetted by the incursion of the railroad in this period. Zink notes that in the period of statehood, immigration both from within North-America and abroad produced "a wide variety of racial and ethnic strains" within the state, resulting in "a highly diverse set of ethnic cultures and religions."[9]

The mountainous southeastern part of the state is, in many respects, a geographic and cultural extension of the Arkansas-Missouri Ozarks. But set in the middle of the region, and forming its urban focal point, is Tulsa, an oil barons' town with distinguished early-twentieth-century architecture and the Philbrook, one of the outstanding art museums west of the Mississippi. Much of northern Oklahoma is different again. Here one enters the Midwest (as one also does in the Texas panhandle). Many of the Sooners who claimed the flat, fertile plains of this part of the state had roots in Kansas and Nebraska, places that did not look to the Southeast for their cultural paradigms. Others came from Europe—from Wales, the Austrian Empire, Germany, Poland, Ireland, and many other European nations. In its capital, Oklahoma City, the varied cultures of the state—Native American, mountain South, Midwestern, European, and African American— meet and mingle to produce what even many of its own citizens characterize as a least common denominator of Okie culture. Religiously, Oklahoma is a state that can propel to prominence both Oral Roberts, the fundamentalist faith healer of the airwaves, and Frank Keating, a Republican Catholic former governor who gained national attention in 2003 when, as head of a lay commission formed to investigate the sexual abuse crisis in his church, he characterized some American Catholic bishops as akin to Mafiosi.

Missouri is no less complex. Despite its early history of extensive slave holding, the state did not choose to secede from the Union. But like Arkansas to its immediate south, it was deeply troubled by fratricidal feuds during the Civil War. Missouri produced the James brothers, whose outlaw activities were an expression of antipathy to the Northern victory in the Civil War—and who, it must also be remembered, operated in Oklahoma for much of their career as guerilla bandits. Like many other Missourians, their family had emigrated from Kentucky before the war and identified strongly with the Confederate cause.

Yet like Texas and Oklahoma, Missouri is a border state, tilting geographically and culturally toward the Midwest. And like Louisiana, to which it had strong political and cultural ties early on, it was initially dominated by a French Catholic presence and later drew a large number of German and other Catholics, many of whom passed through New Orleans and then up the Mississippi to settle in St. Louis or seek farmland elsewhere in the state, confirming the status of St. Louis as "one of the strongly Catholic cities in America."[10] Little wonder that Mississippi-born Tennessee Williams both felt at home as a boy in this gateway city of the South and at the same time saw himself living in exile from the South—a key theme of his autobiographical play "The Glass Menagerie."

Religious Adaptation and Clash

In the Crossroads the religious patterns of the Old South have been exaggerated, and new patterns have taken on new shapes. They all have been supplanted in response to cultural forces not present in such force and such a configuration in the Southeast. It is also a region in which religious conflict has been pronounced, as boundary meets and clashes with boundary. In the Crossroads, new religious movements, many of them unknown to the Southeast until imported there, have proliferated, while at the same time an intransigent insistence on holding the line and defending "that old-time religion" has been a dominant feature of both public and religious life.

The essays that follow will demonstrate the manifold ways in which the Crossroads region is Southern with a difference. These essays suggest that the venerable New England divine Cotton Mather may have been correct in his famous prediction that, if allowed to "jump the fence" of the mountain chains separating the Eastern Seaboard from the interior of the continent, westward migrants would become unruly without the restraining hand of Eastern divines to hold them in check.

To a great extent, the story told in the essays that follow will be about what happens as the Old South and the West (including the Midwest) converge. That is, it will be a story about a theme that has run through American literature from its beginning: the lure of the exotic West, the lawless West, the West in which all things can potentially be made new. The religious history of the Crossroads is replete with examples of the process of adaptation-exchange and culture clash that occurred as Eastern religious bodies moved west.

Take the case of the Presbyterians. As Bill Leonard's chapter indicates, they are well represented in the Carolinas but just a tiny minority in the Crossroads, even though the Carolinas contributed many settlers to the regions. Like Episcopalianism, which also lost adherents (especially to Methodism) in the westward migration, Presbyterianism demanded an educated ministry and looked askance at the emotional "excesses" of the revivalism that throve on the Southern frontier. With a call to ministry that required no formal education, and with circuit-riding patterns, Baptist and Methodist churches were portable religions more suited to frontier conditions than the parent religions of the East. So within a generation, a large proportion of the Presbyterian families who reached the Crossroads from the Carolinas in the early nineteenth century had become Methodists or Baptists. If I may be permitted an autobiographical aside, my maternal lineage can be traced to at least one Presbyterian elder in the Carolinas, and my father descends from such noted Scottish Presbyterian families of the Southeast as the Calhouns and the Lauderdales. Yet in the small Crossroads towns where both of my parents grew up—my father's in northwest Louisiana, my mother's in southeast Arkansas—only Methodist and Baptist churches were to be found, and that went for blacks as well as whites. To be sure, the supplanting of Episcopalians and Presbyterians by Methodists and Baptists happened all across the South, but in the Crossroads it happened with a vengeance.

Alongside this flattening of the Southeast's religious diversity in the Crossroads, the region has spawned numerous new varieties of religion, including a large number of Pentecostal groups. Springfield, Missouri, is the world headquarters of the Assemblies of God, the largest white Pentecostal denomination in the United States and the one to which one-time Missouri senator and governor, and current U.S. Attorney General John Ashcroft belongs. Pentecostalism, which grew out of the Holiness movement of the late nineteenth century, is exceptionally strong in the religious make-up of the Crossroads region, from where it has spread to the Southeast, Midwest, and indeed throughout the world.

In recent years Pentecostal, Holiness, and Restorationist groups such as the Church of Christ have found common ground with evangelical Protestants in what is often represented as a holy war for the soul of the nation. Historically, however, the relationship has been exceptionally volatile and full of flash points. When Pentecostalism emerged in the region in the late nineteenth and early twentieth centuries, it was bitterly contested by many Baptists and Methodists, who resented its siphoning of their members and its tendency to condemn the lukewarmness of evangelicals who had lost the "first blessing." The distrust between Pentecostals and Baptists is longstanding in the Crossroads, and remains alive today. Similarly, Restorationist groups like the Church of Christ, which are well represented in the Crossroads in a belt running through north-central Arkansas into Texas, have long existed in an uneasy (and sometimes openly hostile) relationship with their mainline Protestant neighbors. I know of Church of Christ families in Arkansas today who vote the straight Republican ticket along with their Southern Baptist neighbors, and who agree with those neighbors that God has uniquely blessed the Republican party as a bulwark against such abominations as gay marriage, but who refuse to attend the funerals of these political allies, because their funeral rites are being held in churches that cannot lay claim to unbroken succession from the church of the New Testament.

Finally, it is important to underscore once again another significant factor that has historically contributed to religious adaptation and clash in the Southern borderlands and continues to do so today. This is the significant demographic representation of Catholicism in much of the Crossroads region. Not only has the long historic presence of Catholicism in much of Louisiana, Texas, and Missouri given these states a distinctive cultural and religious flavor, one that sets them apart from the Southeast, but there is convincing empirical evidence that the Catholic influence in parts of the Crossroads cuts against the grain of the dominant paradigm of social and political conservatism in some key respects, and may feed religiously based cultural showdowns in the region over such hot-button issues as treatment of illegal immigrants and social welfare.

For instance, though the Religious Right actively courts Latino voters nationwide, key indicators suggest that many Latino voters in Texas reject the ideology and agenda of that religio-political movement, as do many Catholic voters in south Louisiana, whose vote was decisive in the hotly contested 2003 gubernatorial election battle between a conservative Republican son of Indian immigrants, Bobby Jindal, and a liberal Democrat of Cajun background, Kathleen Blanco. Historically, the Catholic presence in the Crossroads has created strong religious tensions, particularly in areas in which evangelical Protestant borderlines meet Catholic ones. The volatility and unpredictability of the Catholic vote, at a time in which the Religious Right has actively sought to mute historic Catholic-Protestant differences by seeking to build alliances around "family" issues such as abortion and gay rights, points to the probability of increasing socio-political strains as the Latino presence in the region expands.

Religion and Public Life in the Crossroads

In the essays that follow, readers will encounter striking illustrations of the interaction of diverse cultural models—in particular, those of the Southeast—as various groups settled the Crossroads region and built its religious institutions. The collection is organized thematically around dominant religious groups of the area, with an initial essay analyzing the demographic data on which various essayists depend for their analysis of the interplay of religion and public life in the region today.

All of the essays that follow draw in various ways on Bill Leonard's demographic analysis of religion and public life in the region. Leonard provides empirical evidence for many of the points made throughout this collection of essays—for instance, for the dominance of evangelical Protestantism, as well as for the pronounced socio-political conservatism of the area. Leonard concludes by examining a number of signposts to the future of the region: as he reminds us, Crossroads culture is not fixed, but remains in flux, and the story of religion and public life in the area is still being written. Above all, the rapidly burgeoning Latino population of all Crossroads states promises to rewrite the story of religion and public life in the mid-South, so that the essays in this collection tell a story whose outcome is yet to be decided, and which will depend very strongly on how the Latino presence is incorporated into Crossroads culture in the coming decade.

Andrew Manis's essay on evangelical Protestantism reminds us of the predominance of that religious group (or, more precisely, of these groups) throughout the Crossroads, except in the sizable Catholic pockets of the region. Manis notes the truculence of Crossroads evangelicals, their historical tendency to assert distinctive and competing doctrines in a milieu of shifting, conflicting boundaries. He relates this tendency to a socio-political conservatism that, as demographic indices demonstrate, is more pronounced in the Crossroads than anywhere else in the nation. Manis's essay underscores how the religious diversity of the Southeast has been significantly flattened out in the Crossroads, such that evangelical Protestantism—especially the Southern Baptist church—tends to exercise, virtually unchallenged, not merely religious but also socio-political dominance in much of the region.

Jane Harris's essay on Holiness/Pentecostal groups reminds us, however, of how the mix of cultures found in the region has also spawned entirely new religious groups—in particular Pentecostalism, which emerged from Holiness movements seeking to reclaim Wesley's doctrine of entire sanctification. Harris demonstrates that, though small in numbers, Holiness/Pentecostal adherents are proportionately more numerous in the Crossroads states than elsewhere in the nation and wield undeniable influence on American public life, particularly through their institutional headquarters in places such as Springfield, Joplin, and Kansas City, Missouri. As Harris concludes, it is impossible to study these traditions at a national level without paying careful attention to their Crossroads roots and manifestations. Harris notes that, though many surveys tend to lump Holiness/Pentecostal believers together with evangelical Protestants—and, indeed, in many respects they do reflect the socio-political views of evangelicals—in some important respects, they diverge from evangelical viewpoints: for example, these groups are more likely to welcome women to ministry (though often with restrictions).

Kathlyn Breazeale's essay traces the interesting trajectory of Crossroads Catholicism from its beginnings as the only (and only lawful) religion of much of the region to its present status as a minority presence throughout most of the region, save for areas in which it has been traditionally dominant. As she notes, in much of the Crossroads, Catholicism has long been involved in an adaptive process as it interacts with the evangelical Protestant culture of the region. In key ways, it has come to mirror the conservatism of the Crossroads (e.g., in opposing abortion and gay marriage), but in other significant regards, it diverges from the pattern of the dominant culture—e.g., in supporting welfare and advocating for the rights of non-legal immigrants.

Cheryl Kirk-Duggan's essay is an impressive reminder that Native-American and African-American religiosity has long been a salient feature of Crossroads culture and religion. Kirk-Duggan shows that, for both groups, non-European cultural carryovers have exerted undeniable influence on the spiritual outlook of church members and non-religionists alike. She also indicates that in African-American culture, the church has been and remains a refuge in the storm, a bulwark protecting African-American self worth in a hostile majority culture deeply imbued by historic racism. Kirk-Duggan's essay provides abundant illustrations of the way in which Native-American and African-American religion has pulled against the dominant culture of the region, resisting the tendency of that culture to take political and socio-economic stances that have often been harmful to those on the margins of Crossroads society.

In general, all of the essays demonstrate the tendency of border clashes in the Crossroads to generate religious adaptation as well as religious conflict, both of which color the public life of the region in important respects. As all essays suggest, key battles of American religion and public life are being fought today in the Crossroads region with pronounced acerbity—an acerbity rooted in long historic patterns of the region. For instance—and this will be discussed at length in the Conclusion of this volume—gender and family issues are being contested in the

Crossroads region today with a forcefulness that is perhaps unmatched in any other region of the country.

As both Leonard and Manis make clear, Southern Baptists in Texas are sharply divided over cultural issues, including the role of women in church and society. This is a battle that has come to open warfare in the state, where leading national-level adherents of both the fundamentalist and moderate wings of the Southern Baptist Convention are well-represented. Texas Baptists have provided shock troops for the fundamentalist takeover of the Southern Baptist Convention, and at the same time have contributed significantly to the development of alternative structures, including a seminary designed to circumvent the fundamentalist domination of the Convention.

Similarly, one of the leading centers of the movement resisting the ordination of openly gay clergy and bishops as well as the celebration of gay unions in the Episcopal church is an Episcopalian megachurch in Plano, Texas. Yet not a few Texas Episcopalians are strongly in support of greater inclusion of gays and lesbians in the church, and the Episcopal bishops of Arkansas, Oklahoma, and Missouri all voted to confirm New Hampshire bishop Gene Robinson as the denomination's first openly gay bishop.

This is a region that relishes its battles and gleefully elevates to iconic status the bad boys and bad girls who carry on those battles, regardless of whether the showdowns are political, religious, or literal shootouts. Though both the James boys and Bonnie and Clyde were feared through much of the Crossroads as they plied their trade of robbing banks, their daring escapades (and ability to make fools of "the law") have also long been lionized in Crossroads songs. Many Arkansans of the 1950s—including those who were secretly appalled at his crudeness—took a certain pride in Orval Faubus's in-your-face defiance of federal authority during the Central High crisis, at the same time that they celebrated J. William Fulbright's insouciant stand against McCarthyism. Huey Long and his outlandish political shenanigans have come to be shorthand to the nation at large for the rocking and rolling political life of Louisiana and are still celebrated by tall tales told by Louisianans who cherish their folk heroes—including the native son Jimmy Swaggart, who, after all, was only following Luther's dictum that if one is to sin at all, one should do so gloriously.

And the legacy continues: as I write this introduction, large billboards with a picture of Bill Clinton playing the saxophone have sprouted all over the city of Little Rock. They are advertising a local radio station and carry in bold letters the inscription, "Carry on wayward son." Anyone who recalls the original lyrics of this song by the rock group Kansas (several of whose members later joined a Christian rock band) will recall that it ends by informing the wayward son, "Surely heaven waits for you...."

Endnotes

1. Richard Pillsbury, "Landscape, Cultural," in Charles Reagan Wilson and William Ferris, *Encyclopedia of Southern Culture*, (Chapel Hill: University of North Carolina Press, 1989), 534.

2. The unpublished diary is in the possession of a descendant in Riverside, California; a photocopy is in my possession. Dr. Wilson Bachelor was an uncle of the Edward E. Batchelor of Glover, OK, discussed above.

3. Lafcadio Hearn, "A Creole Courtyard," in S. Frederick Starr, *Inventing New Orleans: Writings of Lafcadio Hearn* (Jackson, MS: University of Missippi Press, 2001), 146-7; see also 186-8, 287.

4. "Autobiography of Marshall Harvey Twitchell," 91-97, as cited in Ted Tunnell, *Crucible of Reconstruction: War, Radicalism, and Race in Louisiana, 1862-1877* (Baton Rouge: Louisiana State University Press, 1984), 183.

5. Alison Cook, "The Texas Food Manifesto," in *Texas Monthly* 11,12 (December, 1983), 253-4. Charles Reagan Wilson uses both environmental/ climactic and cultural factors to identify the two distinct cultures: see "Southwest," in *Encyclopedia of Southern Culture*, 561-563.

6. Cook, "Texas Food Manifesto," 252. On the fusion of Deep South and Spanish influences in Texas speech patterns, see Ralph Blumenthal, "Speech Study Explores Distinctions of Texas Twang," *Arkansas Democrat-Gazette* (Nov. 29, 2003), 5A, reporting on a recently released study of Texas Speech by Guy Bailey and Jan Tillery, sponsored by the National Geographic Society.

7. *Life on the Mississippi* (New York: Harper, 1899). On the remoteness of Arkansas due to difficulties early settlers encountered in entering the state from the east, see Donald P. McNeilly, *The Old South Frontier: Cotton Plantations and the Formation of Arkansas Society, 1819-1861* (Fayetteville: University of Arkansas Press, 2000), 19-22; Arkansas Writers' Program of the Works Projects Administration, *Arkansas: A Guide to the State* (New York: Hastings House, 1941), 37; and John Gould Fletcher, *Arkansas* (Chapel Hill: University of North Carolina Press, 1947), 67.

8. H.L. Mencken, "The South Begins To Mutter," *Smart Set* (August, 1921), 141; see also Bob Lancaster, *The Jungles of Arkansas: A Personal History of the Wonder State* (Fayetteville: University of Arkansas Press, 1989), 126-147; and E.J. Friedlander, "'The Miasmatic Jungles': Reactions to H.L. Mencken's 1921 Attack on Arkansas," *Arkansas Historical Quarterly* 38 (Spring, 1979), 63.

9. James K. Zink, "Oklahoma," in *Encyclopedia of Religion in the South*, 563-4.

10. Richard M. Pope, "Missouri," in Samuel Hill, *Encyclopedia of Religion in the South*, (Mason, GA: Mercer Univeristy Press, 1984) 496.

RELIGIOUS AFFILIATION IN
THE SOUTHERN CROSSROADS AND THE NATION

The charts on the following pages compare two measures of religious identification: self-identification by individuals responding to a survey and adherents claimed by religious institutions. The charts compare regional data for the Midwest and national data for both measures. The sources of the data are described below.

On page 24
Adherents Claimed by Religious Groups

The Polis Center at Indiana University-Purdue University Indianapolis provided the Religion by Region Project with estimates of adherents claimed by religious groups in the Southern Crossroads and the nation at large. These results are identified as the North American Religion Atlas (NARA). NARA combines 2000 Census data with the Glenmary Research Center's 2000 Religious Congregations and Membership Survey (RCMS). Polis Center demographers supplemented the RCMS reports with data from other sources to produce estimates for groups that did not report to Glenmary.

On page 25
Religious Self-Identification

Drawn from the American Religious Identification Survey (ARIS 2001), these charts contrast how Americans in the Southern Crossroads and the nation at large describe their own religious identities. The ARIS study, conducted by Barry A. Kosmin, Egon Mayer, and Ariela Keysar at the Graduate Center of the City University of New York, includes the responses of 50,283 U.S. households gathered in a series of national, random-digit dialing, telephone surveys.

Adherents Claimed by Religious Groups
Southern Crossroads

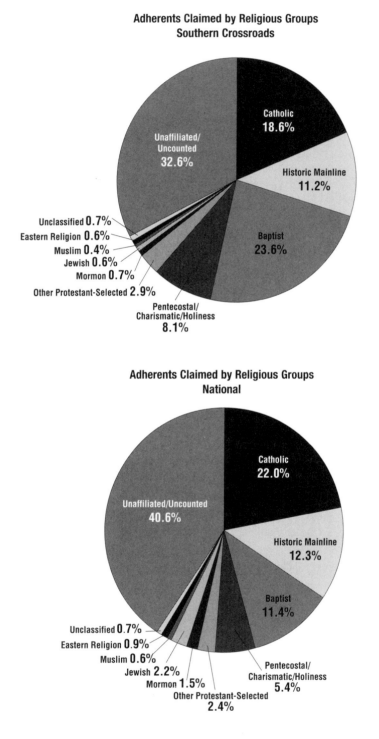

Adherents Claimed by Religious Groups
National

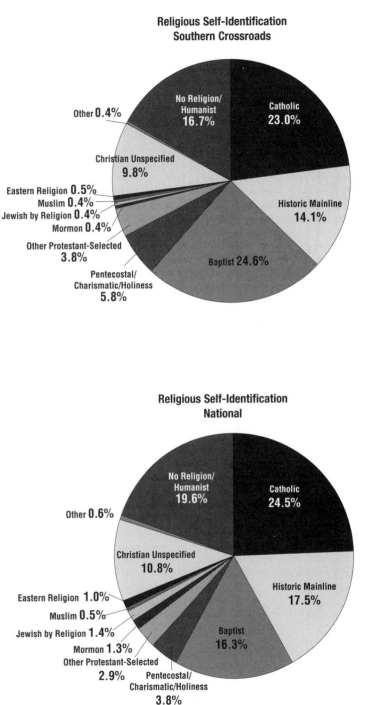

Religious Self-Identification
Southern Crossroads

No Religion/Humanist 16.7%
Catholic 23.0%
Other 0.4%
Christian Unspecified 9.8%
Eastern Religion 0.5%
Muslim 0.4%
Jewish by Religion 0.4%
Mormon 0.4%
Historic Mainline 14.1%
Other Protestant-Selected 3.8%
Baptist 24.6%
Pentecostal/Charismatic/Holiness 5.8%

Religious Self-Identification
National

No Religion/Humanist 19.6%
Catholic 24.5%
Other 0.6%
Christian Unspecified 10.8%
Historic Mainline 17.5%
Eastern Religion 1.0%
Muslim 0.5%
Jewish by Religion 1.4%
Baptist 16.3%
Mormon 1.3%
Other Protestant-Selected 2.9%
Pentecostal/Charismatic/Holiness 3.8%

CHAPTER ONE

THE SOUTHERN CROSSROADS:
RELIGION AND DEMOGRAPHY

Bill Leonard

In his 1950 book, *The Burned-Over District,* the sociologist Whitney Cross described the religious phenomena that characterized a particular region of New York State in the early nineteenth century. Cross wrote:

> Across the rolling hills of western New York and along the line of DeWitt Clinton's famed canal, there stretched in the second quarter of the nineteenth century a "psychic highway." Upon this broad belt of land congregated a people extraordinarily given to unusual religious beliefs, peculiarly devoted to crusades aimed at the perfection of mankind and the attainment of millennial happiness. Few of the enthusiasms or eccentricities of this generation of Americans failed to find exponents here.[1]

The region was swept so frequently by religious euphoria that it seemed "burned-over" again and again, fostering movements that anticipated sectarian pluralism in a nation moving west. In the burned-over district traditional churches were rejuvenated and new faith communities were initiated. The district witnessed the birth of Charles G. Finney's brand of revivalism, Joseph Smith's Mormonism, Ann Lee's Shakers, John Humphrey Noyes' Oneida communitarianism, the spiritualism of the Fox sisters, and the apocalyptic millennialism of William Miller. It became, in Cross's words, a "case study" of the ways in which "religious forces were the driving propellants of social movements important for the whole country in that generation."[2]

Many of these groups and the ideas they espoused spread extensively with westward migration, significantly affecting religion in the new nation. They promoted revivalism, millennialism, perfectionism, and biblical literalism that influenced a number of religious traditions in the "district" and on the larger frontier. Their charismatic leaders offered Americans a variety of spiritual responses to the personal, communal, political, and economic difficulties of frontier life. Many perpetuated the idea of America as a "chosen nation" with a special role in the divine plan.

This exploration of demography in the Southern Crossroads suggests that the region may well represent a twenty-first century burned-over district, an area so rife with dynamic religious movements, old and new, and so touched by immigration, pluralism, and populist traditionalism, that it constitutes a regional "psychic highway" akin to (though not entirely reflective of) the nineteenth century burned-over district. While parallels are not absolute, the burned-over district is, for several reasons, a helpful metaphor for understanding the contemporary religious ethos of the Southern Crossroads.

First, amid twenty-first century technology, urbanization, and multiculturalism, significant segments of the region retain a peculiar *frontier* mentality evident in approaches to law and order, firearms, entrepreneurial economics, and a continuing desire to "conquer the culture" for Christ (or other "saviors"). That church life in the Southern Crossroads is big business is evident, not only in so-called megachurches, but also in huge mainline congregations, television ministries, and storefront congregations whose pastors keep the blueprints for a larger "church plant" in their hip pockets. Evangelistic endeavors represent continuing efforts to "win" people to Christ, the church, and traditional morality. Indeed, statistical evidence of church growth has long been a method for evaluating the effectiveness, sometimes the truth, of viable religious communions. Crossroads pastors who cannot "grow" their churches are sometimes sent packing—like football coaches who cannot sustain winning seasons.

Second, individuals and congregations in the Southern Crossroads are *conservative but decidedly modern* in theology and ethics—ironically so, considering their stress on old-time religion, juxtaposed with their alacrity in using contemporary cultural vehicles of music, drama and marketing in an effort to attract secular "seekers" to traditional faith. As in the earlier burned-over district, Crossroads religion has a strong adaptive tendency: it is willing to refashion traditional worship or doctrinal forms to meet the needs of new generations of believers. Many individuals and churches see themselves in the tradition of revivalistic conversionism born of the nineteenth-century frontier; yet they recast the nineteenth-century model in modern (or postmodern) media, thereby reshaping the religious landscape of America in a new millennium. Others retain a religious traditionalism while attempting to relate to the "seeker-sensitive" culture. For instance, Crossroads Presbyterian, United Methodist, and Lutheran churches may simultaneously offer "high church" liturgical options and "praise bands."

Though the Southern Crossroads is home to some of the largest of the mainline congregations in the United States, and many such churches are beating the odds of decline and fragmentation evident elsewhere in these denominations without adopting the megachurch model, the region probably has more megachurches per square mile than any other segment of the country. A megachurch is a congregation of several thousand members, led by a founder-preacher-CEO-authority figure, providing special ministries to target constituencies, and organized around intentional marketing techniques. In a sense, megachurches are mini denominations, providing in one huge congregation services and activities previously offered through regional or national denominational connections. They often develop their own schools, mission agencies, literature, and venues of theological education.

In the Southern Crossroads, megachurches are an increasingly normative way of defining and participating in the church. Lakewood Church in Houston, a racially diverse charismatic-oriented faith community pastored by Joel Osteen, is a prime example: with over 35,000 members, it is perhaps the largest congregation in the United States.

The Southern Crossroads states also comprise innumerable television and other media ministries based in one geographic setting but beaming their ideologies around the world. Tulsa and Baton Rouge are home to the ministries of two iconic figures of televangelism, Oral Roberts and Jimmy Swaggart. In Houston, Second Baptist and Lakewood churches send out their services across the nation, reaching individuals and congregations far beyond their geographic range. The Fort Worth–Dallas region is also a seedbed of religious broadcasting, ranging from T. D. Jakes' Potters' House, a ministry that is reshaping African-American religious life in the United States, to the "prosperity" gospels of Creflo Dollar and Kenneth Copeland. The area is also the operational center of the Baptist-evangelist-gone-charismatic James Robison, as well as Fellowship Church.com, led by Edwin Young, Jr. The Fort Worth–Dallas region is perhaps unsurpassed in the nation in the number and influence of its religious television broadcasters.

A third parallel to the burned-over district is that many religious leaders in the Southern Crossroads claim a strong *urgency* to stem the tide of American "barbarism," which in their view consists primarily of preserving traditional religious values against the onslaught of godless secularism, immorality, worldliness, and unbelief. Such evangelistic zeal to save an embattled culture was also strongly apparent in the nineteenth-century burned-over district. As a result, the Crossroads is in many ways a bastion of conservatism amid the "culture wars" of the late twentieth and early twenty-first centuries. In 1980, Dallas was the scene of a now famous meeting of the Religious Roundtable, one of the seminal efforts to organize the so-called New Religious Right, with its strategy of compelling conservative religionists to participate more explicitly in the American political process. Ronald Reagan's address to the group marked its tacit endorsement of his presidential candidacy and the beginnings of a continuing link between religious conservatives and the Republican Party. Southern and Independent Baptists throughout the region have constituted major segments of the Moral Majority and other New Right organizations. These groups were strong supporters of Reagan and George Bush— as they are of George W. Bush—and vehement opponents of Bill Clinton.

More recently, the Southern Crossroads has been the scene of extensive reaction by conservative Episcopalians to the consecration of Gene Robinson, an openly gay clergyman, as bishop of New Hampshire in 2003. Christ Church Episcopal in Plano, Texas, has become a national center to rally those opposed to the consecration of openly gay bishops, going so far as to threaten schism if the hierarchy of the Episcopal Church does not heed its call to turn back movements to recognize openly gay clergy. Its rector, Reverend David Roseberry, is a founding member of the Network of Anglican Communion Dioceses and Parishes, a coalition formed following Robinson's consecration. Roseberry and his vestry released a resolution shortly after the consecration declaring that the elevation of a "practicing homosexual male" to the episcopacy "runs counter to centuries of orthodox and biblical teaching."[3]

Fourth, like those groups present in the earlier burned-over district, religious communions in the Southern Crossroads have pioneered *numerous morphologies* to describe the process of religious salvation. Revivalism, a major characteristic of the burned-over district, remains an important method for securing converts in the Crossroads. Some churches continue to use seasonal revivals focused on mass conversions just as Finney did in the nineteenth century. For such evangelists, conversion involves a radical moment of repentance and renewal, often occurring at the "invitation" or "altar call" given at the climatic moment of a revival meeting.

It should be noted, however, that reflecting its tendency to adapt innovative forms of church life—a tendency also present in the earlier burned-over district— an increasing number of Crossroads churches are forsaking the traditional revival format for retreats, renewal weekends, and "contemporary" worship services aimed at "seekers" in need of salvation. It is not unusual to find contemporary Crossroads preachers employing psychotherapeutic language about salvation, equating salvation with deliverance from a poor self image and calling individuals to receive salvation in order to assure both eternal life in the next world and material prosperity in this one.

Many groups in the Crossroads insist on the need for a baptism of the Holy Spirit that empowers the redeemed to live the Christian life—often echoing traditional theological language of Wesleyan Holiness or Pentecostal groups that distinguish justification (entering into faith) from sanctification (continuing in grace). This theological approach parallels the perfectionist emphasis of many groups of the nineteenth-century burned-over district. Believers who follow this theological path tend to emphasize charismatic gifts that may involve glossolalia (speaking in tongues), healing, and ecstatic religious experience. Some are classic Pentecostals of denominations such as the Assemblies of God, United Pentecostal, or Church of God. Others are charismatics who experience Spirit baptism within mainline Protestant or Catholic communities.

These varied morphologies and a tendency toward "switching" denominations or churches mean that many groups debate the nature of conversion, the constituency for conversion, the process of conversion, and the requirements for those who claim conversion. Many Crossroads churches employ conversionist language, but it is not uncommon for this language to have meanings so varied from denomination to denomination as to seem contradictory. Revivalism, conversionism, and evangelicalism are all present and continually being redefined inside the Southern Crossroads.

For example, many Crossroads evangelicals continue to question whether Catholics are actually "saved," given their devotion to sacraments, pope, and the Virgin Mary. Some Pentecostals voice doubts about whether certain charismatic Christians have actually had the "born-again" experience that must precede Spirit baptism. Some insist that the health/wealth gospel of certain Crossroads evangelists is a worldly substitute for genuine conversion, while others demand a certain doctrinal litmus test—belief in the Virgin Birth, biblical inerrancy, or the substitutionary atonement of Christ, for example—as a standard by which to measure whether a conversion is valid.

Finally, the Southern Crossroads mirrors the burned-over district in that it is an area in *transition*. During the first half of the nineteenth century, the burned-over district of western New York was never static in its religious and cultural identity. Immigration, increasing population, schisms, political and economic influences and an abiding sense of religious experimentation permeated the region. So it is today in the Southern Crossroads. The region is one in which immigration, particularly an increasing Latino presence, is reshaping cultural and religious life with each new decade.

In the contemporary Crossroads, religious communions old and new find themselves in competition with one another, as well as with the ever-increasing influence of such perceived enemies as secularism and materialism. Non-Christian religions, still a tiny minority, are also inexorably expanding their presence and influence throughout the region, offering challenges to the "established" Christian groups. As demographic studies indicate, divorce, poverty, and religious "non-affiliation" also strongly mark the contemporary culture of what many believe to be the buckle on America's Bible Belt. While preachers of the

Southern Crossroads profess delight today at how mightily the Spirit is moving in the midst of their churches, they may secretly be running scared as changes beyond their control have begun to reshape the region's cultural and religious ethos at the beginning of the twenty-first century.

In summary, though the Crossroads states of Louisiana, Oklahoma, Arkansas, Missouri, and Texas have much in common with their neighbors in the Deep South, in key respects they are more akin to the frontier region of upstate New York that spawned unique religious movements during the first half of the nineteenth century than they are to the Southern states east of the Mississippi. Like the earlier burned-over district, many Crossroads faith communities exhibit an "emotional religion" that is a "congenital characteristic" of the region's religious ethos, and that sets it apart from other regions of the country.

Unlike the burned-over district, however (and also in contrast to the Southeast), Crossroads culture and religion demonstrates a marked propensity for showdowns and cultural or religious contention. I have noted the historic tendency of Crossroads religionists to debate the minutiae of salvation and conversion. A cursory glance at the religious history of the region shows that these debates have occurred with a particular ferocity in the Crossroads—a ferocity matched by the frontier rowdiness of its culture in the formative period of the region.

Today, as demographic studies demonstrate, the showdown mentality may be more apparent in the region's approach to sociocultural issues (for example, the question of gay rights noted above) than to theological issues dividing one religious group from another. Indeed, there is significant demographic evidence that the diverse religious groups of the region are tending today to downplay theological dividing lines that have split one religious group from another in the past, as—under the influence of the Religious Right—more and more Crossroads religionists turn the sharp edge of their frontier hostility against the perceived threat of secularism, with its attendant evils of women's liberation, gay rights, and political liberalism.

However, even within this growing tendency of Crossroads religious groups to coalesce around a shared political agenda and to mute religious differences, one can note an interesting tendency that both sets the Crossroads apart from the Southeast and also reflects patterns in the earlier burned-over district. Just as the burned-over district generated a movement now significant in both American and world religions—the Mormons—the Crossroads has generated a number of religious movements with a pronounced emphasis on transforming culture to make it conform to religious ideals. Like the Mormons, these groups are a minority within both the national culture and the culture of their own region. Yet they are a significant presence within the Crossroads region and are exerting growing influence on both the region's political life and that of the nation as a whole. These include those groups born of the perfectionist movements within American Methodism in the nineteenth century (including the Holiness churches and the Church of the Nazarenes), as well as of the various Pentecostal churches whose theology has been heavily influenced by the holiness movements. As with Mormonism, these religious groups have an intense interest on evangelizing the world and, at the same time, a community-centered ethic that seeks to perfect members of the religious group, thus to transform the culture at large through community-based movements of religious change.

Cultural Profile

The 2000 Census showed that there are 37,040,061 people (26,953,195 adults) in the Southern Crossroads region. Louisiana (population 4,468,976) is the most densely populated with 102.5 people per square mile, followed by Missouri (population 5,595,211; 81.2 people per square mile), Texas (population 20,851,820; 79.6 people per square mile), Arkansas (population 2,673,400; 51.3 people per square mile), and Oklahoma (population 3,450,654; 50.2 people per square mile).

The male population in each of the states hovers at 48-49 percent while the female population stands at 50-51 percent.

Texas and Louisiana are the most racially diverse states in the Southern Crossroads, as seen in Table 1.1. Missouri, perhaps the state of the region least marked by the frontier mentality, is also the most "Caucasian" of the five states. Louisiana reflects a greater demographic Southernness with its significantly larger African-American population, while the Latino presence in Texas far exceeds that of the other Crossroads states.

While the states in the region retain strong farming traditions, the 2000 census shows that a population shift is evident in the growing urban population. Texas is the most urban Crossroads state, with 82.5 percent of its population residing in urban areas, followed by Louisiana (72.6 percent), Missouri (69.4 percent), Oklahoma (65.3 percent), and Arkansas (52.5 percent). Given the expanse of Texas, the high percentage of its urban population is significant. Of the five states, only Arkansas reflects a near 50/50 urban-rural population.

Educationally, three of the states fall below the national average (80.4 percent) for those with high school diplomas: Texas (75.6 percent), Arkansas (75.3 percent), and Louisiana (74.8 percent). Oklahoma matches the national average (80.6 percent), while Missouri betters it modestly (81.3 percent). All of the states are below the national average for those who have attained a bachelor's degree or higher. Nationally, 24.4 percent of the population over 25 years old has completed a baccalaureate degree, compared with 23.2 percent in Texas, 21.5 percent in Missouri, 20.2 percent in Oklahoma, 18.7 percent in Louisiana, and only 16.6 percent in Arkansas.

Table 1.1   Racial Composition of the Southern Crossroads Region
(percent of population) (2000 U.S. Census)

State	Caucasian	African American	Hispanic
Arkansas	79.9	15.6	3.2
Louisiana	63.9	32.4	2.4
Missouri	84.8	11.2	2.1
Oklahoma	76.1	7.5	5.1
Texas	70.9	11.5	31.9

The concern of the region's citizens for a particular type of law and order evident in incarcerations and executions is also statistically demonstrable. Texas, Oklahoma, and Missouri are among the four states with the highest execution rates in the nation since 1976 (Virginia is second to Texas).

While the religious and ethical ideals of the Southern Crossroads often appear more conservative than other regions, traditional institutions do not always measure up to conservative ideals in the Crossroads. Nowhere is this more evident than in divorce statistics in the region. For example, divorce statistics in Massachusetts (8.3 percent), New York (7.8 percent), and even California (9.5 percent) are lower than those of Oklahoma (11.6 percent), Arkansas (11 percent), Missouri (10.7 percent), Louisiana (10.2 percent), and Texas (9.7 percent). While the region's Catholic and Protestant churches often talk a good game regarding the sanctity of marriage, the importance of family, and the need for marital fidelity, they have not been able to stem the tide of divorce. Indeed, many traditional churches have had to come to terms with divorces of church leaders and not simply with the moral lapses of worldly souls outside the church's scope.

Religious Identities

North American Religion Atlas (NARA) data reveal three statistically dominant traditions. Baptists and Catholics compete for the top position, claiming 29 percent and 28 percent respectively of all church members in the region. When measured by religious self-identity their rank order is reversed: 22 percent of all respondents to the American Religious Identification Survey (ARIS) gave Catholicism as their religion while 20 percent identified themselves as Baptists. Since a majority of black Protestants are Baptists, however, the overall Baptist population would represent well over 20-25 percent. Historically African-American Protestant denominations constitute the third largest religious family in the region, claiming 15 percent of all church members; 9 percent of those sur-

Table 1.2. Adherents in the Southern Crossroads by Religious Family (NARA)

Family	# of Adherents	% of Total Population	% of all SX Adherents
Baptist	7,315,724	19.8	29.3
Catholic	6,893,128	18.6	27.6
Historically African-American Protestant	3,775,825	10.2	15.1
United Methodist	1,911,250	5.2	7.6
Other Conservative Christian	1,302,693	3.5	5.2
Holiness/Pentecostal	1,194,889	3.2	4.8
Confessional/Reformed/ non-UCC Congregational	398,279	1.1	1.6
Presbyterian USA	326,290	0.9	1.3
Episcopalian	271,700	0.7	1.1
Christian (Disciples)	287,344	0.8	1.1
Mormon	252,025	0.7	1.0
Jewish	213,465	0.6	0.9
Eastern Religions	217,095	0.6	0.9
Lutheran (ELCA)	205,811	0.6	0.8
Muslim	155,597	0.4	0.6
Orthodox	117,450	0.3	0.5
United Church of Christ	73,614	0.2	0.3
Other Mainline Protestant	50,389	0.1	0.2
Pietist/Anabaptist	24,016	0.1	0.1
Total	25,040,584	67.6	100.0
Unafiliated/Uncounted	12,053,477	32.5	

veyed by ARIS gave one of the historically African-American denominations as their religion. Together, these three groups account for approximately 50 percent of the region's population, as illustrated in Table 1.2.

The Southern Crossroads hosts one of the largest populations of Latino Protestants in the United States, second only to the Pacific region. Eighteen percent of all Latino Protestants in the United States reside in the Southern Crossroads region—mostly in Texas, whose population is almost one-third Latino. This compares with 5 percent of Oklahoma, 3 percent of Arkansas and 2 percent of Louisiana and Missouri. In total, Latino Protestants constitute about 4 percent of the region's population, according to ARIS data. Half of all Catholics in the region are Latino, according to ARIS.

Among the mainline Protestant denominations, United Methodists have the largest constituency in the Southern Crossroads with more than half of all mainline Protestants in the region.

The Presbyterian and Episcopal numbers are particularly telling when compared to the South. The South is home to 28 percent of all adherents to the Presbyterian Church (USA), while the Southern Crossroads has only 9 percent of the nation's Presbyterian population. Twenty-five percent of the Episcopalians in the United States live in the South, but only 9 percent live in the Southern Crossroads. While the Crossroads region has 21 percent of the Disciples of Christ communions (the third largest segment nationwide), they make up only .4 percent of the region's religious population.

Religious pluralism relative to non-Christian religions is not as prevalent in the Southern Crossroads as in the rest of the country. Indeed, the Crossroads region is the only segment of the United States where statistics for Jews, Muslims, Buddhists, and Hindus are all .5 percent or less in the ARIS data.

The Protestant Landscape: Baptist Dominance

Baptists dominate the Protestant landscape of the Southern Crossroads states. Those who wish to understand the religious ethos of the region must give attention to the role and history of the Baptists. In many respects they represent a case study in dynamics affecting numerous religious groups in the region; in a way that is paradigmatic for the entire region Baptists today struggle to balance the often conflicting demands of traditional theology, moral rigor, denominational conflict, and waning hegemony over the entire region's culture. Nonetheless, as the twenty-first century begins, in many Crossroads towns and cities Baptists of various types represent an almost *de facto* religious establishment—an unofficial "official" religion so intricately related to the culture that it sets religious, moral, and even political agendas implicitly and explicitly. No one who is serious about religious issues in the Southern Crossroads can fail to take seriously the Baptist ethos in the region, with particular attention to Southern, Independent, and African-American Baptists.

Southern Baptists

The Southern Baptist Convention is the largest of the Baptist groups in both the region and the nation. Southern Baptists in the South and Southern Crossroads have been the focus of extensive media reporting since the 1970s, much of it related to the controversy between so-called moderates and conservatives over issues of biblical inerrancy, denominational control, women's ordination, homosexuality, and various political differences. The denomination's very public battles have been the subject of innumerable newspaper stories, books, and documentaries. When Larry King wants a perspective at the far-right end of the

Table 1.3. **SBC Growth and Population Growth in the Southern Border, 1930-1990** (Smith: *The Rise of Baptist Republicanism*)

State	% Population Growth	% SBC Growth	% SBC>POP
Louisiana	59	77	18
Arkansas	39	78	39
Texas	70	79	9
Missouri	29	63	34
Oklahoma	32	80	48

theological spectrum, he frequently brings in a Southern Baptist leader such as Albert Mohler, president of the Southern Baptist Theological Seminary.

In 2003 Southern Baptists reported a total membership nationwide of 17 million in over 40,000 churches. However, early in the twenty-first century, the Southern Baptist Convention was showing some signs of strain. The denomination acknowledged significant declines in denominational funding and programs, and in 2003 the denomination's International Mission Board eliminated some 60 jobs in a cost-cutting measure attributed to declines in the stock market and in designated mission offerings.

A 1997 study of Baptist Republicanism by Oran P. Smith suggests that after a "steady climb" in Southern Baptist membership from 1930 to 1960, the denomination saw declines in its southern market share through the 1990s. Smith concludes that there may be "some credibility to the claim that Southern Baptists behave as they do because they have lost ground culturally."[4] In other words, much of the denomination's political grandstanding on behalf of causes beloved by the Religious Right may be nervous muscle-flexing, as Southern Baptists lose control of the culture of many Southern and Southern Crossroads states.

However, Smith also notes that, while in most Southern states the SBC has "merely kept pace with population growth," membership grew steadily in relation to the population in the Southern Crossroads region from 1930 to 1990 (Table 1.3). Oklahoma showed the greatest spurt, with the Oklahoma Baptist Convention growing 48 percent faster than the population of the state. During the same period, Arkansas Baptists grew 39 percent faster than the population of their state; Missouri Baptists 34 percent faster.

Independent Baptists

Southern Baptists are far from representing *all* Baptists in the Crossroads. One of the more fascinating Baptist communities of the region is the Independent Baptist movement, a collection of independent congregations loosely related through fellowships and pastors' conferences. These churches are especially strong in Texas, Oklahoma, Arkansas, and Missouri. Born of schisms in the Southern Baptist Convention in the 1920s, Independent Baptists are unashamed fundamentalists, some even affirming a strong separatism that eschews any connection with churches that smack of liberalism ("to know a liberal is to be a liberal"). They reject denominational alignments, promote theological conservatism, and have been strong anti-communists and supporters of the political Religious Right. The Baptist Bible Fellowship, perhaps the largest Independent Baptist fellowship, is headquartered in Springfield, Missouri.

Often overlooked by the media, except as represented by Jerry Falwell, Independent Baptists are a serious presence in the region and have become a major constituency for the Republican Party. In recent years some of their leaders, such as Falwell, have cemented alliances with the conservative wing of the SBC and have assisted the latter in making those of a less conservative bent unwelcome in the denomination. Others continue to reject the denominationalism of the SBC system of church polity, and will have nothing to do with Baptists of the SBC. No other region of the country has more Independent Baptists than the Southern Crossroads.

African-American Baptists

As seen in Table 1.1, historically African-American Protestant denominations represent the third largest religious family in the region. In the Southern Crossroads, as in the rest of the United States, Baptists claim the largest segment of African Americans.

African-American Baptists dominate their communities throughout the region, promoting a religious identity that is in many congregations a powerful blend of charismatic spirituality and social consciousness. Three African-American Baptist groups maintain the largest African-American religious communions in the region: the National Baptist Convention, USA, the National Baptist Convention in America, and the Progressive National Baptist Convention.

Subregional Patterns

The broad regional data discussed above hide strong subregional patterns that have profound effects on public culture in the Southern Crossroads. Maps 1-3 demonstrate that the three dominant faith groups in Table 1.1—Baptists, Catholics, and African-American Protestants—exist in three distinct corridors where they reign supreme.

A Baptist corridor runs east to west, including the southern part of Missouri, all of Arkansas, the northern half of Louisiana, the southern counties of Oklahoma, and the northern part of Texas. A Catholic corridor runs east to west

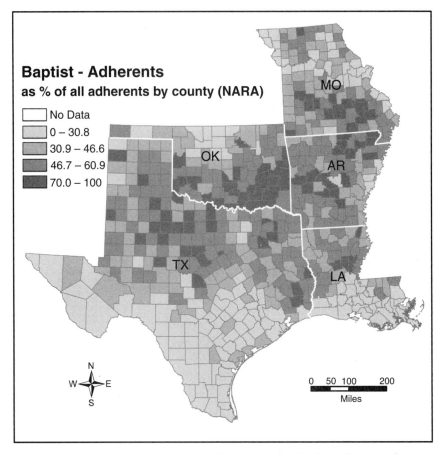

Map 1.1: *Concentrations of Baptist Adherents in the Southern Crossroads*

across the southern parts of Louisiana and Texas, with a notable pocket of Catholic concentration in the vicinity of St. Louis, Missouri. Looking at Map 3, we find a subregional stronghold of historically African-American Protestant denominations that goes from southern Arkansas and northern Louisiana across into east Texas.

To give but one example of how these concentrations affect public life in the Southern Crossroads, one can note that virtually all of the remaining "dry" counties in the region occur within the boundaries of the Baptist corridor.

If one were to broaden the lens to a national scope, it would reveal why the region can be aptly characterized as a "crossroads." The region stands out as

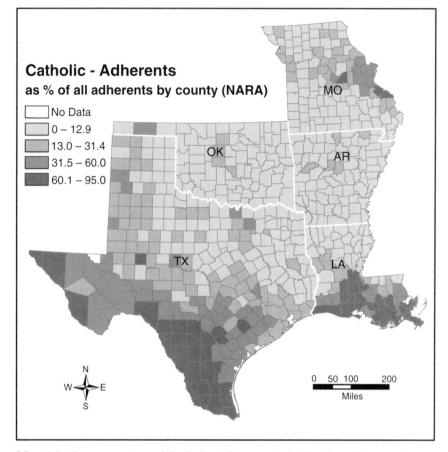

Map 1.2: *Concentrations of Catholic Adherents in the Southern Crossroads*

containing the westernmost part of the Baptist belt that extends across the Southeastern United States; the western part of an African-American Protestant belt that extends across the southern-most parts of those states (with the exception of Florida); and the easternmost part of a Catholic belt that begins in southern Louisiana, extends through southern Texas, and continues into the Southwest before moving up the coast of California.

In fact, one can pinpoint the Houston area as the place where the three traditions converge before going their separate ways. As Helen Rose Ebaugh and Janet Saltzman Chafetz have demonstrated, Houston is a distinctively diverse subregion where a wide variety of new immigrant religious groups are also making inroads to the United States.[5]

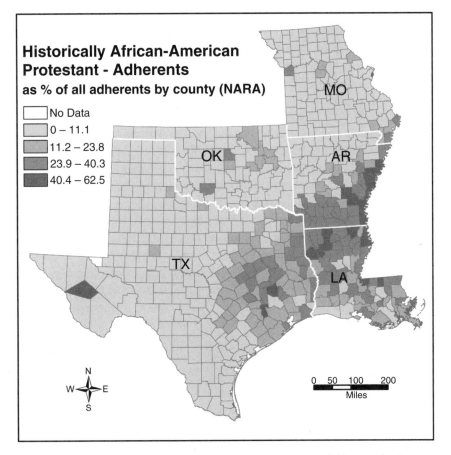

Map 1.3: *Concentrations of African-American Protestant Adherents in the Southern Crossroads*

The States: Arkansas, Louisiana, Missouri, Oklahoma, and Texas

While general characteristics apply to the entire region, data collected by the Association of Statisticians of American Religious Bodies (Glenmary) allow us to examine differences among individual states in the region.[6]

Arkansas

The 2000 Census indicates that the total population of the 75 counties in Arkansas was 2,350,725 in 1990 and 2,673,400 in 2000, a 13.7 percent increase. The Glenmary data show some 1,959,998 adherents to specific religious traditions. A comparison of these data with those reported in the 1990 Glenmary survey reveals declines and increases among select religious groups.

The total Catholic population of the state increased from 72,952 in 1990 to 115,967 in 2000, a rise of 59 percent. Catholics represent 5.9 percent of all religious adherents in the state and are 4.3 percent of the total population. Baptists (not including African Americans) claim 900,510, some 45.9 percent of all adherents in Arkansas and 33.7 percent of the total population. Southern Baptists numbered 617,524 adherents in 1990 and 665,307 adherents in 2000, an increase of 7.7 percent. Baptists represent the largest segment of the religious adherents in Arkansas, with no real competitors on the horizon. African-American Protestants in Arkansas claim 403,686 adherents. These are 20.6 percent of all adherents and 15.1 percent of the state's population. A substantial portion of these people are Baptists, further contributing to the Baptist hegemony in the state.

Holiness/Wesleyan/Pentecostal adherents number 127,603, or 6.5 percent of all adherents and 4.8 percent of the total population. However, their increases between 1990 and 2000 are substantial. For example, the Church of God (Cleveland, Tennessee) claimed 7,408 adherents in 1990 and 9,339 in 2000, an increase of 26.1 percent. Adherents in the Assemblies of God numbered 55,438 in 1990 but showed a 21.2 percent increase in the 2000 total of 67,187 adherents. "Independent charismatic" is a category that increased dramatically, with the number of adherents moving from 5 congregations with 2,065 adherents in 1990 to 7 congregations with 15,374 adherents in 2000. This increase of 644.5 percent gives some hint of the growth of so-called megachurch congregations that attract large numbers of persons to individual churches.

In contrast, mainline churches in Arkansas saw declines or limited growth during the decade 1990-2000. Episcopalians claimed 13,845 adherents in 1990 and 13,956 in 2000, an increase of .8 percent. Episcopalians represent .7 percent of all adherents in Arkansas and .5 percent of the state's population. The Presbyterian Church, USA showed 28,947 adherents in 1990 and 25,345 in 2000, a drop of 12.4 percent. This parallels a similar decline in numbers related to the more conservative Presbyterian Church in America. Between 1990 and 2000 it lost 2 congregations (from 10 to 8) and membership dipped from 944 to 805, a 14.7 percent decline.

United Methodists in Arkansas also revealed a decline in adherents, dropping from 197,402 in 1990 to 179,383, a loss of 9.1 percent. Methodist congregations decreased from 778 to 747, a loss of 41 churches. In 2000 Arkansas United Methodists had 9.2 percent of all adherents and 6.7 percent of the entire population of the state.

In each state of the Southern Crossroads, the Salvation Army showed amazing growth, jumping from 1,041 in 1990 to 2,153 adherents in 2000 in Arkansas, an increase of some 106.8 percent. The growth of the Salvation Army is a significant development in the decade.

Arkansas Mormons showed a significant increase in adherents and congregations. In 1990 there were 43 Latter-day Saint churches with adherents numbering 10,446; in 2000 there were 52 congregations with 14,916, an increase of 42.8 percent. Mormons represent .8 percent of all religious adherents in the state and are .6 percent of the total population.

Non-Christian religions in Arkansas are well worth noting. The number of Jews in Arkansas declined from 2,380 in 1990 to 1,600 in 2000, a 33 percent loss. There are 2,044 Muslim adherents, a figure that represents only 0.1 percent of all religious adherents in Arkansas and 0.1 percent of the total population. There are six mosques or other gathering places for Muslims in Arkansas.

Metropolitan areas also reveal changes in Arkansas' religious landscape. In the four counties that make up metropolitan Little Rock the Catholic population grew from 25,485 to 39,353, an increase of 54.4 percent. This increase added only one new church, from 19 to 20. Southern Baptists, the largest group in the city, increased from 125,785 to 129,583, for a growth of only 3 percent. United Methodists are the second largest religious communion in Little Rock, numbering 49,171 in 1990 and 47,182 in 2000, a decline of 4 percent.

Roman Catholics in the Fayetteville-Springdale-Rogers section of the state showed a huge increase in the decade 1990-2000. Catholics in that metropolitan area grew from 7,590 in 1990 to 18,909 in 2000, increasing by 149.1 percent. Even with that substantial numerical expansion, Catholics added no new churches. The nine congregations present in 1990 had to accommodate the increase. Mormons in the area grew by 103 percent, from 1,534 to 3,114, in a decade. Southern Baptists in the area also grew significantly, from 48,428 in 1990 to 63,597, an increase of 31.3 percent. United Methodists in the Fayetteville area also increased, bucking their denomination's trend toward decline. They had 15,787 adherents in 1990 and 18,185 in 2000, a 15.3 percent increase.

Louisiana

As might be expected, Louisiana reveals a historic Catholic presence, particularly in the southernmost part of the state. The 2000 Census listed Louisiana as having a total population of 4,468,976; Glenmary found 3,568,036 religious adherents. Catholic adherents are 1,382,603, or 38.7 percent of all religious adherents and 30.9 percent of the total population. Catholics in Louisiana showed only a 1.0 percent increase between 1990 and 2000. Southern Baptists, the second largest group, showed a similar percentage increase of 1.4 percent, growing from 757,639 adherents in 1990 to 768,587 in 2000. Catholics maintained only 625 churches, while Southern Baptists claimed 1,435 congregations. Overall, Baptists (not including African Americans) in Louisiana numbered 799,907 and were 22.4 percent of all religious adherents in the state. Baptist adherents represent 17.9 percent of the total population.

As in Arkansas, Pentecostal/charismatic faith communities showed dramatic growth. For example, adherents related to the Church of God (Cleveland, Tennessee) increased by 1,653 (6,919 in 1990 to 8,572 in 2000), for a growth rate of 23.9 percent. Likewise, Independent charismatic Christians increased from 12,000 in 1990 to 23,625 in 2000, a growth rate of 96.9 percent. That those adherents were found in only 9 congregations is further evidence of megachurch influences during the last decade. The Church of the Foursquare Gospel, another Pentecostal communion dating from the early twentieth century, saw 324.5 percent growth, moving from 159 adherents to 675 in 2000. Vineyard churches, also charismatic-related, were not even listed in the Glenmary Study of 1990. In 2000 Vineyard adherents numbered 2,864. The Salvation Army, with its Holiness emphasis, increased from 952 adherents to 2,902 persons, a 204.8 percent increase.

United Methodists and Presbyterians experienced losses between 1990 and 2000. In 1990 Methodists had 172,676 adherents but dropped to 160,153 by 2000. This represents a 7.3 percent decline. United Methodist adherents were 4.5 percent of all religious adherents in Louisiana and 3.6 percent of the state's total population. Adherents related to the Presbyterian Church (USA) declined from 27,105 persons in 1990 to 21,142 a decade later, a 22 percent drop. Presbyterians (USA) are only .6 percent of all religious adherents in Louisiana and .5 percent of the entire population.

Jewish adherents in Louisiana increased from 15,625 in 1990 to 16,500 (estimated) in 2000, a 5.6 increase. In 2000 Muslim adherents numbered some 13,050. Jewish adherents are approximately .4 percent of the Louisiana population, while Muslim adherents represent .3 percent and gaining.

The contrasts between two urban areas of the state, New Orleans and Baton Rouge, are particularly telling in terms of the ups and downs of religious communions in the state. While Catholics in New Orleans remain the majority religion, their adherents in the city dropped from 546,806 to 485,163 in the last decade, a decline of 11.3 percent. Catholics in Baton Rouge declined by 2.3 percent with a loss of 3,439 adherents. Independent charismatics increased by 2.9 percent in New Orleans (3,400/3,500) but by 101.9 percent in Baton Rouge (6,600/13,325). Southern Baptist adherents in New Orleans grew by 21.4 percent from 76,528 to 92,931. In Baton Rouge they decreased by 7.1 percent with 102,192 in 1990 to 94,919 in 2000.

Missouri

Missouri, on the edge of the Southern Crossroads, reflects parallels and differences when compared with the other four states. After Texas, Missouri is the largest of the states in the region, with a population of 5,595,211. Missouri has the largest number of people who claim a religious identity but aren't claimed by religious bodies, some 40.2 percent of the total population. Catholics and

Southern Baptists are the two largest groups in the state, with Catholics numbering 856,964, an increase of 6.8 percent from 1990 and Southern Baptists at 797,732 adherents, an increase of 1.1 percent from 1990.

Catholics in Missouri represent 15.3 percent of the total population and 25.6 percent of the state's total adherents. All Baptists (not including African-American Baptists) number 860,703 in Missouri, 25.7 percent of the total religious adherents and 15.4 percent of the total population.

Pentecostal/charismatic groups show mixed results in the 2000 Glenmary Study. Missouri is headquarters to the Assemblies of God, which grew to 95,429 adherents in 2000 from 84,193 in 1990, an increase of 13.3 percent. Independent charismatics, however, declined by 25.5 percent, from 25,940 in 33 churches in 1990 to 19,315 in 22 churches in 2000. The Church of God (Cleveland, Tennessee) increased by 40.4 percent with adherents numbering 9,327 in 2000. Salvation Army adherents increased to 10,508, a growth of 233.9 percent over 1990.

Presbyterians (USA), Episcopalians, and United Methodists in Missouri all declined during the decade 1990-2000. Episcopalians saw a 7.6 percent (26,846) decrease, while Presbyterians (USA) declined by 19.2 percent (64,277); and United Methodists by 11.2 percent (226,578). United Methodists still represent 4 percent of the total population of Missouri and 6.8 percent of all adherents. Adherents in the United Church of Christ declined 22.9 percent (51,490). Again, mainline churches in Missouri generally reveal a decline in adherents during the past decade.

Jewish presence in Missouri showed an increase of 17.4 percent in 2000 with estimated adherents at 62,315, 1.9 percent of all adherents and 1.1 percent of the total population. Muslims in the state number 19,359, or .6 percent of all adherents and .3 percent of the total population.

The metropolitan areas of Kansas City and St. Louis reflect differences in religious communities. In Kansas City evangelical Protestants, mainline Protestants, and Roman Catholics are statistically comparable. Catholics in Kansas City number 273,234, a 36.8 percent increase from 1990. Southern Baptists in Kansas City claim 159,858 adherents, a .2 percent increase over the decade. United Methodists are the third largest group in Kansas City with 78,684 adherents, a decline of 2.7 percent since 1990. During the last decade the Presbyterian Church, USA lost 5,253 adherents for a decline of 14.5 percent to 30,947.

In St. Louis Roman Catholics represent the largest religious constituency. However, Catholics declined by 0.7 percent in 2000 with a total number of adherents listed at 645,700. Southern Baptists, the second largest religious group, saw a decline of 2.7 percent with 175,994 people claimed in the 2000 Glenmary Study. Pentecostal/charismatic groups also registered losses, with the Assemblies of God churches in St. Louis posting a 12.7 percent decline for a total of 16,794 adherents. Independent charismatic communions listed 17 churches with adherents numbering 14,310 in 1990, but only nine churches with 5,900 adherents in 2000, a loss of 58.8 percent of their adherents in a single decade. This shift is surely related to identities in particular churches that changed over a decade. The Evangelical Free Church in St. Louis increased at a rate of 108.9 percent for a total of 3,013 persons. Jews in St. Louis were estimated at 54,200 in 2000, an increase of 2 percent. As in Kansas City, United Methodists, Presbyterians (USA), Episcopalians, and the United Church of Christ (UCC) saw declines in adherents between 1990 and 2000. Methodists declined by 12 percent, Presbyterians (USA) by 21.4 percent, Episcopalians by 12.5 percent, and UCC by 19.4 percent. The Lutheran Church, Missouri Synod, a bastion of Missouri conservatism, declined by 5 percent in the decade 1990-2000, with adherents numbering 93,300.

Oklahoma

In Oklahoma the groups generally designated as evangelical Protestants dominate the religious landscape. The 2000 Census listed the state's population at 3,450,654. Glenmary shows 2,398,392 religious adherents and a religiously unclaimed group of 30.5 percent. Baptists in general and Southern Baptists in particular are by far the largest religious communions in the state. Baptist adherents (not including African Americans) are listed at 1,027,362, or 42.8 percent of all religious adherents and 29.8 percent of the total population. Southern Baptists embody the lion's share of those statistics, claiming 967,223 adherents, for a growth of 0.3 percent over the decade 1990-2000. American Baptist Churches, USA increased 108 percent, an expansion of 2,609 over the decade.

Pentecostal/charismatic Christians in Oklahoma showed significant growth during the decade. Church of God (Cleveland, Tennessee) increased by 38.6 percent with adherents numbering 7,758. Independent charismatics grew by 25.7 to 28,170, adding 5,758 people. The International Church of the Foursquare Gospel increased 173.4 percent to 2,791 adherents, and Holiness/Pentecostal churches claimed 28,192 adherents, a growth of 68.3 percent. Holiness/Pentecostal/Wesleyan adherents offer a total of 225,997 adherents, representing 9.4 percent of all religious adherents in Oklahoma and 6.5 percent of the total population.

Roman Catholics in Oklahoma comprise 168,625, 7 percent of all adherents and 4.9 percent of the total population. Catholic adherents increased by 17.4 percent between 1990 and 2000. Jewish adherents in Oklahoma are estimated at 5,050 or .1 percent of the total population; Muslims number 6,145 or .2 percent of the total state population. United Methodists number 322,794 adherents or 13.5 percent of all religious adherents and 9.4 percent of the state's total population. This is the largest percentage of Methodists in the Southern Crossroads region. United Methodists declined by 1.1 percent between 1990 and 2000. Episcopalians in Oklahoma showed a 2.3 percent increase in adherents in 2000, while Presbyterians (USA) posted a decline of 15.4 percent.

A comparison of metropolitan areas such as Oklahoma City and Tulsa shows Catholics in a minority in both cities, though obviously increasing, with a 24.1 percent increase in Oklahoma City and an 11.9 percent increase in Tulsa. Southern Baptists, the largest religious group in both cities, increased by only 4.7 percent in Oklahoma City and declined by 1.5 percent in Tulsa. Adherents connected to the Salvation Army in Oklahoma City increased by 646.9 percent and by 1,388.9 percent in Tulsa. The Tulsa Army grew from 404 adherents in 2 locations in 1990 to 6 locations with 6,015 adherents in 2000. Pentecostal/charismatics in both cities grew at substantial rates, but Tulsa Independent charismatics lost 10,662 adherents and two congregations for a decline of 67.6 percent. However, these churches are difficult to categorize using traditional denominational labels and may have been counted elsewhere. United Methodists in both cities showed growth, with a 4.6 percent increase in Oklahoma City and an 8.5 percent increase in Tulsa.

Texas

As the largest state in the region, Texas provides a case study in religious diversity and regional conservatism. Dallas, Fort Worth, and Houston have become seedbeds for megachurch growth and activity, evident in congregations such as Prestonwood Baptist (Dallas), Potter's House (Dallas), Fellowship Church.com (Grapevine), and Lakewood (Houston). Each draws thousands of people to weekly services. With 31.9 percent of its population Latino, Texas has by far the largest concentration of Latinos of any state in the region (Oklahoma, the runner-up, is only 5.1 percent Latino). The burgeoning Latino population has effected the Catholic and, in many cases, the Pentecostal populations.

Numerous mainline churches in Texas have stemmed the tide of their denominational declines to develop substantial growth during the last decade. Presbyterians and Episcopalians in the state have been torn apart by debates over doctrine and ethics, particularly questions regarding homosexuals in the church. Southern Baptist-related churches have divided between support for the Baptist General Convention of Texas and the national Southern Baptist Convention. Controversies abound in religious communions in the state.

Census figures for 2000 put the Texas population at 20,851,820. Total religious adherents include 13,716,712 people. The religiously unclaimed group rests at 34.2 percent of the population. Evangelical Protestants show a slight increase over Roman Catholics. Catholics now represent the largest religious group in Texas with 4,368,969 adherents representing 31.9 percent of all religious adherents and 21 percent of the total state population. Baptists, long the majority, are second with adherents totaling 3,727,242. They comprise 27.2 percent of all adherents and 17.9 percent of the population.

Pentecostal/charismatics, who number about 300,335 in Texas, are represented in numerous groups. These include the Assemblies of God (26,016 adherents), Church of God (Cleveland, Tennessee) (10,431), Independent charismatic (159,449), International Foursquare Gospel (12,501), Pentecostal Holiness (4,748), Pentecostal Church of God (11,592), Salvation Army (25,070), and Church of Nazarene (50,528). While those numbers are nowhere near those of the Southern Baptists, they indicate the presence of a substantial and ever-increasing constituency. Likewise, the fact that independent non-charismatics claim 145,249 adherents offers evidence of the impact of non-denominational evangelical churches in the state.

Among the mainlines, United Methodists claim a significant constituency, with 1,022,342 adherents who make up 7.5 percent of all religious adherents and 4.9 percent of the total population. United Methodists increased by 1.8 percent in 2000 and claimed 2,110 churches. Episcopalians in Texas also increased their adherents by 5.2 percent for a total of 177,910. The Christian Church (Disciples of Christ), a denomination experiencing significant declines nationwide, grew in Texas by 5.5 percent with 111,288 adherents in 2000. While significant, this is a smaller number than Texas Mormons who claimed 155,451 adherents and grew by 39.7 percent. The Presbyterian Church, USA declined, however, by 10.3 percent with adherents numbering 180,315.

Jewish adherents in Texas are estimated at 128,000, or 0.6 percent of the total population, the same percentage as Texas Muslims who number 114,999. Eastern Religions (Hindu, Sikhs, and others) make up .7 percent of the Texas population with a total of 146, 014 adherents. This suggests that there are more Jews, Muslims, and representatives of Eastern Religions in Texas than there are Episcopalians.

Metropolitan areas of Texas provide an intriguing case study in religious transitions, growth, and decline.

Catholics showed a dramatic rise in each of the urban areas, especially when compared to Southern Baptists, the largest Protestant group in the state. Indeed, Catholic growth in the four cities far outstripped Southern Baptist growth in the decade 1990-2000 (Table 1.4).

United Methodists in the four major metro areas showed impressive growth during the last decade in contrast to their overall national numbers (Table 1.5).

The Presbyterian Church (USA) declined in three of the cities, but increased by 19 percent in Austin. Episcopalian adherents increased in three metro areas with only a slight decline of .7 percent in San Antonio. Pentecostal/charismatic churches, both denominationally and non-denominationally affiliated, increased in all the four metropolitan areas.

Muslims in these Texas cities also show significant numbers of adherents in two metro areas and a much smaller number in the other two (Table 1.6).

Table 1.4. Catholic-Baptist Growth in Four Urban Areas (Glenmary)

	1990	2000	% Increase/ Decrease
Austin/San Marcos			
Catholics	114,838	230,358	100.6
S. Baptists	114,517	127,903	11.7
Dallas/Ft Worth			
Catholics	363,085	808,167	122.6
S. Baptists	768,487	855,680	11.3
Houston/Galveston			
Catholics	644,857	850,496	31.9
S. Baptists	555,402	692,355	24.7
San Antonio			
Catholics	477,488	617,262	29.3
S. Baptists	137,660	139,368	1.2

Southern Crossroads: Political and Ethical Issues

Religious communions in the Southern Crossroads address moral and political issues in a variety of ways. The statistical data reveal an abiding conservatism on most issues, often demonstrating more conservative opinions than those evident in the South.

Ideology: Liberal/Conservative/Moderate Views

The National Surveys of Religion and Politics (NSRP) collected by John Green and his colleagues at the Bliss Center at the University of Akron show that high-commitment evangelicals (those who attend church at least once a week), low-commitment evangelicals, and high-commitment mainline Protestants in the Southern Crossroads are ideologically similar to comparable groups nationally. High-commitment evangelicals nationally are 66.1 percent in the conservative camp, with 68.8 percent conservatives among the same group in the Crossroads. Low-commitment evangelicals nationally are at 46.7 percent, with 47.9 percent of Crossroads respondents claiming conservative ideology. One statistic suggests the powerful influence of religion on public life in the region: nationally, 35 percent of those who claim no religion say they are ideologically conservative while the plurality (38 percent) identify themselves as liberals; in the Southern Crossroads, however, the plurality of these "secular" respondents (44 percent) identify themselves as conservative while only 31 percent describe themselves as liberal.

Politics: Party Preference

Party preference and its relationship to religious groups are particularly intriguing in the Southern Crossroads. Voter registration itself parallels the

Table 1.5.   **United Methodist Growth in Four Urban Areas** (Glenmary)

	1990	2000	% Increase/ Decrease
Houston/Galveston	216,922	232,031	7
Dallas/Fort Worth	262,234	294,185	12.2
Austin/San Marcos	35,296	44,296	25.5
San Antonio	44,244	49,132	11

national average with 80 percent claiming to be registered and 20 percent unregistered. The percentages that claim affinity for Republican, Democrat, and Independent connections are about even, (Republican, 30 percent; Democratic, 32 percent; Independent, 29 percent).

There are clear choices, however. More white Catholics in the survey chose the Republican Party over the Democrats, as did, somewhat surprisingly, those who identified with the so-called mainline churches. White Baptists in the region are clearly in the Republican camp (41 percent), about the same percentage as white Methodists (39 percent). Baptists claiming Democratic or Independent affiliation number 27 percent of those surveyed, and thus Democrats do no better than Independents. This is offset by the fact that black Protestants show 69 percent affiliation with the Democrats and only 9 percent with Republicans. One might surmise that white and black Baptists are generally divided over party affiliation.

These statistics generally reflect those of similar religious groups in the Southeast, with one significant exception. In the Southeast, Latino Catholics indicated a preference for Republicans over Democrats by 41 percent to 34 percent. In the Southern Crossroads, statistics for Latino Catholics indicate that only 16 percent preferred the Republicans while 47 percent chose the Democrats. This suggests a general preference for Democrats among Latino Catholics in Texas. Republican attempts to make inroads among black and Latino voters through use of "faith-based funding" (permitting churches to apply for government funds while retaining some of their ecclesial "convictions" regarding hiring and church affiliations) will perhaps change these patterns in the coming years.

Voter registration figures surely point toward considerable indifference to voting among certain groups. Latinos (Catholic and Protestant), Pentecostals, and those who claim no religious affiliation are less likely to be registered voters. This also may suggest that efforts of the new political religious right have influenced party preference toward the Republicans among existing voters but have not necessarily translated into actual voter registration that would at least enable participation in elections. Pentecostal and evangelical groups show a lower registration in the Southern Crossroads than in the nation at large.[7]

Table 1.6.   Muslims (Estimated) in Four Urban Areas (Glenmary)

Houston/Galveston Muslims	54,220
Dallas/Fort Worth Muslims	48,366
Austin/San Marcos Muslims	3,914
San Antonio Muslims	3,182

Abortion Issues

In the Bliss Center data on abortion attitudes, respondents from the Southern Crossroads parallel the national averages with a few telling exceptions. The conservatism of "secularists" is clearly evident in the Southern Crossroads, where 36.6 percent of that group consider themselves "pro-life" (anti-abortion), as opposed to 26 percent nationally. Adherents of non-Christian religions, likewise, are more conservative here than nationwide.

Gay Rights

The Bliss Center data reveal an overall rating of 49.7 percent among those interviewed who could be considered "pro gay rights" in the Southern Crossroads region, while 35.1 percent indicated "anti gay rights." This differs from the national average of 58.7 percent pro gay rights and 28.7 percent anti gay rights.

The Bliss Center data suggest that residents of the Southern Crossroads across the religious spectrum are more conservative on gay-rights issues than nationally. As in the case of abortion, non-Christians and seculars in the region are considerably more conservative than those groups are nationally. In fact, on the matter of gay rights, the Southern Crossroads survey was the most conservative of all the regions investigated.

The Southern Crossroads: Statistics and the Future

Current statistical studies related to the Southern Crossroads reveal many trends that were underway well before the decade 1990-2000. Mainline churches have been in decline for several years. The population of the Crossroads region has long been a bastion of religious and social conservatism. The shift from Democratic Party affiliation to the Republican Party first became evident with the election of Ronald Reagan in 1980, and appears to be ongoing throughout the region.

Another statistically significant shift in the region over the last decade of the twentieth century is the dramatic rise of Roman Catholicism in many segments of the region, as well as the marked increase in Pentecostal/charismatic influences in a variety of communions. Immigration, particularly evident in the Latino presence in Texas, promises to make major changes in the religious, political, and economic context of the nation's second most populous state. Protestant, particularly Baptist, hegemony in that region is also likely to face significant challenges in light of burgeoning Catholic influence and numbers. While megachurches seem to be claiming an increasingly significant segment of the Protestant community, it remains to be seen if they can sustain what seems an unending expansion of facilities, programs, and marketing techniques. Are they the church of the future, or a transitional phase on the way to structures not yet on the ecclesiastical horizon? In short, how much scorched earth can the new burned-over district accommodate? Current statistics demand increased study, not simply for trends of growth and decline, but for questions related to theological differences, cultural accommodation, internecine disputes, and ethical imperatives.

Through it all, I would contend that the Southern Crossroads of the United States remains something of a new burned-over district, with new religious groups continuing to take shape within traditional denominational forms, as certain older groups redefine themselves. Crossroads religious ministries continue to utilize media opportunities—television, radio, Internet—to communicate their views across the culture. Religious conversion remains a powerful personal imperative for a significant number of individuals in the region, and evangelical religion continues to set agendas. Though the expansion of Catholicism throughout the region may change its cultural and religious make-up in ways yet to be seen, traditionalist Catholics and Protestants continue to be determined to stand in the breach against secularists, supporters of choice regarding abortion, gays, and, indeed, anyone who challenges traditional views regarding public morality in the region.

To this end, many religious adherents of the region are promoting a variety of political strategies, most of these overtly linked to the Religious Right, to retain what these church members regard as their divinely mandated control of the region's culture. Crossroads preachers and their programs are actively engaging the public square today in an effort to convert sinners, transform society, and conquer culture.

Endnotes

1. Whitney Cross, *The Burned-Over District* (New York: Cornell University Press, 1950), 3. The reference to "psychic highway" is taken from Carl Carmer, *Listen to the Lonesome Drum: A York State Chronicle* (New York: 1936), 115.

2. Ibid, ix.

3. The American Anglican Council Web page, 2004.

4. Oran P. Smith, *The Rise of Baptist Republicanism* (New York: New York University Press, 1997), 77.

5. Helen Rose Ebaugh and Janet Saltzman Chafetz, *Religion and the New Immigrants: Continuities and Adaptations in Immigrant Congregations* (Walnut Creek, CA: AltaMira Press, 2000).

6. Data in this section are from Association of Statisticians of American Religious Bodies (ASARB), *Churches and Church Membership in the United States 1990* and *Religious Congregations and Membership in the United States 2000* (Nashville, TN: Glenmary Research Center, 2002). Available at www.thearda.com.

7. Nationally, Pentecostal/charismatic individuals showed 79 percent registered to vote with 21 percent unregistered. "Other evangelicals" demonstrate 87 percent registration and 13 percent unregistered, the latter a much higher figure than in the Southern Crossroads.

Chapter Two

Protestants: From Denominational Controversialists to Culture Warriors

Andrew Manis

In a volatile evaluation of the mind of George W. Bush, the progressive commentator Michael Lind has attributed the president's right-wing economics, foreign policy, militarism, and civil religiosity to a worldview that was "made in Texas." Lind argues in his articles and book that the southern fundamentalism of East Texas has now come to dominate the thinking of President Bush, the Republican Party, and the national political scene. He describes a "Texanisation of the American right," noting that Bush II was the first truly "conservative Texan president." Further illustrating the religious zeal of conservative Texas Republicans, Lind recoils in horror from the actions of House Majority Leader Tom DeLay, who in 2002 told a Baptist congregation that God was using him to promote "a biblical worldview" in American politics.

As the nation's second most populous state, with some 21 million people, and as the westernmost part of the Deep South, Texas wields tremendous influence not only on national politics. It also provides an important window on the interaction between politics and religion in the region we are calling the Southern Crossroads. The "Texas style" that Lind believes has shaped George W. Bush, however, is wider than the Lone Star State and reflects what has historically been a distinctively contentious mode of religious interaction on America's Southwestern frontier.

Beginning in 1853, a Memphis, Tennessee, Baptist minister and editor named J. R. Graves sallied forth against denominational adversaries for the next 40 years, describing a war between true (Christian) religion and the forces of Romanism and Rationalist Infidelity. Seeing these twin evils as "working silently [for] the overthrow of our republican government and our free institutions," Graves predicted that "the bloodiest battle-ground—the Waterloo of this conflict—will be the valley of the Mississippi."[1] More than 110 years after Graves' polemical pen took its final rest in 1893, it seems that his prophecy has been fulfilled. Graves also called this region the "Great West," including in it the states of Arkansas, Louisiana, Missouri, and Texas, and substituting Florida for Oklahoma, which did not yet exist in Graves' day.

Taking a cue from Graves' view of the "Great West," this chapter argues that the Southern Crossroads was and remains a center of religion controversy and has become the central theater for the nation's "culture wars." Beginning in the nineteenth century, the Protestants of this region bore a spirit of competition and contentiousness that has continued through the twentieth and into the early twenty-first century. Although the issues about which they currently fight have changed from the denominational to the national and from the theological to the cultural and moral, Protestants in the Southern Crossroads have been transformed from doctrinal controversialists in the nineteenth century to the culture warriors of the twenty-first. This change has also been accompanied by an important continuity—the controversialist mentality of those Protestant spokespersons who settled the Southern Crossroads frontier has led it to remain in many ways the most religiously conservative and contentious region of the country, the theater where the fires of the culture wars rage most fervently. Without understanding the cultural and theological contentiousness endemic to this region, one would be hard put to understand the way Protestants in these states fight the "culture wars" of contemporary times.

Throughout this chapter the particular group of Protestants in view might be called the "Crossroads Evangelical Establishment." This set of conservative Protestants is made up of a broad consensus of white evangelicals and fundamentalists, but also includes the region's more conservative members of historic mainline Protestant denominations. This "establishment" thus includes Baptists of various stripes, Methodists, Presbyterians, Disciples, Holiness, Pentecostal, Confessional or Reformed, and other conservative Christians. All these denominational traditions combined give the Crossroads Evangelical Establishment a large influence in each of the states under consideration. They include 51 percent (roughly 1.3 million) of the total population of Arkansas. In Louisiana they amount to 26 percent (1.2 million) of the population. They represent 32 percent (1.8 million) of Missourians, 54 percent (1.9 million) of Oklahomans, and 31 percent (6.5 million) of Texans.

Crossroads Contentiousness on the Nineteenth-Century Frontier

In the nineteenth century, radiating from Memphis in a southwesterly direction into the five states of the Southern Crossroads region, the Protestant denominations that settled the Southwestern frontier arrived in the early national and antebellum periods when the "democratization of American Christianity" was in full swing. In their formative phases, at least four traits were encoded into the DNA of these states. One was the essential toughness necessary for taming the frontier areas west of the more settled South. A second was a fervent revivalism spawned by the Second Great Awakening in Kentucky and Tennessee, which in turn fostered a third trait, a firm biblicism. The fourth and perhaps most important trait was the denominational competition created by the religious voluntaryism in which these Protestants found themselves. The liberty-induced market situation forged a democratized Christianity where denominational spokespeople "contended for the faith" against other Christian controversialists. These rugged frontier territories fostered contentious denominational controversies as Baptists, Methodists, Presbyterians, Disciples of Christ, and the Churches of Christ competed with each other to win voluntary converts by arguing that their theological traditions best represented or reconstituted true New Testament Christianity.

Arguably, J. R. Graves embodied this southwestern spirit of controversialism and influenced the region more than any other figure. Of course, Graves needed worthy opponents, and found them mostly in the followers of John Wesley, Alexander Campbell, and Barton Stone. The latter two sought to win volunteers by arguing that their Churches of Christ were not denominations but rather restored the true primitive faith, while the Methodists promoted their own forms of baptism and polity. Episcopalians, influenced by the Oxford movement, followed the logic of the Catholic Church in locating their authenticity in their succession of bishops.

Trumping them all, however, Graves advanced an ecclesiology called Landmarkism, which claimed that, never having been a part of Catholicism, Baptists were not Protestants and could trace their origins through a succession of rightly constituted congregations. A true Christian church, he argued, was made up of believers who had been properly baptized—as believers rather than as infants (proper subject), by immersion (proper mode), by a Baptist church (proper authority), by a Baptist minister (proper administrator), and in a baptism that declared but did not procure or effect salvation (proper symbolism). Graves countered Episcopal succession with a fanciful historical construct—a succession of Baptist congregations holding these beliefs going back through the medieval sects to the time of Jesus. As such, Graves argued, Baptists had no need to restore true Christianity because they had preserved and perpetuated it throughout the centuries.

Graves' contentiousness and his unshakable conviction of embodying true Christianity influenced friend and foe alike as he spent more than 50 years debating denominational opponents in the mid-South. James E. Tull, the foremost historian of Landmarkism, summed up Graves' controversialism this way: "During his long career Graves waged war upon every major denomination in the Great

West and upon many of the lesser ones." As editor of *The Tennessee Baptist* and founder of his own publishing company, Graves influenced what has been called the "Landmark Belt," which includes Tennessee, parts of Kentucky, Arkansas, Mississippi, Texas, Louisiana, Oklahoma, and southern Missouri.

In 1851 a Baptist visitor from Virginia commented on the belligerence of denominational contests of Graves and his contemporaries: "Theological champions meet with burnished swords and cut and hew each other to the wondrous gratification of their respective partisans, who gather in hundreds for successive weeks to these scenes of religious combat.... Our brethren of Tennessee neither bury the sword nor allow it to rust in the scabbard." He also noted that Graves infused a "fearless and uncompromising" spirit into these doctrinal debates. Tull noted, "The region had not seen such an adroit, convincing debater since Alexander Campbell had come among them a quarter of a century before."[2]

More important for our focus on public issues, however, Graves promulgated throughout the region a powerful form of "Christian Republicanism" that turned his doctrinal controversialism into a public theology reminiscent of that of contemporary culture warriors. Graves anticipated democratic "civil revolutions" throughout Europe like that in the United States, designed to crush "kingly and clerical absolutism." Writing in the era of Manifest Destiny, he saw America as "the hope of the world" and "pre-eminent among the nations of the earth," asserting further: "Here is Paradise regained—man is restored to the full enjoyment of all his long lost rights—emancipated from every foe but sin." Christian citizens, Graves believed, were given a sacred trust to help America to "exert an influence" upon the nations "in favor of Republicanism and Christianity." Confident of God's protection of the United States, he feared no external conquest, but warned against "the gradual and imperceptible undermining of the foundation upon which we rest. The glory of a nation can only be maintained by perpetuating, uncorrupted, the principles by which it was acquired."[3]

For Graves, America's most dangerous ideological enemies were Catholic hierarchicalism and German Rationalism. He viewed the latter as worming its way into American theological schools and churches "to effect within what it has found impossible to effect from without—to corrupt her doctrines, and emasculate Christianity of its spirituality, and thus stab her through the heart." Against these foes, he admonished, "every Christian and American citizen will be compelled to take sides, or be considered an enemy to religion and republicanism...."[4]

Through Graves' influence this public theology, along with his controversialist style, became a characteristic of Protestants in the Southern Crossroads. As early as 1836, Texas' Declaration of Independence denounced Mexico for establishing a "national religion," and for being supported by a standing army and the priesthood, both being "the eternal enemies of civil liberty." As Protestant missionaries migrated with other southerners into East Texas, their churches clashed with those of their competitors as denominational strife surged even beyond that in the colonial period. The following year Baptist, Methodist, and Presbyterian ministers formed an "Ecclesiastical Committee of Vigilance for Texas" committed to exposing religious imposters. One of the first Baptist ministers in Texas, the Reverend Z. N. "Wildcat" Morrell, brought with him from western Tennessee doctrinal debates with the Campbellites, and the first Baptist congregation in the state was an anti-missionary church that opposed all human organizations. By 1848, when the Baptist General Association of Texas was formed, Landmark influence permeated the state's Baptists.

Landmark tendentiousness erupted into open battle on several occasions during the nineteenth century, two of which had Texas connections. In the early 1890s Samuel A. Hayden, editor of the *Texas Baptist*, advocated Landmark practices for the Baptist General Convention of Texas (BGCT) and competed with the *Texas Baptist Standard*. After a number of lawsuits designed to regain Hayden a voice at convention meetings (most settled out of court), Hayden's followers left the BGCT in 1899 to form the Baptist Missionary Association. The most significant Landmark controversy involved the failure of the church historian William Whitsitt to teach the Landmark view of Baptist origins at the Southern Baptist Theological Seminary in Louisville, Kentucky, where he was president. Among his staunchest opponents was the Texas leader B. H. Carroll, who later founded Southwestern Seminary as a more conservative alternative to Southern. Whitsitt's foes eventually forced his resignation from the Louisville seminary.

Anti-mission and anti-Campbellite controversies also followed Baptist settlements in Arkansas. Arkansas Baptists who tangled with the Disciples of Christ considered Graves their most important leader, and upon its founding in 1848 the Arkansas Baptist Convention recommended Graves' newspaper as the "Journal of Arkansas Baptists," while a number of associations recommended that their churches fight Campbellism by developing Landmark libraries. By the end of the century, Arkansas politics was divided by the New South leadership of Governor James P. Eagle, a leader in the Arkansas Baptist Convention, and the populist (and also Baptist) leadership of attorney general, governor, and eventually U.S. Senator Jefferson Davis. Eagle led the educated, progressive element among Arkansas Baptists, while Davis represented backwoods Arkansans highly influenced by Landmark thought. An effort toward centralized missionary activity by the convention antagonized many who distrusted such efforts, favoring instead the work of individual congregations. In 1902, under the leadership of Ben Bogard, the Landmarkers formed their own American Baptist Association, which today numbers 527 congregations compared to 1,435 churches affiliated with the Arkansas Baptist State Convention.

Landmark views also marked the Baptists of Louisiana, where the *Tennessee Baptist* served for a number of years after 1869 as the state's official newspaper. One commentator after the Civil War wrote that Louisiana's Baptists were firm Landmarkers, "contending earnestly for one Lord, one Faith, one Baptism and the only true and evangelical church and ministry." Another commented that the churches in Louisiana "reject Campbellite and Pedobaptist immersions and would not commune with a church which would tolerate them."[5] Landmark influence among Baptists in Louisiana also spread through the influence of John T. Christian, for many years professor of church history at the New Orleans Baptist Seminary (originally called the Baptist Bible Institute).

Missouri and Oklahoma are similarly religiously conservative states, influenced by southerners who migrated there in their territorial eras. Missouri's first white settlers, who migrated mostly from the upper South—Kentucky, Tennessee, Virginia, and North Carolina—included large numbers of Baptists, Methodists, Presbyterians, and Disciples. In addition, the early twentieth century saw the rapid growth of the Assemblies of God churches, centering in and around Springfield. Independent Baptists have also grown to prominence in Missouri due to the influence of the Baptist Bible Fellowship. The Fellowship-sponsored Baptist Bible College (also in Springfield) is best known for its most famous alumnus, the Reverend Jerry Falwell.

Missouri Baptists, both Southern and Independent, are conservative and strongly influenced by Landmark ideology. Protestant denominations in Missouri have often divided over various issues, including concerns with Darwinism and liberal theology. Liberal-conservative tensions among Disciples led to a threefold division of Churches of Christ, Independent Christian churches, and the Christian Church (Disciples of Christ). Lutherans, Presbyterians, and Episcopalians in the state all experienced tensions in the nineteenth century over how fully to accommodate to modern culture. Those concerns remain a significant part of Protestantism in Missouri. Currently, white conservative Protestant congregations make up almost 73 percent of all religious congregations in the state, according to the North American Religion Atlas (NARA). It is thus no surprise that culture warrior and U.S. Attorney General John Ashcroft is a product of conservative Missouri Protestant culture.

Oklahoma, which became a state in 1907, has no nineteenth-century history. Nevertheless, having been settled by many emigrants from Texas, its Protestant churches share the theologically conservative sentiments of the rest of the region.

The influence of the nineteenth-century controversialists Alexander Campbell and J. R. Graves thus combined with the competitive and often harsh realities of the Southwestern frontier to create a region where contentious conservatism has few equals elsewhere in the United States. As modern America began to dawn, however, the contentious conservative Protestants of the Southern Crossroads joined their coreligionists in other regions to battle theological forces of a different nature. Defenders of denominational faiths who had squared off valiantly against each other in the nineteenth century came to share a more powerful enemy in twentieth-century modernity. This new Goliath was fearful enough to cause erstwhile opponents to make common cause, ignore their former, mostly doctrinal, differences, and take up their theological cudgels in a united front against a foe that threatened them all equally, and in their view threatened Christian civilization in America most of all.

Twentieth-Century Controversies

With precursors in the last 20 years of the nineteenth century, twentieth-century modernity created a warfare with certain American Protestants that continues to today's culture wars. Conservative Protestants in the Southern Crossroads joined with other religious conservatives across the nation to greet the arrival of "modern" America with varying degrees of suspicion. George Marsden and other scholars of fundamentalism have pointed to the years after World War I as a pivotal moment for Protestants fearful that German biblical criticism and sociological forces unleashed by the war might eat away at the foundations of "Christian America." Before the war, most American Protestants believed that America's strength came from its Christian (read Protestant) roots. The war hardened their reaction into a fundamentalist movement that saw German modernistic barbarism arrayed against America's Christian heritage.

The rising secularization of American culture, which began in the 1920s and accelerated rapidly after World War II and the rise of television, marked what some religious historians have called the "second disestablishment." This glacier-like process is in many ways still in progress, as conservative Protestants, recently allied with conservative Catholics, continue the effort to regain the dominance over American culture they once enjoyed. The "acids of modernity," as Martin Marty has often noted, created a "two party system" within American Protestantism, wherein all denominations were divided between factions open to modernity and those unalterably opposed to it. Anti-modernist Baptists, for example, had more in common with anti-modernist Methodists and Presbyterians than they did with pro-modernist Baptists. The Southern denominations, however, and especially those in the Southern Crossroads, were almost completely dominated by their anti-modernist parties. As the twentieth century unfolded, and as modernity and its corollary, pluralism, increasingly threatened them, Crossroads Protestants came to lead the fight against these twin enemies.

Dating from before the Civil War, the South has had a long history of combating the forces of change. In 1969 the historian Sheldon Hackney wrote that southerners are typically most conscious of their southernness "when they are defending their region against attack from outside forces: abolitionists, the Union Army, carpetbaggers, Wall Street and Pittsburgh, civil rights agitators, the federal government, feminism, socialism, trade-unionism, Darwinism, Communism, atheism, daylight-savings time, and other by-products of modernity."[6] Southern identity has often been equated with a need to protect a "peculiar institution" from external threats. The peculiarly southern institution needing protection in the nineteenth century may have been slavery, but for most twentieth-century Protestants in the Southern Crossroads region the institution needing preserving has been the "old-time religion."

One of the most influential twentieth-century crusaders in the Southern Crossroads was J. Frank Norris (1887-1952), the militant fundamentalist pastor of First Baptist Church in Fort Worth, Texas. While he mostly fought the as-yet miniscule theological liberalism in the SBC, in the 1920s Norris more generally assailed "this present godless, commercialized, pleasure-gone-mad, Sabbath-breaking, idol-worshipping, hell-bound age." Eventually leading his congregation out of the SBC, he later formed his own seminary and fellowship of independent Baptist churches, of which the Baptist Bible Fellowship (Springfield, Missouri) is a part. His most recent biographer, Barry Hankins, has correctly argued that Norris viewed himself as the leader of "the southern theater in a national war on modernism." Ahead of his time in seeing the threat of pluralism to Protestant dominance in the South, Norris believed the South was theologically purer and less pluralistic than the North. He thus hoped to "preserve and defend the South" from the encroachments of northern modernism. By preserving the South, Norris believed the nation as a whole might be salvaged. According to the political scientist Oran P. Smith, Norris thus foreshadowed the "militant, individualistic, Texas brand of fundamentalism" that later in the century would come to dominate the "traditionalistic SBC."[7]

Like the denominational debates of the nineteenth century, these controversies over modernism may appear to be arcane, internecine theological disputes with little connection to public issues of the current culture wars. This view is a fatal error because it overlooks the way crusaders from J. R. Graves to J. Frank Norris saw theological orthodoxy as imperative for the survival not only of their denominations, but also of the entire nation as well. Even when denominational spokesmen engaged in doctrinal debates with other denominational leaders, their sectarian debates were built on a historical interpretation of the United States as a Christian nation and a deep belief that a truly Christian America could survive intact only by remaining theologically true to those roots.

Thus, to take an example from the 1920s, although seemingly a mere churchly debate over the proper interpretation of Genesis, the evolution controversy boiled over and out of strictly ecclesiastical debates into the state legislatures. Antievolution bills introduced in Maine, New Hampshire, Delaware, Missouri, Minnesota, North Dakota, and California did not win approval in a single legislative house. In the South and Southwest, however, such bills were taken up often during the 1920s: once in Arkansas, Mississippi, and Louisiana; twice in Alabama, Georgia, Kentucky, North Carolina, Oklahoma, and Tennessee; and three times in South Carolina, Florida, and Texas. In 1923 the Texas House of Representatives voted 71 to 34 to outlaw teaching "that man evolved from an ape" in public schools.

When the bill, which was approved by a senate committee, was never brought to a vote on the floor, the house passed a resolution 81-9 that teaching Darwinism in the public schools was "improper and subversive." In 1927, when the Arkansas state legislature failed to pass an anti-evolution law, the Landmark Baptist pastor Ben Bogard led an effort to pass such a law by initiative and referendum. The initiative drafted by the Bogard forces proposed to outlaw evolution in the public schools along with the use of any textbooks that propounded it. When Arkansans voted the measure into law by a majority of 108,991 to 63,406, the state superintendent of instruction interpreted the statute to outlaw the use in school libraries of the *Encyclopedia Britannica*, the *World Book Encyclopedia*, and *Webster's International Dictionary*.

In the 1930s and 1940s Northern fundamentalists also began to build networks in the South through Bible prophecy conferences stressing premillennialism and the development of Bible schools modeled after Chicago's Moody Bible Institute. The historian William R. Glass argues that the South (and especially the Southwest) provided Northern fundamentalists a region where their conservative interpretations of Christianity and of the United States still dominated the culture. Fighting modernism in their region but nonetheless losing control of their denominational institutions, Northern fundamentalists began to create in the South new institutions to replace those they had lost to denominational modernists. Finding such fertile ground in the Southern Crossroads region, this wing of fundamentalism established an influential beachhead at Dallas Theological Seminary.

The school was founded in 1924 by Lewis Sperry Chafer, a Congregationalist minister who had previously taught and raised money for the Moody schools in Northfield, Massachusetts. His travels led him to cross paths with Cyrus I. Scofield, famous for popularizing dispensational premillennialism through his publication of the Scofield Reference Bible. Eventually becoming the pastor of the Scofield Memorial Church in Dallas, Chafer was inspired to found a seminary independent of any denominational control. Since he believed denominational seminaries were becoming increasingly influenced by modernism, he envisaged a school where future pastors would be trained in biblical exposition, dispensationalism, and other forms of fundamentalist apologetics. Chafer led the seminary from its beginnings until 1952, followed by John Walwoord, who led the school for 34 years. During the tenures of its first two presidents, Dallas Seminary became a central piece of the fundamentalist movement in the South. Today, 40 percent of its graduates who work in Christian vocations serve within the Southern Crossroads region. Schools like Dallas helped create a fundamentalist constituency in the South for their movement, which wages culture war by arguing for the Christian origins of the United States and for its viewpoints in American public life.

The period after World War II, and particularly the tumult of the 1960s, exacerbated Protestantism's uneasiness with the secularizing tendencies of the now postmodern America. Morton Sosna believed the post World War II South was "an arena where the forces of good and evil, progress and reaction, rapid change and seemingly timeless continuity were about to engage in a battle of near mythological proportions." In the mid-1960s, the sociologist Alvin Bertrand saw the rural South in a long-term "confrontation with mass society," which he predicted would last another quarter century.[8] Both predictions have been fulfilled, as the South has, according to Nancy Ammerman, become 50 percent less rural between 1941 and 1981 (63.3 percent in 1940 to 33.1 percent in 1981). In the same period members of Southern Baptist churches have gone from 62.1 percent living in rural areas to 25.3 percent rural.

Their cultural hegemony challenged early in the century, by 1950 conservative Protestants still saw enough of America's Christian heritage to continue thinking of their country as an American Zion. The 1960s and '70s, however, brought racial, religious, and cultural pluralism to the South in ways that challenged the region's traditionalists as never before. After *Brown v. Board of Education* eventually put African Americans into the South's white public schools, after *Engle v. Vitale* took ritual prayers (and, according to conservatives, God) out of the public schools, and after *Roe v. Wade* made abortions legal, conservative Protestants began to feel they no longer were part of a backslidden American Zion, but had been turned into aliens in an anti-Christian Babylon. Advancing this interpretation, Barry Hankins has recently argued that deeper changes in post-World War II America had begun, at long last, to infect even the formerly pure South with diversity, pluralism, and secularism. In response, conservative Protestants, especially in the Southern Crossroads, began to mobilize politically. For fundamentalists in the Southern Baptist Convention, this meant launching an effort to gain control of the denomination. For the Churches of Christ, it meant modifying their tradition of "nondenominationalism," to join with other conservative Protestants to do battle with a more fearful common enemy.

As in previous discussions of Restorationism, the historian Richard T. Hughes clarifies this situation among the Restorationist/Primitivist churches, a tradition into which he lumps both the Churches of Christ and the Disciples of Christ. While this "denominational" tradition is small in numbers compared to Southern Baptists or mainline Protestants, it combines with the Landmark Baptist tradition to be very influential in the Southern Crossroads, where it is stronger than in any other region of the country. Throughout the nineteenth century the Churches of Christ continued to maintain the sectarian insistence that it wasn't a denomination. Criticism often rained down upon Church of Christ members who referred to "*other* denominations."

Though theologically conservative, the Churches of Christ also maintained a sectarian pacifist strand of thought. Beginning after World War I, however, Church of Christ spokesmen came to share Protestant fundamentalism's fear and loathing of German biblical criticism and evolution, viewing German culture as a threat to the Christian foundations of the United States. Losing much of its sectarianism, the Churches of Christ became more like the "other denominations" in interpretations of both itself and the nation. "If the heresies," Hughes explains, "that separated America from the rule of God were foreign rather than domestic, then was it not reasonable to infer that America, in its essence, was a clear manifestation of the kingdom of God?"[9]

This trend continued into the 1980s, when in reaction to the secularizing changes of the 1960s Church of Christ leaders strengthened their political alliance with fundamentalism and the Religious Right. Hughes cites a survey of Church of Christ ministers by an Abilene Christian University sociologist. This research found 76 percent of these ministers identified themselves as political conservatives, compared to only 5 percent who saw themselves as liberals. Seventy-four percent identified with the Republican Party, while not one minister identified himself as a "strong Democrat." Ninety-five percent voted for Ronald Reagan in the 1984 presidential election, and 82 percent agreed or strongly agreed that "it would be hard to be both a true Christian and a political liberal." A large majority of these ministers agreed with the agenda of the Religious Right, although they remained reluctant to participate in religio-political organizations.

Church of Christ culture warriors have more recently overcome this reluctance. Kenneth Starr, the Religious Right's hero of the Clinton impeachment, sponsors a series of ultra-conservative speakers at his alma mater, Harding College in Searcy, Arkansas. Sometimes dubbed the "Vatican of the Church of Christ," Searcy in 2001 managed to drive the Books-A-Million bookstore chain out of the city for selling gay-affirming literature.

There is little question that one of the most important controversies of the late twentieth century, and one that would have been impossible without important players in the Southern Crossroads, was the fundamentalist takeover of the Southern Baptist Convention. Much scholarly analysis has already provided useful narratives and explanations of this controversy, making unnecessary any major reinterpretation here. Instead, this discussion highlights the crucial role played by the Southern Crossroads in the SBC takeover. From the late nineteenth century the advent of biblical criticism at the Southern Baptist Theological Seminary (SBTS) in Louisville, Kentucky, created concerns in some quarters about liberalism. The founding of Southwestern Baptist Seminary in Fort Worth, led by B. H. Carroll with the assistance of J. Frank Norris, was related to doctrinal concerns about the instruction at Southern.

In the 1920s, the SBC faced controversy over evolution, but moderate leaders like SBTS president Edgar Y. Mullins managed to steer the denomination away from a full embrace of Norris' fundamentalist demands. Mullins could accomplish this partly because of his political savvy and partly because the convention and SBTS, both shaped by the conservative but not fundamentalist South, had too little real modernism to be perceived as a credible threat. The SBC and its flagship seminary were *culturally* conservative, and although their theological pluralism would eventually grow to dangerous proportions, in the 1920s the danger was only potential. Their basic conservatism made Norris's accusations look wildly irresponsible, and his viewpoint was temporarily discredited.

During the three decades after 1930 Norris's followers bided their time, surviving the Depression and another world war, building their megachurches and other fundamentalist institutions while awaiting new leaders and catalyzing events. There were minor leaders of this fundamentalist discontent during this period, like E. P. Alldredge, director of the SBC's department of Survey, Statistics, and Information, but no major events to galvanize the disgruntled into a movement until the 1961 Elliott controversy, in which the Southern Crossroads played a particularly significant role.

In the meantime, less visible developments gave greater power to the Southern Crossroads in SBC affairs. By the 1950s annual meetings of the SBC had grown too large to be held in churches, and only the largest American cities had arenas large enough to accommodate the meetings. Before 1950 conventions never met outside the traditional SBC territory, but since that time conventions have met in expansion areas almost 30 percent of the time. In those meetings, Southern Baptists' "pioneer areas" have generally created more conservative annual meetings. In addition, Landmarkism enjoyed a resurgence as Southern Baptists moved into the Far West. In these pioneer areas Southern Baptist evangelistic efforts were aided by the Landmark view that only Baptist churches were truly orthodox. These pioneer areas played a central role in the Elliott controversy.

Ralph Elliott, a young Old Testament professor at the SBC's new Midwestern Theological Seminary in Kansas City, Missouri, came under fire when the SBC's Broadman Press published his book, *The Message of Genesis*. The conservative

Missouri pastors W. Ross Edwards and Mack R. Douglas; a Houston lawyer named Paul Pressler; Jack L. Gritz, editor of the [Oklahoma] *Baptist Messenge*; and K. Owen White, pastor of the First Baptist Church of Houston, Texas, led efforts to have Elliott fired and Broadman Press cease publication of Elliott's book. When Elliott sought another publisher for it against the wishes of the seminary trustees, the seminary dismissed him for insubordination.[10]

In the wake of the Elliott controversy, the historian Samuel S. Hill's 1963 analysis of the Southern Baptist Convention proved prescient as he underscored the importance of what we are calling the Southern Crossroads region. Pointing to "a new ultraconservative power bloc" in the southwest, Hill detected the formation of a coalition of Baptists in the southwestern states and the "frontier states" of Kentucky, Tennessee, Illinois, and Missouri. Such a coalition, combining the self-assurance and drive of the southwestern Baptists with the Landmarkism of their frontier brethren, would, according to Hill, be characterized by exclusivism, aggressiveness, and emotional persuasiveness. Hill then speculated that the moderate faction might solidify its tenuous hold on the denomination "if the conservative coming-to-power can be forestalled for 15 or 20 years."[11]

Hill's predictions could hardly have been more accurate, as exactly 16 years later the Texans Paul Pressler and Paige Patterson launched their plan to elect a succession of inerrantist SBC presidents, who in turn would appoint only inerrantists to denominational leadership positions. The fundamentalist uber-pastor W. A. Criswell (First Baptist Church, Dallas, Texas) began his pastor's conference sermon and the takeover crusade itself with his ringing endorsement of the political machinations designed to elect Adrian Rogers, pastor of Memphis's Bellevue Baptist Church, as SBC president. Beginning with Rogers' 1979 election, the fundamentalist cabal, largely but not completely dominated by players from the Southern Crossroads, gradually took control of the SBC. By 1990 moderate Southern Baptists had been marginalized and the SBC was firmly, apparently permanently, in the ultra-fundamentalist camp. Having re-established orthodoxy within the SBC, the fundamentalists were poised to enter the American culture wars "standing at Armageddon and battling for the Lord."

One might be tempted to find the roots of the crusade in Texas alone. Clearly, the Lone Star State has a disproportionate influence in the region and in the larger SBC. Many of the key figures in the takeover were Texans. As Harold Bloom has noted, many of them embody the dogmatism and triumphalism of precursors like Graves and Norris. Clearly, the political leadership of Pressler and Patterson, the spiritual leadership of W. A. Criswell, and the strategic leadership of many prominent Baptist Texans would lead Michael Lind to add the new SBC to his "made in Texas" category. The example of the aforementioned "big three" led Jesse Fletcher, author of the SBC's 1995 sesquicentennial history, to "give credence to the view that Texas was the seedbed" of the SBC takeover. Even Pressler's autobiography seems to bear this out. He wrote, "As I traveled throughout the spring of 1979, I compiled a list of people who were interested in our concerns. Most of them lived in Texas." Table 2.1 demonstrates the disproportionate influence the Southern Crossroads region, especially Texas, has on the Southern Baptist Convention, as demonstrated by the percentage of the time a Texan has held the presidency of that organization.

All in all, these trends suggest that Texan and Southern Crossroads power in the SBC grew significantly in the twentieth century, especially the second half. Perhaps the safest conclusion to draw is that although there would probably have been no successful movement without its Texas leadership, the SBC fundamentalists' movement can more accurately be called a phenomenon of the Southern Crossroads.

Culture-War Battlefields

At the crossroads of the new millennium conservative Protestants, especially in the Southern Crossroads, have found participation in the Religious Right as an effective entrance into the culture wars. The close association between conservative Christians and the Republican Party has been well documented since the rise of the Moral Majority and the Christian Coalition in the 1980s. By 2002 John C. Green and Kimberly H. Conger had documented the degree to which state Republican parties across the nation had been influenced by the Christian Right. Interviewing 395 informants from all 50 states, Green and Conger showed that the Christian Right had gained influence in 15 states and declined in eight. Eighteen state Republican parties had strong Christian conservative contingents, the same number as in 1994, while those state parties in the moderate category grew from 13 in 1994 to twice that in 2000.

In the Southern Crossroads region the Texas and Oklahoma Republican parties had strong Christian Right factions in both 1994 and 2000, while Arkansas went from moderate to strong in the same period. Missouri remained in the weak category and Louisiana's Christian conservatives weakened from strong to moderate. Based upon these findings, it is possible to compare the overall strength of the Christian Right in each region. Ranking and averaging Green and Conger's judgments indicates that the Southern Crossroads is tied (2.6 out of 3.0) with the Pacific Northwest for first place in Christian Right influence of their state Republican parties. The South, Mountain West, and Midwest are tied (2.4) for third place, followed by the Pacific (2.0), Mid-Atlantic (1.5), and New England (1.2) regions. These comparisons again suggest the Southern Crossroads as a primary theater of the culture wars.[11]

Looking more closely at the Christian Coalition's efforts in the Southern Crossroads states where it is strongest, Green speculated in 2001 that the Texas

Table 2.1   SBC Presidents from Texas and the Southern Crossroads
2002 Annual of the Southern Baptist Convention, 458-60.

Presidents from Texas

1845-1900:	0 percent of the time
1901-1949:	16 percent of the time
1950-1978:	25 percent of the time
1979-2003:	32 percent of the time

Presidents from the Southern Crossroads (including Texas)

1845-1900:	0 percent of the time
1901-1949:	44 percent of the time
1950-1978:	71 percent of the time
1979-2003:	77 percent of the time

Christian Coalition (TCC) was probably the strongest of six or eight southern and western state organizations, partly because of its connections with President Bush and then-House Majority Whip Tom DeLay. The TCC wields powerful influence within the state Republican Party, which in turn "controls virtually the entire state political establishment." While nationally the Christian Coalition slipped in its influence, largely because of the departure of Ralph Reed as director, the TCC has fared much better. Although in 2001 it failed to block passage of a hate crimes bill, which it opposed because of its perceived "special protections for homosexuals," and could not gain approval for the Defense of Marriage Act that would have banned same-sex marriages, the TCC nonetheless has used its influence with the state board of education to oppose sex education and textbooks teaching evolution or multiculturalism. Most importantly, while still working to expand its appeal to the growing Latino and minority population of Texas, the TCC-influenced Republicans hold every statewide elected office and control the state senate. "Those who predicted the Christian Coalition would no longer be a power don't live in Texas," noted Charlotte Coffelt of the Houston chapter of American United for the Separation of Church and State in a *Fort Worth Star-Telegram* article on Christian Coalition strength. By January 2003, for the first time since Reconstruction, Republicans had gained control of the top three political offices in the state (governor, lieutenant governor, and house speaker), and were poised to push their agenda more successfully.

In 2000 the Oklahoma state legislature was awash in controversy when a number of Republican house members sparked skirmishes over several culture war issues, seeking to protect the people of the state against the "encroachment from a secular world that they believe controls too much of their lives." Representative Bill Graves, who authored a bill allowing voluntary school prayer, argued that "I don't think we ought to exclude God and his laws from government." Another house member, Jim Reese, sponsored a bill requiring that state science books acknowledge "that human life was created by one God of the universe." Graves also supported the anti-evolution measure, arguing that its opponents "want evolution taught as fact. By teaching that you're actually trampling on people's religious beliefs."

In addition, with the support of the Oklahoma Christian Coalition, Graves and his colleagues introduced measures requiring public buildings to display the Ten Commandments. Representative Tim Pope agreed with the bill, opining that the First Amendment was intended to keep government out of religion, not vice versa. "Not only have we demoralized our citizenry by taking any mention of God out of our schools," Pope said, "we've created an immoral society because we've taken morality out of our schools." Democratic state senator Bernest Cain, however, objected to Republican efforts to promote religion in a multicultural society. Defending his own religious convictions, Cain told reporters he resented having others' religion pushed on him. "Lawmakers," he said, "should be less interested in promoting a particular religion than in prohibiting barriers to religious freedom," he told the *Tulsa World*. Willing to grant freedom while wishing to favor Christianity, Graves replied, "If somebody wants to be a Muslim, they can do that. But that doesn't mean we have to downgrade Christianity."

Later that year, the Oklahoma Christian Coalition (OCC) influenced the outcome of a state senate race when its voter guide implied that Democratic state senator Lewis Long supported the legalization of sodomy and bestiality. A 12-year incumbent, Long lost the election by 265 votes to first-time Republican candidate Nancy Riley. A week after the election Long's attorneys filed a libel suit against the OCC, charging the organization with "actual malice," with knowledge that their charges were untrue. Long had voted at least twice *against* bills that proposed to drop anti-sodomy and anti-bestiality language from state laws. The previous year saw state senator David Herbert bring a similar libel suit against the OCC for negative statements in their 1998 voter guide. Herbert eventually lost his case when the Oklahoma Supreme Court agreed with the district court that the senator had not proved actual malice. Undeterred by the outcome of the Herbert case, Long proceeded with his suit, even using campaign funds to pay for his efforts. For its part, the OCC issued an apology, acknowledging that its statements regarding Long were mistaken. In February 2003 the Tulsa County District Court found in favor of the OCC, and on the following July 18, the Oklahoma Supreme Court affirmed the lower court ruling as it did in the Herbert case.

For its part, Arkansas seems in recent years to be the national headquarters for Southern Baptist pastors going into secular politics. Between 1996 and 2002, two former ministers, Mike Huckabee and Tim Hutchinson, both fundamentalists involved with the Christian Right, served the state as governor and U.S. senator respectively. This is unusual in that, while many Southern Baptist laypersons serve in elective office, few ministers do so. Traditionally both the Baptist insistence on separation of church and state and the preference of particular congregations made even socially conscious pastors reluctant to enter elective politics. By the late twentieth century, the emergence of the Religious Right and the high-profile 1984 and 1988 presidential candidacies of the Reverends Jesse Jackson and Pat Robertson opened doors into politics that had in earlier years been closed.

Mike Huckabee had left Southwestern Seminary without graduating to take a job directing the television ministry of Fort Worth, Texas, evangelist James Robison. In 1980 Robison helped launch the Religious Right into the national limelight by spearheading a national affairs briefing of the Religious Roundtable. It was Robison who suggested the famous line in which Ronald Reagan won over Christian conservatives by saying, "I know this is non-partisan, so you can't endorse me, but I want you to know that I endorse you." Later Huckabee became a pastor in Texarkana, Arkansas, and at one time president of the Arkansas Baptist State Convention.

As governor, Huckabee's strategy has been to provide a counter-example to that set by his fellow Arkansan, Bill Clinton. As president and first lady, Bill and Hillary Clinton became lightning rods for the Christian Right's culture war, and Huckabee has availed himself of many opportunities to criticize them. In 1997, speaking at the Southern Baptist Theological Seminary, Huckabee took a swipe at Mrs. Clinton's views on raising children. "I quite frankly, in all due respect," the governor asserted, "don't believe that it takes a village to raise a child after all, but takes the character found in mothers and fathers who pass that character on to the children nurtured by the community values, by a church where values are undergirded rather than uprooted." Later that year, a few months before the White House became embroiled in the Monica Lewinsky scandal amid conservative assaults on Clinton's character, Southern Baptist Convention's publishing house, Broadman/Holman, brought out Huckabee's book, *Character Is the Issue.*

Although he was re-elected in 2002, Huckabee's performance has been strongly criticized by some Arkansans for stonewalling on requests that he reveal a full list of his financial contributors; his penchant for secrecy also attracts critics. Some critics who are familiar with Baptist ways, like the former Little Rock pastor Fred H. Findley, liken his administrative style to fundamentalist ministers who often wield virtually dictatorial power over their congregations. In addition, Huckabee has occasionally been burned by the appointment of a former religious associate to a state agency, often with little experience in the area he or she was to direct. For example, he influenced the appointment of Diane O'Connell as the director of the Division of Children and Family Services. O'Connell had no background or experience in social work, but had made a name for herself in Baptist churches for having arisen from a troubled background. She had attended the same church and seminary as Huckabee, earning the Master of Divinity degree, and had served as director of the Baptist Student Union at the University of Arkansas at Little Rock for 11 years. Announcing her appointment, the department's spokesman, Joe Quinn, acknowledged her lack of social work expertise but praised her "management background" and "sense of compassion." Twenty months later, with her department suffering from a $1.6 million budget deficit, O'Connell resigned.

Also a former Baptist minister, Tim Hutchinson represented Arkansas in the U.S. senate for one term. Hailing from a farm in northwest Arkansas, he has his roots in the ultra-right wing, Texas-influenced section of the state that is also fertile ground for the Landmark churches of the American Baptist Association. According to Tony Woodell, past president of a moderate group called Arkansas Baptists Committed, northwest Arkansas is both the fastest-growing section of the state, influenced by Wal-Mart and Tyson Industries, and the heart of the Christian Right in the state. During Hutchinson's college days, he left Arkansas to attend Bob Jones University. Entering the Senate in 1996, he was a key voice calling for Bill Clinton's impeachment. He later divorced his wife of 29 years and married one of his assistants. Hurt by the scandal in his 2002 re-election campaign, the candidate of "family values" was defeated by Mark Pryor, son of the former senator David Pryor. Currently, Hutchinson serves as a spokesman for an organization known as Family Life America and God (FLAG).

Of course, the culture war is fought on battlefields of denominational as well as secular politics. The United Methodist Church (UMC), like most mainline Protestants denominations, has found itself for the last 30 years in the middle of a culture war zone. Several movements within United Methodist have developed to foster conservative theological and moral positions within the denomination. First among these is Good News, an organization advocating "reformation and renewal" within the UMC. Begun in 1967, the group continues to be organized around *Good News Magazine,* published by James Heidinger III. In 1968 the magazine published a scathing critique of the UMC's adult Sunday school curriculum, which was held to be bereft of biblical theology and the message of spiritual rebirth. Readers of the magazine rallied themselves to action in a 1970 national convocation in Dallas. The UMC's 1974 doctrinal statement on "theological pluralism" sparked more criticism from the Good News faction, particularly a blistering address by the Texas evangelist Ed Robb, Jr. and a task force that prepared a statement calling for "Scriptural Christianity" in the denomination.

While *Good News* is strongly Midwestern in orientation, there is also a strong southern flavor to its activities and personnel. According to the magazine's Web site (www.goodnewsmag.org), although 12 Midwesterners make up 35 percent of the magazine's board of directors, the South and Southern Crossroads combined hold 16 (47 percent) board seats. In 2001, in a move partly indicative of the Southwestern flavor of the movement, *Good News Magazine* named President George W. Bush its "Layman of the Year." In doing so, Good News not only honored the UMC's most politically prominent member, but also contrasted the president with the Methodist Board of Church and Society, Council of Bishops, and the Women's Division, all of whom the magazine said gave "a skewed view" of how most Methodists felt about the September 11 attacks. In contrast, said Good News president James Heidinger, "President Bush represents the mainstream of United Methodism—and indeed historic Christianity—in a way that many denominational leaders do not."

Even in more official circles, some have argued that the Southern jurisdictions wield disproportionate power in the UMC. In November 2000, the pastor Keith Pohl wrote a two-part commentary in the *Michigan Christian Advocate* complaining that the Southeastern and South Central jurisdictions "now hold enough delegates to sway the General Conference to their agendas." The combined membership of the two Southern jurisdictions is more than the total of the other three combined. He also noted that six of the 10 legislative committees had chairpersons from the Southern parts of the UMC. Membership of the church's Judicial Council included one Westerner, one non-American, three from the Southeast, three from the South Central, but no members from the Northeast. Further, a motion to mandate at least one member from each of the five jurisdictions was defeated. Several months earlier the 2000 General Conference changed the formula determining the allocation of delegates to each annual conference. Pohl contended that the new legislation would strengthen what he called the "southern captivity" of the UMC. He concluded his complaints by noting that his experience had taught him that, apart from their theology of baptism, Methodists in the South have "more in common with the Southern Baptists than with United Methodists in the North."

Whether or not the Southern jurisdictions really do constitute a "captivity" of the UMC, there is no doubt that Good News continues to work privately to help elect traditionalists to UMC positions. In particular, Good News has allied itself with the "Confessing" movement to halt what it views as the church's drive toward tolerance of abortion and homosexuality. Like the other mainline denominations, every quadrennial General Conference of the UMC since 1972 has struggled with the church's position on homosexuality.

As for the denominational culture wars among Southern Baptists, the fundamentalist takeover has now spread to the state conventions, especially in the Southern Crossroads region. Most of these conventions are now controlled by the conservative or fundamentalist factions in those states. In evenly divided Arkansas, fundamentalists were able to elect one of their own as state president by only seven votes in 1999. They have continued to hold the presidency ever since. In 2000, after the SBC made another historic lurch to the theological right by amending its Baptist Faith and Message (BF&M), Arkansas fundamentalist Baptists pushed the convention to follow the SBC's doctrinal example. Fundamentalists were unable to muster the two-thirds vote necessary to change the convention constitution and adopt the 2000 BF&M as its own doctrinal statement. The following year, however, the conservatives did manage to make the change, significant because the 2000 BF&M eliminated language that made Christ rather than the Bible itself the focus of divine revelation. With regard to public issues, Arkansas Baptists passed resolutions condemning the "anti-Christian" and "pro-witchcraft" materials in the Harry Potter books. The Southern Baptists of Arkansas are thus now firmly in the fundamentalist camp, with little chance of reversing that trend in the near future.

Other than in Texas, which has provided as many moderate as fundamentalist leaders, all of the state Baptist conventions of the Southern Crossroads have now come under the control of the Christian Right. In the 1980s Louisiana fundamentalists, led by Ron Herrod, then a New Orleans-area pastor, assailed Louisiana College for allowing rock music groups on campus, for allowing Mormons to hold meetings, for allowing Catholics on the faculty, and for giving an honorary doctorate to an Episcopalian who imbibed alcohol. Eventually the school's president promised to develop new policies on alcohol and honorary degrees. Like the SBC, the Louisiana Convention fell victim to biennial contests over the election of its president. In 1997 and 1998 fundamentalist and moderate factions agreed to support consensus candidates, but the following year a fundamentalist candidate was elected. Since then the convention has stayed under fundamentalist control.

Missouri Baptists have been inundated with controversy over the political activities of the right-wing activist and leader of the Missouri Baptist Laymen's Association, Roger Moran. The organization is known for using guilt-by-association tactics against its opponents. For example, Moran sounded an alarm among Texas Baptists by implying that David Currie, president of Texas Baptists Committed, has dangerous views because he sits on the board of Interfaith Alliance with pro-gay-rights advocates. Answering Moran's charges, Currie said that in his four years of attending Interfaith Alliance meetings, homosexuality had never been mentioned. Moran also led a political effort called Project 1000, which is credited with helping conservative candidates win the Missouri Baptist Convention presidency. In these capacities, he has led efforts to induce the convention to stop funding the liberal organization Americans United for Separation of Church and State.

His main complaint against Americans United is the views of its director, Barry Lynn, on homosexuality and abortion. In 2000 Moran's group supported the distribution of some 200,000 voter guides by the Missouri Pastor Council to some 1,500 churches on the Sunday before the election. Critics charged the guides with distorting the records of Al Gore and the deceased senatorial candidate Mel Carnahan. In a related issue, some members of the Missouri convention objected to a resolution sending sympathy to Carnahan's widow. The late governor, argued some opponents of the resolution, deserved no such sympathy because he was a "baby murderer." At the same time, for the third consecutive year, another Project 1000-backed conservative was elected as convention president.

In 1999 and 2000 the Southern Baptists in Oklahoma bypassed any major controversy, largely because of solid support for the rightward turn of the SBC. After the SBC added to the BF&M a controversial article on the family that asked women to "graciously submit" to their husbands' authority, the Oklahoma convention endorsed the new article of faith. The following year, Oklahoma directors of missions endorsed the new BF&M and encouraged local churches to do likewise.

Beginning in 1994, Baptist moderates thwarted fundamentalist efforts to duplicate in the Baptist General Convention of Texas (BGCT) what they had accomplished in the SBC. Failing to stop the BGCT from allowing congregations to contribute financially to the Cooperative Baptist Fellowship, 400 dissident fundamentalist Baptists, led by Miles Seaborn, created a new organization called Southern Baptist Conservatives of Texas (SBCT) on November 20, 1997. Key issues separating the two Texas conventions are the BGCT's disapproval of the fundamentalist takeover of the SBC, biblical inerrancy, women's ordination, and homosexuality. By their second official annual meeting in 1999, the SBCT endorsed the new "family" article in the BF&M. Richard Land, director of the SBC's Ethics and Religious Liberty Commission, referred to the group as the "real Texas Baptists," adding, "I cannot have fellowship with those who do not believe the Bible is the inerrant word of God...who believe in culture over conviction...who believe it's alright to murder babies in the womb." In addition, the group adopted resolutions against abortion and euthanasia, and in favor of student prayers at sporting events, and the posting of the Ten Commandments in public buildings. As the SBCT continues to travel the trail blazed by the SBC, there is little doubt that these culture warriors will continue to cross swords with both secularized American culture and with their separated Baptist brethren in the Lone Star State.

The culture war will thus continue to rage for some time at the Southern Crossroads, as well as across the nation. There are, of course, many social issues that make up the key ideological battlefields of this conflict. Among these are abortion, school vouchers, prayer in the public schools, and support for the nation's current war on terrorism. One issue, however, towers above the others as the venue for the bloodiest battles and the fiercest fighting of the culture wars: the related issues of homosexuality, same-sex marriage, and "the gay agenda."

As the region and the nation approached the 2004 presidential election the culture wars were destined to continue between the red (pro-Republican) and the blue (pro-Democratic) states. Significantly, a Texan was running for re-election, with the Religious Right or the "Crossroads Evangelical Establishment" as his base. The lynchpin of his efforts to shore up his base was an appeal to the most volatile and most symbolic issue of the culture wars—a proposed constitutional ban defining marriage as between one man and one woman. With a war on terrorism abroad and a culture war at home, it was no wonder that the man from Crawford, Texas considered himself a "war president." Don't be surprised if his campaign speeches borrow a line from an earlier "cowboy president," Teddy Roosevelt: "We stand at Armageddon and we battle for the Lord."

Endnotes

1. J. R. Graves, *The Watchman's Reply* (Nashville: Tennessee Publication Society, 1853), 20, 60.

2. James E. Tull, *High Church in the South: The Origin, Nature, and Influence of Landmarkism* (Macon, GA: Mercer University Press, 2001), 10-12.

3. Graves, *Watchman's Reply,* 14-15.

4. Ibid., 54, 59-60.

5. Quoted in Penrose St. Amant, "Louisiana," in Samuel S. Hill, *Religion in the Southern States* (Macon: Mercer University Press, 1983), 123-145.

6. Sheldon Hackney, "Southern Violence," *American Historical Review* 74 (1969); 924-25.

7. Kenneth K. Bailey, *Southern White Protestantism in the Twentieth Century* (Gloucester, MA: Peter Smith Reprint, 1968), 45; Allyn Russell, *Voices of American Fundamentalism: Seven Biographical Studies* (Philadelphia: Westminster Press, 1976), 39-40; Barry Hankins, *God's Rascal: J. Frank Norris and the Beginnings of Southern Fundamentalism* (Lexington, University Press of Kentucky, 1996), 3-4, 176; Oran P. Smith, *The Rise of Baptist Republicanism* (New York: New York University Press, 1997), 33-34.

8. Sosna quoted in James C. Cobb, *Redefining Southern Culture: Mind and Identity in the Modern South* (Athens: University of Georgia Press, 1999), 43; Alvin L. Bertrand, "The Emerging Rural South: A Region Under 'Confrontation' by Mass Society," *Rural Sociology* 31 (December 1966): 449-457.

9. Richard T. Hughes, *Reviving the Ancient Faith: The Story of the Churches of Christ in America* (Grand Rapids, Mich.:William B. Eerdmans Publishing Company, 1996), 252-253, 256-258.

10. Ralph H. Elliott, *The "Genesis Controversy" and Continuity in Southern Baptist Chaos: A Eulogy for a Great Tradition* (Macon: Mercer University Press, 1992); Bill J. Leonard, *Baptist Ways: A History* (Valley Forge: Judson Press, 2003), 414.

11. Kimberly H. Conger, John C. Green, "Spreading Out And Digging In: Christian Conservatives and State Republican Parties," *Campaigns and Elections* (February 2002), 18-21.

CHAPTER THREE

HOLINESS AND PENTECOSTAL TRADITIONS: MAKING THE SPIRIT COUNT

Jane Harris

If the Southern Crossroads is a latter-day Burned-Over District, then its prime representatives are the members of Holiness and Pentecostal congregations. In small chapels on country roads and massive megachurches on interstate highways, from television screens to the corridors of power, they have kept the fires of the Holy Spirit alive with a vigorous religiosity that has made their presence felt in the public life of the region and the nation.

In the 1980s, members of these intertwined religious families most familiar to Americans were controversial media celebrities: Oral Roberts, Jimmy Swaggart, Jim and Tammy Faye Bakker, and Pat Robertson. In the first years of the twenty-first century, the most prominent were U.S. Attorney General John Ashcroft; the African-American megachurch pastor and best-selling author T.D. Jakes; and James Dobson, head of Focus on the Family, the most influential national organization of the Christian Right. Other than Robertson and the Bakkers, they are all Crossroads natives, except for Jakes, who moved to the region in the early 1990s.

The Crossroads was where the Holiness tradition gave birth to Pentecostalism and where Pentecostalism established its strongest national presence, spreading its influence across the nation and around the globe. The fastest growing Christian movement in the world, Pentecostalism represents a highly consequential force on the American religious scene—from its worship style and use of mass media to its approach to politics. If the Crossroads is shaping the character of the new culture wars in America, then much of the responsibility belongs to Pentecostalism.

Today, the Pentecostal name covers a movement with as many as 100 million adherents around the world, including millions of Americans belonging to 300 different denominations, most of them tiny. Amidst the diversity, they share the conviction that conversion to Christianity needs to be followed by another life-transforming event known as baptism in the Holy Spirit. Such baptism typically emphasizes the spiritual gifts enumerated in the twelfth and fourteenth verses of Paul's First Letter to the Corinthians, and expresses the disciples' experience of the Holy Spirit described in Acts 2. These include prophecy and speaking in tongues—glossolalia—which from the beginning has made the largest impression on outsiders.

According to the folklorist Elaine J. Lawless, who grew up in southern Missouri where people (including her parents) talked about "Holy Rollers," attitudes toward Pentecostals "were rooted in ignorance and in discomfort about the noise that could be heard for miles on warm summer nights through the open doors and windows of the little Pentecostal churches, which seemed to appear overnight on the dirt roads between the cotton fields in that part of the country. There were many Pentecostal churches, both black and white, and they were feared and misunderstood more than hated."[1] Even today, as Pentecostals join the mainstream of American life, they continue to be widely viewed as unsettling religious curiosities.

Not that they cut a high institutional profile on the national stage. The largest predominantly white Pentecostal denomination, the Assemblies of God, counts about the same number of members—2.5 million—as the Episcopal Church, but attracts nothing like the same amount of attention. When the Assemblies' fiftieth General Council met in Washington, D.C. from July 31 to August 3 of 2003, the 30,000 delegates and non-voting participants were ignored by the news media. All the attention went to the seventy-fourth General Convention of the Episcopal Church USA, which met in Minneapolis at the same time with only a third as many attendees. To be sure, the Episcopalians were wrestling with the issue of their first openly gay bishop, while the Assemblies of God was merely concerned with parochial issues like church growth. But the only time in living memory that the denomination made national headlines was in 1988, when the denomination disciplined the flamboyant Jimmy Swaggart for sexual misconduct.

The Assemblies of God is based in the Crossroads state of Missouri (in Springfield), as are several other important denominations of the Holiness-Pentecostal families: the United Pentecostal Church (in Hazelwood), the Pentecostal Church of God (in Joplin), and the Church of the Nazarene (in Kansas City). And in Memphis, just across the Mississippi from the Crossroads state of Arkansas, is the headquarters of the Church of God in Christ, by far the largest predominantly African-American Pentecostal denomination.

Even in the Crossroads, however, Holiness and Pentecostal Christians constitute a relatively small minority. While nearly a quarter of all Americans who identify with the traditions live in the region, according to the American Religious

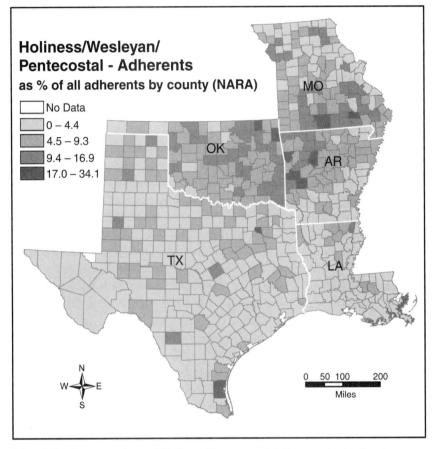

Map 3.1: *Concentrations of Holiness/Pentecostal Adherents in the Southern Crossroads*

Identification Survey (ARIS), this amounts to just 5.8 percent of the region's total population. Pentecostal Christians are most thickly distributed in a band running from southern Missouri down through northwest Arkansas and across eastern Oklahoma. (For a state-by-state and denomination-by-denomination account of Holiness and Pentecostal Christians in the Crossroads, see chapter 1 on the region's demography.)

According to the North American Religion Atlas (NARA), there is but a single Crossroads county where adherents to the Holiness-Pentecostal traditions constitute more than 15 percent of the population—Delaware County in far northeast Oklahoma. In Oklahoma the Church of the Nazarene, the largest Holiness denomination, is proportionately 10 times more populous than in the nation as a whole, but that amounts to only 1.2 percent of all Oklahomans.

Yet these religious families have had more impact on the outside world than their size might suggest. They might even be called the leaven in the lump of American evangelicalism.

Historical Background

The roots of the Holiness-Pentecostal tradition lie in Methodism—in the theology of John Wesley, Methodism's founder, whose doctrine of sanctification sparked the pursuit of Christian perfection that lies at the tradition's heart, and in the itinerant Methodist preachers who in the early nineteenth century established the frontier churches where Holiness took hold. For Methodists, the perfectionist ideal was not something to be pursued by a community of saints walled off from the secular world, but rather an impetus to change the world in its image. The great Protestant crusades of the nineteenth and early twentieth centuries—abolition of slavery, women's rights, and the suppression of alcohol—were an outgrowth of this reform imperative. The campaign for prohibition—what the historian Sydney Ahlstrom a generation ago called "the last great corporate work in America of legalistic evangelicalism"—received its most powerful support from the Methodist churches, which provided across-the-board institutional support and most of the militant leadership.[2]

The Holiness movement itself began in the 1830s in an attempt to revive within American Methodism the doctrine and practice of entire sanctification, which Wesley taught in the eighteenth century but which Methodism set aside as it rose to prominence as the leading Protestant denomination of the 1800s. In "Meetings for the Promotion of Holiness" in New York City, the Methodist laywomen (and sisters) Sarah Lankford and Phoebe Palmer articulated their belief that sanctification was available to all who intentionally consecrated everything to God and believed God's promises. Before the Civil War, the movement spread to other Northeast cities and was taken up by the revivalist Charles Finney, who taught that God commanded holiness and that Christian perfection is possible in this lifetime.

After the Civil War the promoters of Holiness harked back to the roots of American Methodism by reviving the practice of holding camp meetings. At the first such meeting, held in Vineland, New Jersey in July 1867, a Methodist minister named J. W. Horne proclaimed the heart of the Holiness message: "Sanctification is a progressive work, while entire sanctification is the work of but a moment. There is a moment in which the darkness forever ceases; there is a moment in which the dying Adam is dead and the new Adam is alive…there is a moment in which sanctification passes into entire sanctification."[3]

By the 1870s the National Camp Meeting Association for the Promotion of Holiness was advancing the movement into the Midwest, South, and Southwest. Meanwhile, Holiness prayer meetings (modeled after Phoebe Palmer's meetings) were organized in the United States and overseas. As the emphasis on Christian perfection spread—primarily but not exclusively among Methodist churches—controversies erupted within local congregations, causing some preachers sympathetic to Holiness to leave the Methodist church altogether and work independently in small, storefront churches.

In the 1890s, such devotees of Holiness began organizing themselves into formal denominations, and in 1908 the Church of the Nazarene was formed when several of these agreed to merge at a meeting in Pilot Point, Texas, just north of Dallas. In doctrine and practice the denomination to this day preserves its ties to Wesley, particularly in its belief in the sanctification of the believer as a second work of grace subsequent to regeneration or conversion; Nazarene leaders are required to attest to the experience of entire sanctification. Members believe in divine healing but never to the exclusion of medical intervention. The use of tobacco and alcoholic beverages is denounced. Today, the Church of the Nazarene is strongly represented through all the Crossroads states except Louisiana.

As for the camp meeting association, it turned into the umbrella organization for the entire Holiness movement. Changing its name first (in 1894) to the National Association for the Promotion of Holiness (or National Holiness Association) and ultimately to the Christian Holiness Partnership, from its headquarters in Clinton, Tennessee, it today promotes Holiness teaching and practice through 21 different Holiness denominations, three interdenominational missionary agencies, 48 colleges and seminaries, six Holiness publishing houses, and nearly 2,000 camp meetings.

Even as Holiness Christians began institutionalizing themselves, however, they were being swept up in a Pentecostal fervor, a sense of the intense presence of the Holy Spirit, which was breaking out in religious revivals across the nation. A number of early Holiness denominations (including the Church of the Nazarene) initially took the name "Pentecostal," and in many areas of the South Holiness churches came to be regarded as synonymous with Pentecostalism. Not surprisingly: There is evidence that the Holiness tradition played a significant role in these revivals, and in some cases whole Holiness congregations converted to one of the Pentecostal groups. By 1908 the major southern Holiness bodies were firmly in the Pentecostal camp; numerically, the future belonged to Pentecostalism. What might be called the "Greater Crossroads" was the seedbed of this new growth.

Perhaps the key figure in the early history of Pentecostalism was Charles Fox Parham (1873-1929), a sometime Methodist preacher and the founder of Bethel Bible College in Topeka, Kansas. Through his study of the New Testament—and particularly Acts 2:4—Parham became convinced that the apostolic gifts of the Holy Spirit were available to modern Christians. He envisioned the gift of tongues as an essential tool for world evangelism: The baptism of the Spirit would impart, so he thought, knowledge of languages one had not studied (technically known as zenoglossia).

The first supposed occasion of glossolalia occurred at Bethel Bible College in 1901, when Agnes N. Ozman is reported to have asked Parham to pray that she might receive the baptism of the Holy Spirit. Other students at Bethel Bible College had similar experiences over the following days, generating both positive and negative publicity about the phenomenon of tongues. Despite some successful revivals in Kansas and Missouri, Parham could not overcome obstacles—particularly the tragic death of his young son—and his Bible college closed.

He nonetheless continued his revival preaching and faith healing. In the first years of the twentieth century, lead and zinc mining brought an influx of immigrants to the area where Oklahoma, Missouri, and Kansas intersect. The inhabitants of the area responded favorably to Parham's revivals and his new "Apostolic Faith," which included a forswearing of medical care. But in October 1904 a 9-year-old girl, Nettie Smith, died after her father, under Parham's influence, relied upon "the Apostolic Faith method," and the community turned against Parham. Making his way to southeast Texas, where "white hot" Holiness revivals had paved the way for Pentecostalism, he spent three weeks in Orchard, a small community 45 miles west of Houston, then headed north to Missouri to preach and solicit help for a campaign in the Houston-Galveston area. Like his Missouri-Kansas-Oklahoma mission field, Houston-Galveston was undergoing a social and economic sea change—in this case thanks to the discovery of oil.

While Parham was preaching in Houston in the summer of 1905, an entire Holiness church converted to the new Pentecostal faith. By August, he was back in Kansas holding the first Pentecostal camp meeting. Then, returning with his family to the Houston area, he founded a 10-week Bible school to train leaders to spread the Pentecostal message throughout the world.

Among those who took the course was William J. Seymour, an African-American evangelist from Louisiana associated with the Evening Light Saints, a radical Wesleyan sect that espoused entire sanctification, faith healing, and the restoration of the gifts of the Spirit as a prelude to the Lord's return. A few months later, in January 1906, Seymour began a revival on Azusa Street in Los Angeles that lasted for the greater part of three years. According to the historian Grant Wacker, the Azusa meetings began to flourish when "neighboring Holiness missions started to force Pentecostal worshippers out of their midst."[4]

Although the initial group to receive Seymour was black, after only a week the revival meetings were thoroughly integrated, with native whites, blacks, Mexicans, Asians, and eastern Europeans all worshipping together. The Azusa revival has generally been called the catalyst for the entire Pentecostal movement but, as Wacker points out, Azusa appeared to ignite the flames of revival only because so many visitors to Azusa Street in 1906 and 1907 took the message back home with them to gatherings that were well prepared to come under the influence of emerging Pentecostalism.

The most important of these visitors was Charles Harrison Mason (1866-1961), a son of former slaves who had been born outside Memphis and spent his early years in Arkansas. Mason's religious roots were in the Missionary Baptist church, into which he was baptized by his brother in Plumerville, Arkansas, 45 miles northwest of Little Rock. Experiencing a call to preach, he received license to do so from the Mt. Gale Missionary Baptist Church in nearby Preston. He entered the Arkansas Baptist College in 1893, but after three months left because of theological differences, stating that there was "no salvation in the schools and colleges."

In 1895, a Baptist preacher named C. P. Jones of Jackson, Mississippi, entered Mason's life, and the two young men joined forces to conduct revivals in Baptist churches in the Mississippi Delta. Their emphasis upon the Holiness doctrine of entire sanctification prompted the local Baptist association to "disfellowship" them. Undeterred, they continued their revivals and established their first congregation in 1896 in Lexington, Mississippi. A year later, while walking down a street in Little Rock, Mason received an inspiration to call his nascent denomination the Church of God in Christ. From its formal inception in 1897, the Church of God in Christ emphasized Holiness teachings regarding sanctification, abstinence from tobacco and alcohol, modest dress, hard work, and financial responsibility, and developed a worship style involving exultant shouting and "spiritual dancing."

But it did not become explicitly Pentecostal until Mason experienced what was happening on Azusa Street. Hearing reports of the revival, he and several Church of God in Christ elders went to Los Angeles in March 1907, and while worshipping with the Azusa congregation he received the gift of tongues. When he brought the Pentecostal message back to his denomination, which now extended into Tennessee and Arkansas, not all leaders received it gladly, Jones foremost among them. Mason left the denomination, taking half the clergy and laity with him as well as—after a court battle—the denomination's name.

Jones went on to lead the Church of Christ (Holiness) U.S.A., which has remained a very small African-American denomination with approximately 25,000 members in 146 churches. Meanwhile, in 1907 a fully Pentecostalized Church of God in Christ proclaimed that the "full baptism in the Holy Spirit is evidenced by speaking in other tongues." Mason served as the denomination's spiritual and organizational leader until his death in 1961, building it into what may be the largest Pentecostal denomination in America. According to NARA estimates, the denomination (headquartered in Memphis) has 8.5 million members in more than 17,000 churches, which are governed by an episcopacy of diocesan bishops.[5]

Under Mason's principled leadership, the Church of God in Christ did a remarkable job of maintaining the Pentecostal movement's original opposition to barriers of class, gender, and race. The poorest sharecropper could become a preacher or even a bishop within the denomination. Although the denomination initially barred women from ordination, some "church mothers" like Mother Emma Cotton, pastor of a large congregation in Los Angeles, enjoyed a degree of ecclesiastical authority unknown in most other American denominations.

Extraordinarily for a religious body based in the South, the Church of God in Christ was for many years the most integrated denomination in America. Mason's charismatic personality and preaching attracted thousands of whites; in the years before World War I he ordained hundreds of white Pentecostal preachers. "Many denominations have made distinctions between their colored and white members," the denomination declared in its church manual during World War I. "The Church of God in Christ recognizes all its members have equal rights. Its Overseers, both colored and white, have equal power and authority in the church."[6] After the war, the denomination persisted in the fight to keep its interracial character, despite the pressures of life in the Jim Crow South as well as in the urban North, where Southern blacks took the church during the great migration. By the 1930s, however, the Church of God in Christ had become predominantly, though not exclusively, black.

In the meantime, white Pentecostals were increasingly likely to find their home in the Assemblies of God. In the first years of the twentieth century several different groups of Pentecostals, Parham's Apostolic Faith among them, had emerged with a shared understanding of sanctification (Baptism of the Holy Spirit) that rejected Wesley's notion that sanctification eradicated sin from the Christian's life. Instead, they described the trajectory of salvation as a movement from conversion (new birth) to baptism with the Spirit evidenced by tongues.

Beginning in 1912, these separate non-Wesleyan groups began to join together and, in late 1913, organizers ran advertisements in Pentecostal publications calling for a convention. It met in Hot Springs, Arkansas, a Pentecostal hot spot where evangelists Maria Woodworth-Etter and D.C.O. Opperman were holding revivals. In April 1914, a diverse group of 300 men and women convened in the old Grand Opera House on Central Avenue. According to the historian Edith Blumhofer, most of the Assemblies of God founders carried credentials with the Church of God in Christ, while C. H. Mason and his group were only nominally invited to participate in the Hot Springs meeting. He preached and his choir sang. Participants created a structure to conserve "the core of the Pentecostal message and to preserve the movement's sense of history and identity during a brief burst of evangelism that would culminate in Christ's soon return."[7]

Although the Hot Springs delegates may not have intended to start a new denomination, that's what they did. Delegates approved a Preamble and

Resolution of Constitution that declared that the participants were part of the "General Assembly of God." A statement of faith affirmed speaking in tongues, while stating that entire sanctification should be "earnestly pursued" as a "progressive" rather than an instantaneous experience.

This statement placed the Assemblies of God outside the Wesleyan fold. Possibly reflecting Baptist influence, the new denomination departed from the Wesleyan/Methodist roots of some early Pentecostals with the adoption of a congregational form of governance. Delegates also identified Bible and training institutes where Pentecostal ministers would be welcomed for theological education. By the fall of 1914, the Assemblies of God moved its headquarters from Arkansas, first to St. Louis and then to Springfield, Missouri, where today 1,000 employees direct the work of the denomination's churches throughout the United States and around the world.

Like the Church of God in Christ, the Assemblies of God accorded women a significant, if not equal, role in ministry. A resolution on women in ministry passed in Hot Springs in 1914 reflected the stance of the former Southern Baptist preacher Eudorus N. Bell, who led a Pentecostal congregation in Malvern, Arkansas, edited the monthly periodical *Word and Witness*, and preached frequently at camp meetings and conventions. Referring to women as "busybodies," Bell helped create the official position that women ministers "should be permanently attached to some mission and take up some regular and systematic work for the Lord under the proper oversight of some good brother whom God has placed in charge of the work." The General Council not only authorized the licensure of female evangelists and missionaries but also permitted female missionaries to perform baptisms, marriages, funerals, and communion when a man was not available. Those same privileges were extended to female evangelists in the United States in 1922.

Strikingly, there were 142 female evangelists and missionaries among the 512 ministers, evangelists, and missionaries for which the Assemblies of God accepted credentials in the fall of 1914. In contrast to other evangelical groups with whom it is often identified, this Assemblies of God has had a rich history of women in a variety of public ministries, including evangelists. In 2002, 5,502 of the 32,556 ministers in Assemblies of God churches, or 16.9 percent, were female.[8]

If the establishment of the Assemblies of God went a long way towards halting Pentecostalism's experiment in interracial church development, it did not wipe out the movement's tradition of inclusiveness for all time. Today, with 29 percent minority adherents, the denomination is far from lily white. Latino membership totals approximately 193,917 (of 2,627,029 total members) in 1,732 churches (of 12,133 total congregations) nationwide. This Latino presence is significant enough that the denomination has formed Spanish-language districts throughout the United States.

In the Crossroads, 38,865 Latino adherents attend 387 Latino Assemblies of God churches, according to denominational statistics.[9] Moreover, an outsider visiting many Assemblies of God congregations in the Crossroads is likely to be impressed by the diversity of the congregation, when compared with a mainline Protestant congregation in the same locale. At a Sunday worship service in a large Assemblies of God church in Arkansas in the summer of 2003, for example, the congregation included African-American and Asian as well as white and Latino worshippers. In the choir, among the musicians, and on the platform that day, white participants were not the only ones leading in worship.[10]

Race has not been the only source of divisiveness within Pentecostalism. Early on a number of adherents rejected the doctrine of the Trinity in favor of a unitarian view of the Godhead. After a number of denominational sallies these "Oneness" Pentecostals ultimately joined together to form the United Pentecostal Church International. Based in St. Louis, the group has developed into a denomination of autonomous local churches led by officials elected at an annual General Conference. Rejecting trinitarianism and insisting on "Jesus only" baptism, United Pentecostals hold traditional Holiness and Pentecostal views, including the belief that speaking in tongues is the initial sign of the reception of the Holy Spirit.

Statistical data for the denomination are not easy to come by, even from denominational headquarters, but one recent estimate puts the denomination's size at 600,000 in 3,876 churches, over a quarter of which are located in the Crossroads. In a 2003 interview with the author, the Rev. J.L. Hall, director of the group's historical center, estimated that Arkansas and Missouri each has 150 churches, Oklahoma about 100, Louisiana 250-260, and Texas between 400-500 churches. These tend to be small congregations. The only documented megachurch among the nation's Oneness Pentecostals is The Pentecostals of Alexandria, a 2000-plus member congregation in Louisiana founded in 1950.

Celebrities

Throughout its history, Pentecostalism has shown a propensity to produce larger-than-life characters, figures who were at once media celebrities and institution builders. This pattern was set by the most famous woman evangelist in American history, Aimee Semple McPherson, a.k.a. Sister Aimee. Born in 1890 in Ontario, Canada, to a Methodist father and a Holiness mother who was a leader in the Salvation Army, McPherson was converted as a teenager in a Pentecostal revival conducted by Robert Semple, whom she subsequently married. After being ordained in the North Avenue Mission in Chicago, she went with her husband in 1910 as a missionary to China. Three months after their arrival Robert Semple died. After giving birth to their daughter a month later, Amy Semple returned to America to work with her mother in the Salvation Army in New York City. There she met and married Harold Steward McPherson, giving birth to a son in 1913.

McPherson's restlessness in her roles as wife and mother, and a renewed sense of calling as an evangelist, led her to take her children to her father's home in Ontario and begin her ministry as an itinerant evangelist. From 1916 to 1918, Harold McPherson joined his wife in a series of revivals up and down the East Coast, from Maine to Florida, where she drew large crowds to hear sermons, ordinary in content but extraordinary in delivery. Her "illustrated sermons"—sermons given to the accompaniment of staged tableaux—as well as her faith healing, would become the sources of her fame. Between 1918 and 1923, McPherson evangelized throughout the United States, crossing the country eight times. By 1918, she had separated from her husband (divorcing him in 1921) and settled in Los Angeles, where she remained for the rest of her life.

Ordained as an Assemblies of God evangelist in 1919, in 1920 McPherson became one of a small number of women ever to address the Assemblies of God's General Council. But her relationship with the denomination was rocky—thanks to her dramatic and unpredictable preaching style, her growing fame, and the denomination's ambivalent attitude toward women in ministry. Queried about her doctrine, she replied, "We have no doctrine. We believe in real repentance."[11] In 1920 she joined the Hancock Methodist Episcopal Church in Philadelphia; in 1922, she relinquished her ordination credentials and withdrew from the Assemblies of God.

When McPherson opened her permanent headquarters, the 5,000-seat Angelus Temple, on January 1, 1923, Angelinos poured in to witness the performances. As Blumhofer puts it, "Heralded as one who provided 'the best show of all' in a city renowned for its show business, McPherson gave transplanted, entertainment-starved working-class people a rich sampling of theatrical skill. At a time when Pentecostals shunned theatres, she offered an appealing substitute."[12] She did not restrict herself to appearing in person, having already begun recording "sermonettes" that received a ready airing on Los Angeles' new radio stations. In February 1924, radio station KFSG (Kall Four Square Gospel) took to the airwaves from a state-of-the-art studio on the third floor of the Temple; it was the nation's first religious broadcasting station, and McPherson was the nation's first woman to receive a commercial radio license from the FCC. Soon her voice was the most recognizable in the Western United States, reaching hundreds of thousands of listeners.

Like later Pentecostal media celebrities, McPherson was not immune from scandal. On May 18, 1926, the entire country was riveted when she disappeared in an apparent swimming accident, only to reappear August 23 in the Arizona desert with a story that she had been kidnapped. No kidnappers were ever found, and there were widespread rumors—fanned by her clerical enemies and pursued by the press—that she had been enjoying a secret tryst with her radio engineer. She was even indicted for "criminal conspiracy to commit acts injurious to public morals and to prevent and obstruct justice," though the case was eventually dismissed at the district attorney's request.

The Angelus Temple became the foundation of McPherson's own denomination, the International Church of the Foursquare Gospel. In 1927, when it was officially established, the Foursquare Gospel movement had single women serving as pastors in 18 of its 55 branch churches and married couples overseeing another 16 congregations. While insisting that all clerical offices remain open to women, however, McPherson herself appointed only men as elders at Angelus, baptized converts only in the presence of men, and refused to share her platform with another woman.

Over the years, Sister Aimee's path has been trod by a range of Crossroads Pentecostals. One of the first was Edith Mae (Patterson) Pennington of Pine Bluff, Arkansas, who won a national beauty contest sponsored by the *St. Louis Globe-Democrat* in 1921 (the year before the Miss America contest started). With her title of "The Most Beautiful Girl in the United States," Pennington crossed the country in the capacity of everything from civic-club speaker to fashion model to aspiring Hollywood actress. Then, in 1924, she was converted in a Pentecostal Holiness Church in Oklahoma City and five years later was ordained by the Assemblies of God.

She itinerated as a tent revivalist before founding her own church, the Full Gospel Temple, in Shreveport, Louisiana (now independent of the Assemblies of God), which she pastored until her death in 1974. Her legacy today is the Plant of Renown, Inc., described as an interdenominational ministry and marked by a strange blend of Pentecostalism and Jewish culture, including Hosanna Dancers, a troupe that performs Jewish folk dances.[13]

Pennington did not, however, hold a candle to the two great Crossroads Pentecostal celebrities of the twentieth century: Oral Roberts and Jimmy Swaggart.

Born in Pontotoc county, Oklahoma, in 1918, Oral Roberts grew up the fifth and youngest child of a poor Pentecostal preacher. Despite a bout with tuberculosis and the humiliation of stammering, Roberts sustained an optimistic spirit throughout his childhood. Like Sister Aimee, he realized in time that he was "an evangelist first and last" and a natural preacher.[14] Also like Sister Aimee, Roberts shifted his religious affiliations. He departed from Pentecostalism for a number of years and identified himself as a United Methodist, but in 1984 joined Tulsa's Victory Christian Center, a large independent charismatic church. (McPherson's International Church of the Foursquare Gospel awarded him an honorary doctor of divinity degree in 1988.)

Over the years, Roberts became a businessman, an educator, and perhaps most importantly a pioneer in religious broadcasting, capturing the country's attention in the 1950s by using the new medium of television to conduct

Pentecostal faith-healing revivals. He then adapted the television variety-show format to create religious prime-time specials that were also popular entertainment. His syndicated television programs kept him in the public eye and provided the financial means to build institutions—above all Oral Roberts University (ORU) in 1963—to sustain his legacy.

But in the 1980s, having established a medical school at ORU, Roberts sought to extend his healing ministry through the building of the City of Faith, a medical research center and hospital that was meant to combine scientific medicine with prayer and faith healing. Despite objections that another hospital in Tulsa was not justified, he used his business and political clout in Oklahoma to obtain permission to proceed with construction.

The project's costs grew so huge, however, that neither the television broadcasts nor direct-mail solicitation could raise the $10 million per month needed to keep all the Roberts ministries afloat. At the height of the televangelist scandals in 1986-1988, Roberts made himself a national laughingstock by announcing that God would "call him home" if he did not raise $8 million ostensibly to fund medical-student scholarships at ORU. When his contributors did come up with the cash the City of Faith, awash in debt, was forced to close in 1989. Humiliated and now into his 70s, Roberts withdrew from the public stage, where he had been in the spotlight for over three decades. Today his son Richard presides over ORU and the Roberts ministries, but without the high profile Oral Roberts once cut.

Since McPherson, no American Pentecostal evangelist has had more stage presence or dramatic flair than Jimmy Swaggart, a preacher whose theatrical gifts seem to have been genetically programmed. Born in rural Ferriday, Louisiana, in 1935, he and his cousins Jerry Lee Lewis and Mickey Gilley, early rock-and-roll and country-western stars respectively, all grew up in poor Pentecostal families. While the cousins followed their paths as entertainers, Swaggart, the most pious of the three, became an itinerant evangelist and then established his own ministries in Baton Rouge. Until his downfall in 1988 he broadcast one of the most popular syndicated religious programs ever to air on television. The program captured the atmosphere of old-fashioned revivalism while bearing the marks of a variety show, the cameras alternating between shots of the excited audience, Swaggart, and those of the performers. The Southern tradition of storytelling and the Pentecostal tradition of spontaneous pastoral communication combined in Swaggart to convey electrifying performances that drew millions of viewers and, at its height, generated an estimated annual income of $140 million.

In 1987, the national press was filled with tales of Swaggart's tawdry encounters with a prostitute on a seedy strip outside New Orleans. For several months, his live broadcasts were replaced with previously recorded programs. Then, on February 21, 1988, he returned to the air in a broadcast carefully staged around the theme of forgiveness. In the words of the communications professor Quentin Schultze, "By providing ample shots of his tear-drenched face, the cameras created an intense sense of both the preacher's genuine sorrow and his need for forgiveness from God and the viewers. The eye of the cameras jumped repeatedly to heartbroken congregants, who clearly suffered with Swaggart and held nothing against him. At the end of the show the projected images captured Swaggart hugging and crying with individual supporters."[15] The Swaggart confession and its aftermath was prime media fodder for everything from ABC's Nightline to *Penthouse* magazine. While Swaggart's ministries have continued with the assistance of his son Donny, his popularity and fortunes have ever since been in eclipse.

Relating to the Cultural Mainstream

Like McPherson, both Roberts and Swaggart were people of consequence in their hometowns and significant figures in the Pentecostal community. But on the national stage they seemed, for all their celebrity, to be eccentric representatives of an eccentric religious tradition. At the dawn of the twenty-first century, however, the mainstreaming of the Holiness-Pentecostal tradition is the main story.

To be sure, the lifestyle of Holiness people remains at odds with the larger society. Holiness teaching in both the Wesleyan and Nazarene churches continues to reject dancing, movies, popular music, make-up, ornate clothing, gambling, drinking, and smoking. But the far more numerous Pentecostals are much more engaged in the larger culture if not in important respects accepting of it.

By some measures, the Assemblies of God blends comfortably into the larger cultural environment. Once regarded as outsiders to the dominant American religious and secular cultures, Assemblies of God congregations today look like middle-class America. Visits to several congregations, both urban and rural, during the summer of 2003, revealed lively worship services marked by enthusiastic "praise" music but no discernible glossolalia. Church architecture of some of the largest Assemblies of God churches in the region borrows from contemporary design in a way that tends to efface the distinction between the secular and the sacred. A few examples:

• In Kansas City, Missouri, the 6,000-member Sheffield Family Life Center chose to remain in the inner city and build a new facility there. The $18 million worship complex opened in 2001 with seating for 2,750 people. On the exterior, only the huge cross adorning the entrance prevents one from mistaking the building for a civic auditorium. Inside, the facility was created to enhance participatory worship and to accommodate "a group of praise singers, a full band and orchestra...and the 125-member choir." Adjoining the worship complex, a 60,000 square foot educational building also houses a 400-seat chapel and the church's own broadcast studio, from which its pastor, George Westlake, hosts a weekly television show.[16]

- In North Little Rock, Arkansas, the First Assemblies of God Church, located near shopping malls and office complexes, on a typical Sunday draws an average of 1,800 people to worship.[17] The $5 million structure of glass and steel was built in 1990, paid in full in 1995, and expanded twice since then to create offices, classroom spaces, and a gymnasium.[18] Without the three crosses standing in front of the church, the building would easily be mistaken for another office complex.

- The Calvary Temple Assembly of God in Irving, Texas (suburban Dallas), combines a circular design seen in sports and entertainment arenas with an imposing, asymmetrical tower, topped by a cross. As with its large sister churches in neighboring states, Calvary's design communicates an easy accommodation to the designs of public spaces in the dominant culture and an enviable prosperity that makes expansive building projects possible.

To be sure, there are Pentecostal church structures that communicate an entirely different relationship to the larger culture. Many small congregations throughout the region meet in buildings that make their ecclesiastical purpose plain. A grandiose example of this is the new 69,000 square foot sanctuary of the First Pentecostal Church of North Little Rock, Arkansas, a so-called "Free Pentecostal" congregation (i.e. one independent of denominational affiliation). Sheathed in marble and adorned with a large dome and a steeple reaching 193 feet into the air, it fairly shouts "church" to the thousands of commuters who drive by it each day on Interstate 40. When I attended services there in the summer of 2003, a member related that theirs is "an old time religion." Indeed, unlike worshippers at neighboring Assemblies of God congregations, the folks at First Pentecostal speak openly in tongues, shout, dance, and become slain in the Spirit.

As a rule, however, the larger Pentecostal congregations in the Crossroads, whether Assemblies of God or Free Pentecostal, seem like typical American megachurches (whether or not they meet the megachurch rule of thumb of having 2,000 members). They employ state-of-the-art technology for worship; sound equipment, video cameras, and projection screens are more visible than religious symbols. Musical accompaniment is more likely to be provided by a band than an organ or piano, and the singing has more in common with contemporary popular music than with the hymns of Charles Wesley.

Everything, in short, conspires to make worship accessible and enjoyable to both churched and unchurched folks. Of course, technological sophistication and the adaptation of popular cultural forms have been features of Pentecostalism since the days of Sister Aimee. And it was Oral Roberts who, in the 1950s, established the "variety show" style of worship replicated today in "contemporary worship services" throughout America's conservative Christian denominations.

Although the definitive study has yet to be done, it is fair to say that the megachurch style owes more to Pentecostalism than the other way around.

Here it is important to note that Pentecostal influence on contemporary American religious practice also extends to what is often called the "charismatic movement," which has affected individuals, congregations, and networks of churches in denominations not identified as Pentecostal. The Catholic Renewal Movement, for example, began in 1967 "when a handful of students and university theology professors from Duquesnes University in Pittsburgh, Pennsylvania, got together for a weekend retreat." By 1990, this movement claimed to have grown to include 72 million Catholics worldwide, with 15 million in the United States alone.[19] In the Crossroads, there are two Catholic Charismatic Renewal Centers, in New Orleans and San Antonio, while six Catholic churches in Texas and two in Louisiana are identified with the movement.[20]

Among Episcopalians, the charismatic movement and an evangelical impulse took root in 1977 when a group gathered in Chicago called for evangelicals to "rediscover their roots in historic Christianity." The result was the formation of the International Communion of the Charismatic Episcopal Church, which states that it has grown from one bishop and three parishes in 1992 to 1,000 churches with over 200,000 "communicant members" at the beginning of the twenty-first century. These churches identify themselves with the Anglican tradition because it "allows for tremendous flexibility in local expression without compromising the essentials of faith." The churches describe themselves as "wholly orthodox, wholly evangelical, wholly sacramental, and wholly charismatic."[21] The organization disavows schismatic intentions while seeking to incorporate Pentecostal worship styles into the traditional Episcopal liturgy.[22] Twenty-two Charismatic Episcopal churches are scattered across the Crossroads, with 16 in Texas, three in Missouri, two in Arkansas, and one in Oklahoma.

In the Political Arena

While the effects of the Holiness-Pentecostal tradition on Christian worship in America are widely acknowledged, the impact of the tradition in the political arena has gone largely unrecognized. This is hardly surprising. Holiness and Pentecostal Christians represent a small voting bloc, and have been regarded by scholars as more prone to speak in terms of spiritual battles between forces of good and evil than of political and social conflicts and choices.[23] Moreover, early Pentecostal leaders renounced politics and cautioned against involvement in the electoral process.

One such leader was A. J. Tomlinson, the autocratic founder of what is now called The Church of God (Cleveland, Tennessee). Writing in 1913, Tomlinson recalled that in the late 1880s he had embraced secular politics, running (and losing) a race as a populist candidate for auditor in Hamilton county, Indiana. His conversion convinced him to renounce politics; he vowed that he would never vote for anyone except Jesus. Notes Wacker, "In 1908 the Church of God's General Assembly authorized its members to cast ballots—but only if they could do so with a 'clear conscience.' The record implies that very few did."[24]

That this tradition of political non-involvement continues to cast a shadow is evident in the ARIS survey, which shows that 78 percent of Holiness Christians and 79 percent of Pentecostals/charismatics are registered to vote, as compared with 87 percent of those in the evangelical/fundamentalist/nondenominational camp. Among Protestants, only Mennonite/Brethren (68 percent) and Latino Protestants (73 percent) are registered in lower numbers. (Overall, 80 percent of American adults are registered.)

Nor does state public office attract a large number of Holiness and Pentecostal candidates. In the Crossroads, the Arkansas legislature has two representatives who belong to Assemblies of God congregations and one Church of God in Christ member, while in Missouri three legislators indicate Pentecostal affiliations. No more than a sprinkling of Pentecostal legislators is to be found in Oklahoma, Louisiana, and Texas.

Nowadays, however, the signals from the top on political participation are entirely different from Tomlinson's day. "Believers must exercise their God-given privilege and responsibility to vote," the Assemblies of God's general superintendent, Thomas E. Trask, declared in an interview published in the June 13, 2004 issue of *Pentecostal Evangel*, the group's weekly magazine. "I believe that we can make a difference in this nation. But it isn't going to happen by sitting on our hands." By way of example, Task cited Assemblies of God member and U.S. Representative Marilyn Musgrave, the Colorado congresswoman who introduced the proposed constitutional amendment restricting marriage to one man and one woman.

On the issues, the Assemblies of God falls squarely into the camp of social conservatism. It strongly opposes abortion, calling itself "unashamedly pro-life," and likewise has staked out stands against therapeutic cloning, gambling, pornography, and physician-assisted suicide. While urging good stewardship of the environment, it warns that a "major concern for Christians is the overemphasis of the environment at the expense of spiritual issues affecting life and eternity. The Bible's message declares that spiritual matters (those affecting the hearts of mankind) are the priority with God. These and not the environment are the reason He sent His own Son Jesus as a sacrifice to save people."[25]

On matters of sexuality and family, the Assemblies of God declares "homosexuality is sin because it perverts the created order of human sexuality, the heterosexual fulfillment of both man and woman. In creating the first man and woman,

God ultimately established the family consisting of a father, a mother, and eventually children. Society is founded on this social unit which propagates the human race. In total contrast, the lifestyles and practice of homosexual couples establish a social unit that thwarts that process and the creative purposes of God for humanity." The Assemblies of God defines the family as "God's agency for populating the earth with people who would love God and be loved by Him. It is to be formed exclusively through a loving lifelong marriage covenant between a man and a woman."[26]

This view of marriage extends to other members of the Holiness-Pentecostal family. In a February 29, 2004 full-page advertisement in the *Arkansas Democrat-Gazette* five Pentecostal and Holiness denominational leaders signed the message that called for support of Musgrave's marriage amendment. On its official Web site the Church of God in Christ has posted a proclamation on marriage that concludes, "Therefore, in spite of the progressive normalization of alternative lifestyles and the growing legal acceptance of same-sex unions; we declare our opposition to any deviation from traditional marriages of male and female. Notwithstanding the rulings of the court systems of the land in support of same-sex unions; we resolve that the Church of God in Christ stand resolutely firm and never allow the sanctioning of same-sex marriages by its clergy nor recognize the legitimacy of such unions."[27]

Under the circumstances, it is to be expected that, when it comes to party preference, contemporary Holiness and Pentecostal Christians should look more or less like their evangelical cousins. Nationwide, according to the ARIS data, whites calling themselves Pentecostal or charismatic are almost identical to white Baptists: 46 percent Republican, 22 percent Democrat, and 25 percent Independent as compared to the Baptists' 45 percent Republican, 25 percent Democrat, and 25 percent Independent (with the balance answering "don't know" or refusing to say). In the Crossroads, the differential between Democrats and Republicans is almost the same: 35 percent to 23 percent for Pentecostals/charismatics versus 41 to 27 percent for Baptists. (Pentecostals/charismatics count 7 percent more Independents.) For their part, white Holiness Christians are somewhat less Republican nationwide: 40 percent Republican versus 30 percent Democrat. (The ARIS data counts too few Holiness people in the Crossroads to identify them meaningfully by party.)

Blacks in the Holiness/Pentecostal/charismatic camp are politically almost indistinguishable from other black Protestants nationwide: 8 percent Republican, 64 percent Democratic, and 21 percent Independent as opposed to 6 percent Republican, 69 percent Democratic, and 19 percent Independent. Although the ARIS sample in the Crossroads is too small to identify black Holiness/Pentecostal/charismatics meaningfully by party, there is no reason to believe that they look significantly different from Black Protestants as a whole in the region (9 percent Republican, 69 percent Democratic, and 15 percent Independent).

But it is not sufficient to see Holiness and Pentecostal Christians as merely being brought by their leaders into general conformity with the voting behavior of the rest of the evangelical community. Rather, the leadership stance on political involvement should be understood as the reemergence of the reformist impulse embedded in the tradition's perfectionist past. As Trask put it in his interview, "The church was meant to change the culture of the world.... [T]he responsibility for this country's welfare lies at the door of the church and at the pulpit of every minister." No nineteenth-century Methodist leader could have expressed himself more clearly.

This point of view can be usefully contrasted with the more cautious, evangelistically based views of conservative Baptists. For example, the section headed "The Christian and the Social Order" in the Southern Baptists' *Faith and Message* reads, in part, "Means and methods used for the improvement of society and the establishment of righteousness among men can be truly and permanently helpful only when they are rooted in the regeneration of the individual by the saving grace of God in Jesus Christ.... Every Christian should seek to bring industry, government, and society as a whole under the sway of the principles of righteousness, truth, and brotherly love. In order to promote these ends Christians should be ready to work with all men of good will in any good cause, always being careful to act in the spirit of love without compromising their loyalty to Christ and His truth."

The different postures can be seen in the political approaches of the two most prominent organizations of the Christian Right in the later part of the twentieth century. The Moral Majority, created by the Baptist Jerry Falwell, presented itself as an organization of individuals of different faiths working for a common social agenda apart from churches or synagogues. The Christian Coalition, founded by the Pentecostal Pat Robertson, not only named itself in overtly religious terms but also devoted much of its energy to church-based voter mobilization. This was most evident through the massive distribution of voter guides prior to state and national elections; beyond that, the idea was to turn conservative churches into sources of political activists—and activism. This was in line with Robertson's initially successful effort to use churches to mobilize primary voters when he sought the Republican nomination for president in 1988.

Over the past generation, there has been no more consequential development in American electoral politics than the shift of white evangelical churches across the Bible Belt—in the South and Southern Crossroads—from being refuges from politics to sources of social transformation. Although the rise of the Christian Right in the churches is a complex story, it is not too much to credit the Holiness-Pentecostal tradition for providing the world-changing theology that has animated American evangelicalism politically in our time.

In the Crossroads itself, this theology dovetails closely enough with the "Christian Republican" dimension of Landmarkism that, as Andrew Manis makes clear in the previous chapter, continues to influence the public theology of Baptists in the Crossroads. But in the rest of America, the moralistic and uncompromising Holiness-Pentecostal summons to political engagement has been critical, if often (and at times purposefully) difficult to trace.

James Dobson is the latest and perhaps most important case in point. Born in Shreveport, Louisiana, he is the scion of three generations of Nazarene pastors. He attended a Nazarene college in California, but rather than go into the ministry became a child psychologist, teaching pediatrics for 14 years at the University of Southern California School of Medicine. Then, reacting to the permissiveness of the 1960s, he published in 1970 a childrearing manual, *Dare to Discipline*, that sold 3 million copies. His own radio show came in 1977, followed by Focus on the Family, a seven-part video series that turned into a full-fledged family ministry.

In 1991 Dobson moved the organization to Colorado Springs, helping to make that city the evangelical Mecca it has become. By the late 1990s the radio show was reaching 4 million listeners daily, his books had sold more than 16 million copies, and his budget was five times the Christian Coalition's. And while he generally kept himself behind the scenes of partisan politics, he would regularly emerge in election years to lecture Republicans on the need to keep to the conservative straight and narrow. In 1998, for example, he roiled the G.O.P. dovecotes on Capitol Hill by threatening to bolt the party unless it gave higher legislative priority to issues like abortion. "If I go I will do everything I can to take as many people as I can with me," he said. At the turn of the millennium he was widely regarded as the most important figure on the Christian Right.

In an evangelical world, where denominational labels matter less and less, at least when it comes to action on the public stage, Dobson did not advertise his Nazarene identity. Yet his ability to seamlessly meld generic conservative family counseling with a political agenda grounded in evangelical piety comes directly out of his Holiness roots—whether his followers know it or not, or care.

A 1998 cover story on Dobson in *U.S. News and World Report* pointed to two paladins of the Christian Right in Congress from the Crossroads as Dobson acolytes. Then U.S. Representative Steve Largent of Oklahoma, a former star football player who served as a volunteer speaker for Focus on the Family from 1990 to 1993, credited Dobson with "sparking my interest in public policy." Missouri U.S. Representative Jim Talent, elected to the Senate in 2002, described pulling off a highway and praying along with Dobson on the radio to become a Christian. "He is the instrument through which I committed my life to Christ," Talent said.

Neither, however, was a Nazarene, or (as evangelicals go) anything close to one. Largent attended the Fellowship Bible Church in Tulsa, an independent evangelical congregation more Baptist than Holiness or Pentecostal. Talent belonged to the Presbyterian Church in America, a small conservative denomination that broke away from the main body of southern Presbyterianism a generation ago in order to establish an old-time Calvinism.

If Dobson was the foremost outside advocate on the Christian Right, the extreme personification of the Crossroads Holiness-Pentecostal style in political office at the dawn of the twenty-first century was George W. Bush's attorney general, John Ashcroft. The son of an Assemblies of God college president and evangelist, Ashcroft grew up in the Assemblies' headquarters town of Springfield, Missouri.

With the encouragement of his father, who was anxious to bring Pentecostals into the mainstream of American life, he attended Yale College on a scholarship and went to the University of Chicago for his law degree. Back in Missouri he rose through the ranks of public office—from state auditor to attorney general to congressman to governor to senator—all the while demonstrating a rigid moralism and a gift for political polarization. He expressed a sacral sense of duty upon assuming high office by having himself anointed with oil—like the ancient Israelite kings. He made it clear that he thought Congress was in the business of legislating morality; his sense that church and state were supposed to cooperate in the public weal led to the one significant piece of legislation he introduced as a senator: a section of the 1996 welfare reform act known as "charitable choice," which was designed to enable religious institutions to use federal funds to provide welfare services without hiding their spiritual lights under a bushel.

Affirmed as U.S. Attorney General on a near party-line vote, Ashcroft proved to be no less polarizing in the Bush administration than he was in Missouri. He did not stint on bringing his straight-laced piety into the Justice department, holding morning prayer sessions and, to the merriment of Washington press corps, erecting curtains in the department's Great Hall to screen the bare breast of a statue representing the Spirit of Justice from public view. The attacks of September 11, 2001, in a sense enabled Ashcroft to freely indulge his worldview.

As Jeffrey Toobin described it in a *New Yorker* profile of Ashcroft in 2002, "[H]e has always been serious about the binary nature of the universe, which for him is defined by right and wrong, good and evil, heaven and hell." Combining the theological vision of his faith with the confrontational style of this region, Ashcroft made showdowns his specialty. Thus, at a notable hearing on the Patriot

Act on December 6, 2001, he made it clear that whoever was not with the administration was on the enemy side. "To those who pit Americans against immigrants and citizens against non-citizens, to those who scare peace-loving people with phantoms of lost liberty, my message is this: your tactics only aid terrorists, for they erode our national unity and diminish our resolve. They give ammunition to America's enemies, and pause to America's friends. They encourage people of good will to remain silent in the face of evil."[28]

Animated by an imperative to moral revival, unburdened by a past that made an icon of church-state separation, and shaped by a regional culture of confrontation, the Crossroads Holiness-Pentecostal tradition is perfectly suited for the politics of today's Christian Right. Yet it is also equipped to make this politics broadly palatable by its historic openness to racial and gender equality. On gender roles the Assemblies of God, for example, states that "females and males are together the complete physical expression of God's image in humanity. God-given gender differences are to be protected and celebrated. God has clearly communicated that neither gender is spiritually or socially superior. The Assemblies of God will continue to give women opportunities to be copartners in the work of the Kingdom. 'God does not show favoritism'."[29] That is a far cry from the Southern Baptist Convention's ongoing effort to stress the patriarchal nature of the family, just as Rev. Lenora Allison's ability to carry on her family's three generation-long ministry as pastor of the Bigelow Assemblies of God church in rural Arkansas is a far cry from anything the Southern Baptists would permit.

Similarly, Holiness and Pentecostal Christians do not, like most other denominations, have to disavow their racial past. It is in line with the origins of Pentecostalism that the white pastor of North Little Rock's First Assembly of God should have been singled out to receive one of the Arkansas Martin Luther King, Jr. Commission's community service awards in 2004. Likewise, the Sheffield Family Life Center in Kansas City, has been recognized for its work in feeding the homeless and reaching out to singles, gays, street prostitutes, prisoners, and gang members. Survey Pentecostal church Web sites, and the lists of outreach ministries in their communities are impressive. Moreover, in their very names, Pentecostal denominations, such as the United Pentecostal Church International, the International Pentecostal Holiness Church, and the International Church of the Foursquare Gospel, look beyond the borders of the United States and claim a connection with their Pentecostal brothers and sisters throughout the world.

From humble but explosive beginnings, the Pentecostal and Holiness movements have maintained a century-long presence in the Crossroads. Their modest structures in rural areas and massive complexes on interstate highways contribute significantly to the material culture of the region. And from their headquarters in the Crossroads and surrounding states, they are quietly rocking the world.

Endnotes

1. Elaine J. Lawless, *God's Peculiar People: Women's Voices and Folk Tradition in a Pentecostal Church* (Lexington, Kentucky: The University Press of Kentucky, 1988), xiii-xiv.

2. Sydney Ahlstrom, *A Religious History of the American People* (New Haven: Yale University Press, 1972), 871.

3. Edith L. Blumhofer, *Restoring the Faith: The Assemblies of God, Pentecostalism, and American Culture* (Urbana: University of Illinois Press, 1993), 26.

4. Grant Wacker, "Pentecostalism,"in Charles H. Lippy and Peter W. Williams, *Encyclopedia of the American Religious Experience*, volume 2 (New York: Scribner, 1988), 938.

5. Because COGIC did not report membership figures to the Religious Congregations and Membership Survey (Glenmary), NARA used the denomination's claim of 8 million members as the basis for its more detailed membership estimate (not shown on the NARA website). However, the ARIS study, based on a telephone survey, arrived at only 1.7 African Americans in the entire category of Pentecostal.Charismatic/Holiness (260,000 in the Southern Crossroads). NARA, by contrast, estimates 1.8 million COGIC members in the Crossroads alone.

6. Quoted in Grant Wacker, *Heaven Below: Early Pentecostalism and American Culture* (Cambridge, Mass.: Harvard University Press, 2001), 229.

7. Edith Blumhofer, *Restoring the Faith: The Assemblies of God, Pentecostalism, and American Culture* (Urbana: University of Illinois Press, 1993), 116-117.

8. These statistics come from the General Secretary's Office, Statistician, General Council of the Assemblies of God, Springfield, Missouri, dated 1/31/03.

9. "Current Facts 2003," produced by the Office of Public Relations, The Assemblies of God (USA).

10. This observation is based upon a visit on July 13, 2003 to the First Assembly of God of North Little Rock, Arkansas.

11. Quoted in Blumhofer, *Restoring the Faith*, 165-166.

12. Ibid., 166.

13. http://www.plantofrenown.org/founder.htm.

14. David Edwin Harrell, Jr., *Oral Roberts: An American Life* (Bloomington: Indiana University Press, 1985), 476.

15. Ibid., 85, 104-105.

16. http://acousticdimensions.com/profiles/sheffield.htm.

17. This figure was obtained from a staff member, Pam Harrell, of the First A/G of North Little Rock, Arkansas.

18. This information was obtained from the church's history, posted on the web site at http://www.firstassemblynlr.com/information/history.html.

19. "Catholic Charismatic Renewal Movement: History," http://religion-cults.com/spirit/charismatic.htm.

20. "Catholic Charismatic Renewal Movement: The Prayer Groups," http://religion-cults.com/spirit/charismatic.htm.

21. http://www.iccec.org/whoweare/index1.html.

22. Ibid.

23. Christian Smith, *American Evangelicalism: Embattled and Thriving* (Chicago: University of Chicago Press, 1998), 43, 142.

24. Wacker, *Heaven Below*, 222.

25. "The Assemblies of God Perspectives—Contemporary Issues: Social, Medical, Political," http://ag.org/top/beliefs/contemporary_issues/issues_00_list.cfm.

26. "The Assemblies of God Perspectives—Relationships, Conduct, and Sexuality," Springfield. Missouri: Assemblies of God Office of Public Relations, http://ag.org/top/beliefs/relationships/relations_00_list.cfm.

27. http://www.cogic.org/marriageproclamation.htm.

28. Jeffrey Toobin, "Ashcroft's Ascent," *New Yorker* (April 15, 2002).

29. "The Assemblies of God Perspectives—Contemporary Issues"

CHAPTER FOUR

NEGOTIATING CATHOLICISM:
RELIGIOUS IDENTITY VS. REGIONAL CITIZENSHIP

Kathlyn Breazeale

In the Beginning — Water

As in its liturgy, with the sacrament of baptism, the story of Catholicism in this region begins with water. On June 18, 1541, Hernando De Soto was probably the first European invader to see the Mississippi ("Great River" as named by the indigenous people). Traveling from the east, De Soto led his group of Spanish men and indigenous women across the water and erected a cross on the western bank near present day Helena, Arkansas. Seven days later, the first recorded Catholic ceremony was conducted by De Soto and the priests accompanying him as the group knelt before the cross and sang a *Te Deum*, a traditional Catholic hymn of praise.

More than 100 years later, the next group of Catholics to enter this region also came via the Great River. In 1673, a Jesuit, Fr. Jacques Marquette, and Louis Joliet, a fur trapper, traveled south from the land the French had claimed as Canada, following the waterway as far as the junction of the Mississippi and Arkansas rivers. They stayed for two weeks, exploring lands inhabited by the Osage and Shawnee that would become known as Perry county, Missouri, and visited a Quapaw village located a few miles north of the mouth of the Arkansas. Nine years later another priest, a Franciscan, Fr. Zenabe Membré, conducted services at this Quapaw village. The Quapaw were known as Akansea to the Illinois and other Algonquian tribes; the French called them Akensas and Akansas. Thus the state of Arkansas derived its name from these earliest inhabitants to encounter Catholicism.

Fr. Membré and his fellow Franciscan, Fr. Anastase Douay, were accompanying Robert Cavalier de La Salle, who followed the Great River south to its mouth and claimed possession of the vast Mississippi valley for France, naming it Louisiana in honor of Louis XIV. In 1718, a city was founded on the banks of the Mississippi in a crescent-shaped bend and named New Orleans in honor of the Duke of Orleans; the plans for the city included a church and presbytery. The first parish church (dedicated to St. Louis) was completed in 1727, and in that same year "the Ursuline Nuns opened an academy that has the longest uninterrupted history of any Catholic school in America."[1] The arrival of the French-speaking and predominantly Catholic Acadians, expelled from Nova Scotia in the mid-1750s, laid the foundations for the Catholic majority culture in southern Louisiana that continues to the present day.

These French foundations were built upon by succeeding groups of Catholic immigrants, including Spanish, German, Irish, Caribbean, Italian, and most recently Vietnamese. Thus Catholicism in south Louisiana has developed as a multicultural affair through extensive cultural interchange within the original French paradigm. For example, many "Cajun" family surnames such as Schexnaydre, Ory, and Hymel are German in origin and became assimilated to the dominant French culture, making them appear to be French names.

Although the Arkansas Post, the first permanent European settlement in the lower Mississippi valley, was established in 1686 by Henri de Tonti, one of La Salle's lieutenants, this area near the juncture of the Mississippi and Arkansas rivers remained sparsely populated by Europeans until the nineteenth century. However, further north, near the juncture of the Mississippi and Kaskaskia (some 80 miles south of present-day St. Louis), a group of French Catholics founded St. Genevieve in about 1735; this area continued to attract French settlers, and St. Louis was established in 1764. In the succeeding decades, St. Louis and New Orleans became intimately interconnected focal points for development of a Catholic presence in this region. There was continual interchange between these two cities as the Mississippi River brought European trappers, traders, soldiers, and families into the Louisiana Territory.

In 1682, the same year that La Salle claimed the Mississippi River valley for France, subjects of the Spanish crown crossed the Rio Grande to establish the first Catholic settlement near present-day El Paso. The Spanish occupation of this territory inhabited by the Apache, Comanche, and other indigenous peoples was led primarily by Franciscans, who established a chain of 36 missions between 1690 and 1794. However, this mission effort was not successful in winning converts; intense conflict ensued between the native people and the colonizers with their missionaries. European diseases decimated the Hasinai and Caddo people of the northeastern area, and the Comanches effectively defended their land against

European settlement on the western plains. By 1794 the mission system was completely abandoned, and the land surrounding some of the missions was "divided among friendly tribes."[2]

Catholic influence in the area now known as Oklahoma began with the friars and priests who passed through this land with Francisco Vasquez de Coronado in 1541 and De Soto in 1542. However, Catholic missionary activity was not conducted again until 1830 by the Jesuits. Between 1830 and 1845, five tribal nations from the southeastern United States—the Cherokees, Choctaws, Chickasaws, Creeks, and Seminoles—were forced to relocate to this area, which had been claimed by the United States as part of the Louisiana Purchase in 1803.

Originally inhabited by Plains Indian peoples including the Kiowas and Comanches, this area was now designated as Indian Territory (I.T.), and U.S. policy guaranteed that the area would be settled only by indigenous people "forever." However, after the Civil War the tribal allotments were reduced, due in part to the tribes' support of the Confederacy, which had promised to admit I.T. as a state if the South was victorious. Many other tribes were then relocated to this territory, and one unassigned area near present-day Guthrie, at the junction of the Cimaron and Chisholm rivers, was opened for white settlement on April 22, 1889. Additional "surplus" lands were made available to white people between 1891 and 1906, after the U.S. government forced the tribal nations to give up land titles and take allotments as individuals. The land made available to whites became known as the Oklahoma Territory. Ironically, the name Oklahoma means "[land for] red people" in Choctaw.

Of the nearly 60 tribal nations that were settled in Indian Territory during the nineteenth century, only the Osage and Potowatomi had been predominantly "converted" to Catholicism. Although permanent missionary activity was reinforced with the arrival of French Benedictines in 1875, "the Church was too late on the scene to do much effective evangelization of Native Americans, who were too disheartened and disorganized to respond to the white man's religion."[3] The Catholic Church throughout Oklahoma would not grow until subsequent decades brought European immigrants including German farmers, Italian and Polish coal miners, and Irish railroad workers. These immigrants arrived via the railroads that became the "new rivers" in the latter half of the nineteenth century. For example, the terminus of the Missouri, Kansas, and Texas railroads at Atoka was the site of the first Catholic church in Oklahoma, built in 1872. The development of Catholicism via the railroads is evident in the number of Catholic settlements that developed in towns along the railroads throughout the Crossroads region, especially in Arkansas and Missouri as well as Oklahoma.

As in Oklahoma, development of Catholicism in other Crossroads states was also assisted when the government of the emerging United States gained ownership of Louisiana, Arkansas, and Missouri with the Louisiana Purchase of 1803, and when the Republic of Texas became a state in 1845. For example, Catholic clergy in Louisiana supported the politics of the new nation; following the U.S. victory over the British at the Battle of New Orleans on Jan. 8, 1815, a *Te Deum* was sung in St. Louis Cathedral at Andrew Jackson's request. However, the change in government meant that now all religions were legal, whereas under the rule of France and Spain, the Catholic Church had been the only approved faith, and Protestants had been prohibited by law from conducting public worship, marriages, and funerals. Furthermore, "financial ruin faced the Church since most institutional expenses and salaries had formerly been paid by the royal governments, a practice that had to end in 1803."[4] The transfer of the Louisiana Purchase dioceses also placed more demands on the understaffed American Catholic Church. Although this region received large numbers of European Catholic immigrants via the port cities of Galveston and New Orleans, the influx of American and European Protestants was greater throughout the nineteenth century. Thus Protestantism became dominant, and to the present day Catholicism has developed as a minority religion except in southern Texas, southern Louisiana, and pockets of Missouri, Oklahoma, and Arkansas.

By 1840, New Orleans was emerging as the fourth largest city in the new nation, and the city's importance as a commercial center instigated a population expansion and period of growth for the Catholic Church as European immigrants traversed the water to find a new home. In 1842, the first Catholic newspaper in Louisiana, *Le Propagateur*, was founded. The large influx of European Catholic immigrants to the city can be traced by the development of new ethnic parishes: St. Patrick's, in 1833, to accommodate Irish and other English-speaking people, and Holy Trinity, to serve German immigrants, in 1847. The Irish grew dominant among New Orleans Catholics; by 1850 they comprised over half the city's Catholic population. These Irish settlers "produced wealthy and powerful Catholic leaders who competed with the Creoles for local political power."[5] However, the Irish influence was mitigated by the assimilation into Creole culture of Irish who came during the 1830s, as well as by the deaths of Irish who came in the famine period due to cholera and yellow fever contracted in crowded, unsanitary living quarters and through the hard manual labor accorded to Irish men digging canals and unloading cotton bales.

European immigrants also settled with the Acadians (Cajuns) and other French-speaking people across the bayous of southern Louisiana to consolidate the Catholic majority population in this geographical area. By 2001, Lafayette had a higher proportion of Catholics (65 percent) than any other diocese in the United States, according to statistics published in the 2003 *New Catholic Encylcopedia*. Although the Church made smaller gains in the central and northern parts of Louisiana, the state's strong Catholic heritage is still evident in the fact that Louisiana is the only state in the country to be subdivided into civil parishes rather than counties.

Water continued to play a significant role in the establishment of Catholicism as large numbers of Irish and German immigrants followed the waterways north to Missouri, and St. Louis "developed into one of the strongly Catholic cities in America."[6] Other centers of Catholic identity developed in Kansas City, on the Missouri River, and in smaller towns such as Perryville. In particular, the Irish Catholic population grew steadily, with many of the women employed as domestic workers and the men laboring on the docks and steamboats along the Missouri and Mississippi. In 1845, the first predominantly Irish Catholic parish in Missouri was established at St. Joseph on the Missouri River. Many of the German Catholic immigrants were farmers who settled near St. Charles county and along the Maries River.

In St. Louis, a number of immigrant Catholics moved into the middle class through political and trade organizations such as the German-Roman Catholic Benevolent Society, and the son of an Irish-born Catholic was elected mayor. The growth of Catholicism in Missouri was also evident in the creation of St. Louis as a separate diocese in 1826 and its elevation to an archdiocese in 1847.

In contrast, little effort was made to promote Catholicism in Arkansas before 1843, when the diocese of Little Rock was established with headquarters in Little Rock, on the Arkansas River. The area had been rapidly overtaken by Protestants after 1803, and the financial challenges confronting Catholic efforts were evident when the bishop of Arkansas, who had arrived in 1844, declared: "Within the whole diocese of Little Rock there exists no means to erect a single altar."[7]

In 1850, a colony of Irish immigrants was brought to Arkansas by the bishop, yet this attempted settlement was unsuccessful as no preparation had been made for these immigrants. They dispersed, with some following the waterways back to New Orleans and further south to the Corpus Christi area, while others headed up the Arkansas River to Fort Smith. However, in 1851 the Irish Sisters of Mercy opened St. Mary's Academy in Little Rock, which today is the oldest continuous educational institution in the state. Irish immigrants were also instrumental in building the railroads, and many of them settled in northwest Arkansas near the railroad that terminated in Fort Smith.

The Arkansas River and the railroads also brought German and Swiss immigrants, who arrived after 1850 with Benedictines who founded Subiaco Abbey south of Fort Smith. These immigrants established Catholic parishes throughout the upper Arkansas River valley between Little Rock and Fort Smith, locating many church buildings on the river so the priest could easily travel between parishes. In the present day, these German communities still celebrate homecoming liturgies by the river to commemorate the first settlement brought upriver.

Italian immigrants also settled in Arkansas via the Arkansas River later in the nineteenth century. They established Catholic parishes along the river south of Little Rock at Pine Bluff, where there had been an early French settlement and thus a well-established Catholic community. They also settled downriver near Lake Village, where they worked as sharecroppers on plantations. Other Italians established Catholic parishes upriver in northwest Arkansas between Little Rock and Fort Smith, while still others followed the railroads to settle in the mountainous area near Fort Smith, where they became vintners. Thus Fort Smith is an example of how both the Arkansas River and the railroads were primary means of Catholic settlement. Northwest Arkansas continues to be the one area of the state where the population includes a significant proportion of Catholics (about a third in Fort Smith).

Similar to the Church's struggle to maintain a presence in Arkansas before 1843, Catholic development in the area now known as Texas suffered due to political upheaval when Mexico won independence from Spain in 1824. The new Mexican government expelled all Spanish priests and confiscated the Church's extensive properties south and north of the Rio Grande, yet its constitution also established Catholicism as the only legal religion. This love-hate relationship between Mexican Catholics and their church developed from the colonial period when indigenous people first encountered Catholicism as the religion of European invaders.

Stephen F. Austin, who arrived in 1821 leading the first group of Anglo-Americans to establish colonies north of the Colorado River in present-day Austin and Washington counties, publicly insisted that his group declare themselves Catholic. However, Austin could not prevent Protestant ministers from entering other areas of Texas, and Mexican officials consistently refused to send priests to the region. Thus, due to the illegality of Protestantism and the lack of Catholic priests, "there was, in effect, no organized religious activity in Texas before it gained its independence."[8]

In 1836, the constitution of the new Republic of Texas indicted Mexico for supporting "a tyrannous priesthood," guaranteed religious freedom for all, and prohibited clerics of any group from holding public office. In response, the Vatican sought to stimulate the "revival of religion" in the new republic by removing Texan Catholics from the spiritual jurisdiction of the bishop of Monterrey, Mexico, and creating the diocese of Galveston that received its own bishop in 1847. This strategy was successful in reviving old parishes and creating new ones to minister to the 30,000 European immigrants, mostly Catholic, who followed the rivers north, west, and south of Galveston to establish their own communities between 1840 and 1860: Irish in Refugio and San Patricio de Hiberniai; Germans in New Braunfels and Fredericksburg; Belgians, French, and Swiss west of San Antonio; and Poles in Panna Maria.

Catholics as a Crossroads Minority: Antebellum to Contemporary Periods

The arrival of large numbers of European Catholic immigrants in the decades preceding the Civil War incited anti-Catholic sentiment throughout the Crossroads region. Faced with increasing threats to their slave-holding society, Southern Protestants became suspicious that Catholic allegiance to the Pope would prevail over loyalty to Southern social order. For example, "tales of Popish plots against the nation's liberty, with immigrants acting as agents, were coupled with fantastic stories of priestly immorality and treachery." Based on these sentiments, the anti-Catholic, anti-foreign Know-Nothing party came into power in the 1850s. In Louisiana, with its high concentration of Catholics, this party succeeded in electing candidates and establishing newspapers such as the New Orleans *Protestant*.[9] The Catholic church at Helena, Arkansas, was burned in 1854, and in the presidential election of 1856, the Know-Nothing candidate, Millard Fillmore, received his strongest support from Southern voters, while anti-Catholic mobs attacked convents in Galveston and New Orleans.

However, with the outbreak of the Civil War, Southern hostility toward Catholics was mitigated by the courageous behavior of nuns on the battlefields. These women, the only trained nurses among Southern women, volunteered their services and opened their convents as hospitals. During the shelling of Galveston in January of 1863, the Ursulines refused to leave the city; rather, they used a lantern to find the wounded on the battlefield and cared for men in gray and blue alike. Similarly, the Sisters of Mercy in Little Rock cared for the sick and wounded of both armies during the battles in September 1863. Although these women were on the losing side at the end of the war, the historians Randall Miller and John Wakelyn point out that the role these women chose to play on behalf of the Confederacy "won over many Protestants to accept Catholics as 'Christian'."

Anti-Catholic sentiment in the South was also reduced by the complicity of the institutional Church with slavery. "By labeling slavery a political issue, the churchmen of the South placed it outside the Church's province. They absolved themselves of any moral responsibility to pass judgment on the social world in which they lived. The Church, rather, was obligated to support the state."[10] In Louisiana most slave owners were Catholic, and the *Code Noir* prescribed that "slaves be baptized and instructed in the Catholic religion." Catholic slaveholders throughout the region were admonished to treat their slaves well and train them to be good Catholics, yet there was no public statement in favor of ending human bondage. With this strategy of supporting the existing social organization of the host society, as mandated by the Church in Rome, the American Catholic Church remained united during the Civil War; in contrast, many Protestant denominations divided over the practice of slavery. In the South as the North, the American Catholic church combated anti-Catholic prejudice by adapting to dominant cultural mores in the region in which it found itself.

Southern Catholic newspapers played a key role in responding to anti-Catholic sentiment by promoting the Church's support of slavery and subsequently the Confederacy. By publishing strong endorsements of "Southern rights" by bishops and prominent lay leaders, these newspapers influenced the laity to display loyalty to their region. Special Irish Catholic units were organized to fight on behalf of the Confederacy, and Irish immigrants in general tended to assimilate willingly to plantation culture. However, not all Catholic laity accepted the Church's official position. For example, German Catholics attending an annual singing festival in San Antonio in 1854 "adopted a resolution that condemned slavery on moral grounds and called for federal assistance in ending the institution in Texas."[11]

After the War, the Church's efforts to grow and strengthen its institutions were hampered by devastation and poverty across the region. Many working-class Catholics in urban centers sought employment in other states, and the arrival of new immigrants during the nineteenth century essentially ceased, with the exception of the thousands of Italians who came to New Orleans. Although the Church maintained its commitment to unity between black and white members, the Church "conducted only a limited ministry among blacks, had few black members, and ordained almost no black priests."[12] Though many slaves in Louisiana were nominally Catholic under the *Code Noir*, after emancipation they tended to join either Baptist or Methodist churches. The significant groups of blacks who clung to Catholicism were Creoles, whose status in the white power structures depended on having lighter skin.

Throughout the Crossroads region, the Church adopted a respectable, low social and political profile as clerics and laity became increasingly conscious of their minority status in the strongly evangelical Protestant South. Continuing its strategy of acculturation, the Church developed segregated parochial schools and distinctively Catholic social-service agencies that reinforced the ghetto posture of Catholics in a hostile environment. At the same time, Catholics became more acceptable to their Southern Protestant neighbors as many adopted the region's general critique of modernism that "idealized a simpler southern past and decried the insidious secularism of industrial, urban America."[13]

However, some Catholic leaders spoke out against the prevailing Southern attitudes and influenced public life regarding desegregation and later Prohibition. Claiming infringement of religion, the Church in Oklahoma protested the 1917 "Bone-Dry Law" that forbade importing alcohol into Oklahoma. The production of beer and wine within Oklahoma had been forbidden by the state constitution. In 1918 the state Supreme Court upheld the Church's protest, and "ironically, this paved the way for national Prohibition, once the precedent for an exception on religious grounds was established in the Oklahoma case."[14]

The Southern practice of segregation was protested by the bishops of St. Louis and New Orleans, two of the region's most Catholic cities. In 1947, almost a decade before the 1954 Supreme Court ruling that decreed segregation unconstitutional, Archbishop Joseph E. Ritter of St. Louis ended segregation in the archdiocese's schools. In 1953, New Orleans Archbishop Joseph Francis Rummel deplored racism in his letter "Blessed Are the Peacemakers." In 1955, he mandated desegregation of Catholic schools in the archdiocese. Today about 22 percent of all children in Louisiana from pre-kindergarten to twelfth grade are enrolled in Catholic elementary and secondary schools.

Rummel further showed his commitment to desegregation by excommunicating Leander Perez, the political overlord of Plaquemines Parish, who resisted desegregation. However, when Perez died in 1969, the excommunication was overlooked and he was buried from the prestigious Holy Name of Jesus church on the Loyola University campus in New Orleans.

The anti-segregation voices of Ritter and Rummel were strengthened by a 1958 papal statement against racism, and during the 1960s the desegregation of Catholic schools and other Catholic institutions occurred more rapidly than in the public sector. Predictably, this shift from accommodating to challenging Southern practice was met with strong resistance by many Crossroads Catholics who despised Rummel, defied Church orders, and joined those opposing integration. Just as white mobs were photographed screaming epithets at black youths trying to integrate Central High School in 1957 in Little Rock, Catholic parents appeared in nationally distributed photographs shortly after exhibiting the same behavior as Catholic schools in New Orleans were integrated. As in other significant respects (e.g., opposition to divorce and later abortion) Southern Catholics easily found common ground with the same evangelical Protestants who had suspected their loyalty in previous generations. In the 1970s, Southern Baptists and Catholics held several regional conferences to "build a consensus for social action" largely focused on defending "family values" against the purported erosion of the family.

In the decades following Vatican II, new waves of immigrants enhanced the Crossroads' Catholic population. In contrast to the predominantly European immigrants of the previous century, these new immigrants were from Mexico, the Caribbean, Central America, and after the Vietnam War from Southeast Asia.

Between 1990 and 2000, the Catholic population in Arkansas grew from 2.5 to 3.4 percent of the total population. Thousands of Vietnamese refugees arrived at Fort Chaffee, Arkansas; a large Vietnamese Catholic community, Mary Queen of Vietnam Parish, developed in New Orleans; Vietnamese parishes were established throughout Texas; and in Carthage, Missouri, a community of Vietnamese priests and brothers established themselves as the Community of the Mother Co-Redemptrix in the 1970s. Currently, only California has a larger Vietnamese Catholic population than Texas and Louisiana.

The Church responded to the growing numbers of Mexican-American Catholics by developing outreach ministries, especially in Oklahoma City, Tulsa, and throughout Texas. In the 1970s advocacy groups were formed such as *Padres*, an organization of Mexican-American priests, and *Las Hermanas*, an organization composed primarily of women religious. In 1978 the first Mexican-American bishop in the United States, Patricio F. Flores, was appointed to the diocese of El Paso and then in 1979 to the archdiocese of San Antonio. Currently, Mexican Americans comprise the largest group of Latino/Latina citizens in the United States.

In summary, the story of Catholicism in the Crossroads is one of a group that has moved from being the first and only legal form of Christianity in the region to finding itself in a defensive posture as a religious minority after Americanization made evangelical Protestantism the unofficial religion of the region. In contrast to their Protestant neighbors, Southern Catholics belong to a religious group that did not sever its ties with religious officials outside the emerging United States. Southern Catholics have been continually challenged to negotiate a perceived chasm between their regional citizenship and religious identity.

Randall M. Miller, a prominent historian of Southern Catholicism, has cogently analyzed how Southern Catholics have managed their dual citizenship/identity: "The accommodation of the Catholic church and its people to southern social and political norms, in addition to the higher religiosity of southern Catholics compared to their northern counterparts, paradoxically reaffirms the evangelical Protestant core of southern culture with its stress on personal religious accountability and conservative social values."[15]

Contemporary Crossroads Catholics and Public Life

Miller's analysis provides an effective framework for examining how contemporary Catholics are negotiating their Southern citizenship and their Catholic identity. Testing Miller's analysis against current voting patterns among Crossroads Catholics shows the input a minority religion can have on public discourse in a region.

The minority status of Catholics in the Crossroads population is clearly evident in data from the North American Religion Atlas (NARA) and from the

American Religious Identification Survey (ARIS). NARA shows Crossroads Catholics as 18.6 percent of the region's total population. In the ARIS data, the percentage of the Crossroads population who self-identified as Catholic is slightly higher, at 22 percent; of this 22 percent, 11 percent are Latino, 10 percent white, and 1 percent black or other minority including Asian and Native American. The fact that less than 1 percent of those surveyed are black reflects the exodus of Africans and African Americans (already a minority) from the Catholic Church in the Crossroads region after the Civil War. The fact that one half of those surveyed are Latino supports the prediction that Latinos will comprise over half of all Catholics in the United States by 2020. In contrast to the 22 percent of the Crossroads population who self-identify as Catholics, 58 percent report themselves as Protestants. The hegemony of Protestantism in the Crossroads region is also apparent in the minimal percentages of the population who self-identify as other than Christian: 1 percent Buddhist and another 1 percent Hindu, and less than 1 percent each Jewish, Mormon, or Muslim.

Of the 58 percent of the Crossroads population who self-identify as Protestants in the ARIS data, almost half—25 percent—are white evangelical Protestants. A sub-group of white Crossroads Catholics who self-identify as politically conservative have aligned themselves with this large group of evangelical Protestants to oppose abortion and to support school vouchers. The conservative ideology of high-commitment (defined as weekly or greater church attendance) white Crossroads Catholics is further demonstrated by the National Survey of Religion and Politics conducted by John Green and his colleagues at the Bliss Institute at the University of Akron. In the Bliss data, 51.5 percent of high-commitment white Crossroads Catholics indicate their ideology as conservative, in contrast to 26.9 percent moderate and 21.6 percent liberal. The percentages for low-commitment white Crossroads Catholics are more evenly distributed, with 37.8 percent conservative, 33.9 percent moderate, and 28.3 percent liberal. (Bliss data are not available for Catholics who do not identify as white.) As Bill Leonard's demographic essay in this collection demonstrates, although this breakdown of data for Crossroads Catholics is not dissimilar to the data reported in the Southeast, the percentage of self-identified conservative Catholics in the Crossroads is significantly higher.

The conservative nature of white Crossroads Catholics is further substantiated by 2000 presidential election exit polls conducted by Bliss. In these, 64.3 percent of white Crossroads Catholics voted for Bush, 33.7 percent for Gore, and 1 percent for Nader. In comparison to white Crossroads Catholics, more Latino Crossroads Catholics voted for Gore—55.6 percent versus the white vote of 33.7 percent—and fewer Latino Crossroads Catholics voted for Bush, 44.4 percent versus the white vote of 64.3 percent. However, both white and Latino Crossroads Catholics favored Bush over Gore in larger percentages than the national Catholic vote. National percentages for white Catholics were 50.2 percent for Bush versus the Crossroads vote of 64.3 percent, while the national Latino Catholic vote was 32.9 percent versus the Crossroads vote of 44.4 percent. These statistics indicate that while Latino Catholics are more liberal than white Catholics within the Crossroads region, both groups of Crossroads Catholics are more conservative than the national average.

In the Crossroads region, the white Catholic vote in the 2000 presidential election essentially paralleled the vote of white mainline Protestants, demonstrating that Crossroads Catholics continue to be politically and culturally similar to Crossroads Protestants. Bush received 64.3 percent of the vote from both mainline Protestants and Catholics, while Gore received 35.3 percent from mainline Protestants and 33.7 percent from Catholics. However, white Catholics were less similar to their evangelical Protestant neighbors, who voted 75.4 percent for Bush and 21.2 percent for Gore.

Examination of Bliss data on a number of social and economic issues, also conducted at the time of the 2000 election, reveals more similarities than differences between white Crossroads Catholics and white evangelical and mainline Protestants. (These data do not allow comparisons between Catholics and Protestants who do not identify as white.) With few exceptions, there was not a difference of more than 15 percentage points between high-commitment Catholics and Protestants, and low-commitment Catholics and Protestants, across the seven issues of abortion, environmental protection, gay rights, help for minorities, national health insurance, school vouchers, and welfare spending.

The exceptions, with the highest percentage-point difference, were among high-commitment Catholics and Protestants on abortion, school vouchers, and gay rights: 66.2 percent of Catholics were pro-life versus 41.2 percent of mainline Protestants and 76.6 percent of evangelical Protestants; 54.3 percent of Catholics were in favor of school vouchers versus 37.5 percent of mainline Protestants and 47.4 percent of evangelical Protestants; 48.9 percent of Catholics were pro-gay rights versus 49.5 percent of mainline Protestants and 24.6 percent of evangelical Protestants. Thus, Catholics were more similar to evangelical Protestants in opposing abortion and favoring school vouchers, yet essentially the same as mainline Protestants in taking a pro-gay-rights stance.

Although these percentages represent less than 50 percent of the members of each group, other striking similarities among the high-commitment groups emerge regarding welfare spending and help to minorities: 37.6 percent of Catholics and 36.5 percent of mainline Protestants favored more welfare spending, while 44.3 percent of evangelical Protestants did so; 26.3 percent of Catholics and 34 percent of mainline Protestants favored more help for minorities, while 26 percent of evangelical Protestants favored more help.

In summary, these statistics suggest that high-commitment white Catholics would be most likely to form coalitions with high-commitment white mainline Protestants to work for gay rights and increase welfare spending, yet this group of Catholics would most likely form coalitions with high-commitment white evangelical Protestants to oppose abortion, support school vouchers, and favor more help for minorities. These data provide some answers as to how Crossroads Catholics negotiate their minority status to affect current public discourse in the region.

It is possible to test these data against data gathered from interviews with newspaper reporters and Catholic clergy and laity in each of the five states in the Crossroads region. These interviews reflect important conversations among American Catholics on key issues and reveal a diversity of perspectives on these issues among Crossroads Catholics.

Texas

The rapidly growing Latino population is one of the key factors shaping the interface of Catholicism and public life in Texas. Currently, Latinos (primarily Mexican Americans) comprise 31 percent of the state's population. Catholics comprise 21 percent of the population, according to NARA data, and 85 percent of Texas Catholics are Latino, according to Br. Richard Daly, Executive Director of the Texas Catholic Conference.[16] This Conference was established by the bishops in 1964 to provide a forum for the state's dioceses to exchange information and coordinate activities regarding government policy and legislation on issues of importance to the Church. In the Southern Crossroads region, Louisiana and Missouri also have state Catholic conferences. Further information about these conferences may be found at www.nasccd.org. Arkansas and Oklahoma do not have state conferences because Arkansas has only one diocese and Oklahoma only two.

Catholic churches in Texas are responding to the growing Latino presence by offering social services and by supporting advocacy groups. Between 1990 and 2000, the largest percentage growth of Catholics in Texas was in the Dallas-Fort Worth area, where the Catholic population increased by 122.6 percent; Houston-Galveston was the site of the second largest growth at 113.8 percent. In both areas, Hispanic in-migration largely accounts for the growth.

Susan Hogan Albach, religion reporter for the *Dallas Morning News,* noted that all priests in Dallas are required to learn Spanish. She described how some parish churches in the area are offering social services to Latinos that are not usually offered in white parishes. For example, churches are conducting job programs, providing after-school care for children, and developing literacy classes for adults. Parish churches are also providing the "organizational backbone" to promote the advancement of Mexican-American issues by offering meeting space, financial support, and leadership and spiritual guidance to community activist groups. Richard Vara, religion reporter at the *Houston Chronicle*, noted that the

Catholic Church is also able to lobby effectively for Latinos on the national and local levels due to the central organization of Catholic bishops in the United States.

The dramatic increase of Latino Catholics in the Dallas-Fort Worth area was also noted by Jim Jones, religion reporter at the *Fort Worth Star Telegram.* As in Dallas, Jones observed that the bishop of Fort Worth has urged all priests to be bilingual. He stated that one of the ways Latino Catholics are affecting public life at the polls is through their loyalty to the Vatican on issues of abortion and birth control. If this observation is correct, Latino Catholics could use their influence and numbers to reinforce rather than challenge the political views of the Protestant Baptist hegemony, as noted by Bill Leonard at the conclusion of his demographic chapter.

However, with 47 percent of all Latino Crossroads Catholics self-identifying as Democrats, according to ARIS, one suspects that Latino fervor for Vatican teaching about these issues of human sexuality may not be so solid as some perceive. As David Gibson's *The Coming Catholic Church: How the Faithful Are Shaping a New American Catholicism* asserts, Latino Catholics may be more likely than Anglo Catholics to ignore such official moral teachings. If Gibson is correct (and the demographic data about party affiliation in the Crossroads suggest he is), Latino Catholics may well join other American Catholics in ignoring the ban on artificial contraception: substantial data show around 90 percent of American Catholics reject the Vatican teaching on birth control.

Br. Daly confirms this tension between official Catholic teaching and individual practice in personal and public life for Catholics in Texas. The Texas Catholic Conference offices are located in Austin, the state capital and the area of the third largest growth in Catholic population between 1990 and 2000, 100.6 percent. Daly stated that because the Catholic Church in Texas is very diverse, there is no uniform agreement on public issues among Church members or Catholic state legislators.

He noted that liberal Catholics were challenged by the Church's teachings regarding human sexuality that forbid abortion and same-sex unions, yet conservative Catholics find themselves at odds with the Church's support for raising taxes to provide universal healthcare. However, conservative Catholics would agree with the Church's opposition to mandatory healthcare coverage for procedures that the Church deems unacceptable, such as the provision of contraceptives.

Daly also emphasized the expansion of the Church's ministries to meet the needs of the growing Hispanic Catholic population. In addition to the social services provided by parish churches, he noted the Church's attempt to support undocumented workers seeking driver's licenses and its insistence that these workers be allowed to contact their government if arrested. Daly was dismayed that in Texas, Mexicans and Central Americans had been given the death penalty and executed without being allowed to communicate with their government's officials. He explained the Church's concern for undocumented workers with the insight that, by proclaiming itself universal, the Catholic Church regards political boundaries to a certain degree as artificial.

Thus the portrait of Catholics and public life emerging in Texas includes a dynamic tension due to ethnic and political diversities. Tension exists between Church members and official Church teachings, as well as among Church members themselves. Catholics in Texas are divided on issues including birth control, abortion, same-sex unions, universal healthcare, and undocumented workers. Differences of opinions on social issues related to ethnic and political diversities are also evident in the growing population of Catholics in Arkansas.

Arkansas

The small Catholic population in Arkansas—4.3 percent of the total population—grew by 59 percent between 1990 and 2000. The tension among Texas Catholics Br. Daly noted was identified as a new racism by Cackie Upchurch, Director of Little Rock Scripture Study, a ministry of the Diocese of Little Rock in partnership with Liturgical Press of Collegeville, Minnesota. She observed that some long-time white residents of Arkansas are resentful of the influx of Latinos from Mexico and Central America in the northwestern section of the state, many of whom take jobs in the area's large chicken factories—jobs many whites do not want. Noting that advocacy for labor is strong in the Church's social teachings, Upchurch believes that the Church in Arkansas should become more involved in lobbying on behalf of these workers.

Concern about prejudice against the new Latino as well as Vietnamese residents of Arkansas was echoed by Monsignor John F. O'Donnell, pastor of Immaculate Conception Church in Fort Smith, south of the Fayetteville-Springdale-Rogers area, in which the Catholic population grew by 149.1 percent between 1990 and 2000. O'Donnell noted that some of the Catholic parishes in this northwestern area of Arkansas are now 75 percent Hispanic. The Church has responded by forming multi-ethnic committees to develop programs and to meet with local police to address issues of racial profiling.

These discussions suggested that the attempt of Arkansas Catholics to grapple with the influx of Hispanics occurs against the backdrop of debates among local Catholics about their minority status. Deborah Halter, a member of the Department of Religion at Loyola University, New Orleans, and former editor of the *Arkansas Catholic Weekly*, noted that Catholics hardly have a public presence in a state where issues are defined by Southern Baptists and other evangelical Protestants. Msgr. O'Donnell indicated that their minority status influences Arkansas

Catholics to be ecumenical, but not overtly political; Upchurch believes that the vibrancy of Catholicism in Arkansas actually derives from its minority status. She asserted that Catholics are eager to know more about their faith in order to dialogue with their friends of other faiths who can clearly articulate their beliefs.

Halter noted that Arkansas Catholics have influenced public life by collaborating with conservatives in opposing abortion and the ordination of women while joining forces with progressives to oppose capital punishment. However, Upchurch indicated that while there were large public demonstrations in Arkansas against abortion, few people show up to protest an execution. She believes that being pro-life does not mean opposing abortion to the exclusion of other life issues including capital punishment, and that the diocese should offer more education on this issue. In contrast, Msgr. O'Donnell stated that some Arkansas Catholics support capital punishment and war despite the American Catholic bishops' position on these issues; he attributed this divergence from official teaching to the fierce frontier individualism of many Arkansans.

Poverty among families headed by women is another concern identified by Upchurch, who believes that the role of women is one of the main issues for the Church and public life. She points to mentoring and welfare-to-work programs in some parishes, yet argues that the Church should do more to support women who are single parents and seek to improve their earning capacity. Upchurch notes that women's leadership has been critical in the growing strength of lay leadership in the Church, and Halter's research shows that Catholics who approve of women's ordination is approaching 70 percent in the United States.

Another important gender-related issue for the Catholic Church in Arkansas is pointed out by Msgr. O'Donnell: namely, that the state ranks first in teen pregnancy and last in education. He described how the Church is working to keep Catholic schools open in spite of rising taxes. Msgr. O'Donnell stated that, in contrast to Catholics in some other areas (including Louisiana), most Catholics in Arkansas oppose vouchers due to fear of government control of curriculum that would be attached to accepting voucher monies.

In summary, although Catholics comprise a minority of Arkansas residents, they influence public life in various ways. Catholics side with conservative Protestants to oppose abortion and the ordination of women, yet with progressives to oppose capital punishment and support welfare. Furthermore, the growing ethnic diversity of the Arkansas Catholic minority is stimulating the Church to address new racial tensions between whites and Latino and Vietnamese residents. And while Catholics are also working to improve education in the state and thus lower the rate of teen pregnancy and the numbers of college graduates who leave Arkansas after graduation, most Catholics oppose school vouchers so as not to compromise their control of Catholic school curriculum.

Louisiana

In contrast to Arkansas, the Church in Louisiana has lobbied vigorously in favor of school vouchers, as noted by Bruce Nolan, religion reporter at *The Times-Picayune*, and Daniel Loar, Executive Director of the Louisiana Catholic Conference, who explained that lobbying for school vouchers is a social justice issue for Catholics. Many inner-city parents receive federal funds from the Temporary Assistance for Needy Families (TANF) program to send their pre-kindergarten-aged children to Catholic schools. The program is designed to move people from welfare to work. These parents have been pleased with the education their children received and want the children to continue attending Catholic schools.

The Church's lobbying efforts were not successful during the 2002-03 legislative session because the Church refused to agree to change curricula to focus on public school standard tests, yet Loar remains optimistic that future efforts will be successful. He noted that 17 percent of all students in Louisiana attend private school, the highest percentage of any state in the country. Furthermore, 85 percent of these private school students attend Catholic schools. He attributed these large percentages to the fact that Catholic schools predate public schools in Louisiana by 100 years, beginning with the Ursuline nuns, who opened their academy in 1717.

Working against the death penalty is also a social justice issue for Catholics in Louisiana. Loar explained that Louisiana and Mississippi have the highest poverty rate in the nation, and the highest percentage of prisoners who receive the death penalty are people living in poverty. Furthermore, after the Supreme Court decision that the mentally retarded cannot be executed, the local Catholic Church is working to have this determination made prior to trial. The Catholic Church in Louisiana is also working in the criminal justice system to establish a restorative justice approach in which victims of nonviolent crimes can choose to meet with the person who committed the crime to work out a plan for emotional and financial restitution. The goal of such an approach is primarily to make the community whole, rather than to punish offenders.

Loar summarizes the stance of the Louisiana Catholic Conference as "pro-life, pro-family, and pro-poor." A pro-family perspective means that the Church joins evangelical Protestants to oppose legislation to legalize adoption by gay and lesbian couples in Louisiana. Diane Hague, religion reporter for *The Shreveport Times,* observes that Catholics unite with evangelical Protestants against progressive Episcopalians who support gay and lesbian rights. These comments from Loar and Hague contradict Bliss data that 48.9 percent of high-commitment Catholics in the region are pro-gay rights. This contradiction may be explained by Deborah Halter, who notes that though south Louisiana appears monolithic due to the strong Catholic majority in the population, the "Catholic vote" stereotype is misleading: among four Catholics, there will be five opinions.

Following the pattern described in Texas and Arkansas, Louisiana Catholics make common cause with either liberals or conservatives depending on the issue at stake. For example, Loar says that the Louisiana Catholic Conference works equally well with the Louisiana Family Forum, a conservative evangelical group, and the Louisiana Interchurch Conference, a mainline moderate to liberal group. This cooperation among religious groups is one way that political differences between predominantly Baptist north Louisiana and Catholic south Louisiana get negotiated in the state capitol of Baton Rouge.

Missouri

Negotiating coalitions as a strategy to influence public life also occurs among Catholics in Missouri, according to Lawrence Weber, Executive Director and General Counsel for the Missouri Catholic Conference. Weber notes that Missouri Catholics have joined with Baptists in St. Louis to oppose abortion, and with mainline Protestants to oppose concealed weapons and the death penalty. Catholic leadership, in its efforts to abolish the death penalty, was affirmed by Helen T. Gray, religion reporter at *The Kansas City Star*. She notes that the Catholic Church has been very active in the ecumenical Western Missouri Coalition to Abolish the Death Penalty. Weber says the Catholic Church in Missouri has been a major voice for incarcerated people, and, as in Louisiana, the Church has been successful in passing legislation to provide community-based alternatives to punishment in the criminal justice system. Catholic coalition-building in Missouri has also included collaboration with the Jewish Federation to provide child protection services in areas where the state system has broken down. Gray stated that the Church had prevented legislation that would have mandated severe reductions in the state's budget for foster care.

Weber sees concern for the condition of the Missouri public school system as another major issue. He describes how the Catholic Church is working to give parents the option to direct the education of their children, particularly in low-income areas. The Catholic effort to provide quality education for children in inner-city Catholic schools is also noted by Patricia Rice, religion reporter with the *St. Louis Post-Dispatch*, who says that these schools also educate Protestant children. Thus, as in Louisiana, the push for school vouchers for Catholic schools is framed as a poverty issue—an attempt to provide quality education to children on the social and economic margins.

Church spokespersons in Missouri also express concern for new immigrants suffering under the Homeland Security and Patriot Act legislation. Weber points to the Church as the only state-level advocate for non-citizens. He explains that the Church endeavors to be a voice of the disenfranchised, of those not present at the table when public policy is negotiated. Similarly, Gray notes that the Catholic Church has expressed concern for Muslim communities in Missouri. Since

September 11, 2001, Catholic high school students have been meeting with Muslim, Jewish, and Protestant students to become acquainted with each other and discuss issues.

Another community receiving particular attention from the Catholic Church in Missouri is the growing number of Latinos. In Kansas City, the number of Catholics grew by 36.8 percent from 1990 to 2000, and the majority of these were Latino, according to Gray. She says that Catholic parishes and Catholic Charities have been very active in providing food, clothing, language classes, and job-placement services for these immigrants. Perhaps one reason Latinos have settled in Kansas City is because of partnering relationships between parishes in the diocese and those in Central and Latin American countries. According to Gray, these relationships have been long term and have included financial assistance from Kansas City parishes to Central and South American parishes.

The Catholic Church in Missouri has also focused on specifying the public role of Catholic elected officials. Catholics comprise a majority of Missouri's mayors and heads of police and fire departments, according to Rice, and over 30 percent of the state legislators, according to Weber. Church leaders encourage these officials to bring their faith to bear on their decision-making, and also encourage Catholics to contact the officials and share their opinions with them. Weber states that the Church is working to encourage all public officials to work for the common good so that every person in Missouri will benefit from public policy decisions.

Oklahoma

The goal of making Catholic voices heard in the public arena is reiterated by Shirley Cox, an attorney and director of social action for Catholic Charities for the Archdiocese of Oklahoma City. Cox conducts parish presentations on "Faithful Citizenship" to educate Catholics about the social teachings of the Church on issues including poverty, housing, healthcare, euthanasia, abortion, and the death penalty. She also described a "Just Faith" nine-month retreat program in which participants study the social teachings of the Church in order to make a difference in public life. After their experience with this program, one group of retreatants formed a legislative lobbying group.

These educational programs are critical for enabling Catholics to be heard in a state in which they are only 4.9 percent of the total population. As with Catholics in Arkansas (who comprise 4.3 percent of the state's population), Oklahoma Catholics want courses and workshops so they can articulate their faith in dialogue with Protestants, according to Nancy Housh, Director of Youth and Young Adult Ministry for the Archdiocese of Oklahoma City. Housh states that, in contrast to previous generations of youth who were afraid to acknowledge their faith in public settings, Catholic youth today are vocal in expressing their faith, particularly in opposition to abortion and the death penalty, and proudly wear Catholic Conference t-shirts.

Being in the minority apparently convinces Oklahoma Catholics of the importance of collaboration with other religious and community groups to influence public life. Following the pattern described in other Crossroads states, Cox says that Oklahoma Catholics have worked with the Baptist General Convention on informed-consent legislation to discourage women from having abortions, and with the Oklahoma Conference of Churches (composed of 18 mainline denominations) and Amnesty International to outlaw the death penalty. The Church is also working with Central Oklahoma Turning Point, a citizen-led coalition for public health improvement that includes the media, non-profit organizations, corporate entities, and local and state governmental agencies.

Caring for the growing number of Latino immigrants is another priority for the Catholic Church in Oklahoma. Carla Hinton, religion reporter for *The Oklahoman,* and Bill Sherman, religion reporter for the *Tulsa World,* both note that more Catholic parishes are now offering Mass in Spanish, and the Church is requiring training for priests regarding Spanish culture. Housh echoed this by stating that bilingual events have been held in Oklahoma City for Latino and non-Latino youths.

Cox describes the Church's legislative efforts on behalf of immigrants in Oklahoma, including promoting legislation to mandate Spanish editions of the state drivers' manual and to allow undocumented workers to obtain a driver's license. Following federal welfare reform legislation that permits undocumented workers to receive food stamps, the Church is working to educate the community and food stamps program administrators about cultural barriers that discourage immigrants from accessing social services. The Church was successful in passing legislation that allows undocumented students to go to college by paying in-state tuition, provided the student has lived in Oklahoma for two years and graduated from a high school in the state. Now the Church is striving to implement this law, which was strongly contested in the state legislature, by working with the regents of Oklahoma State University to insure that all colleges know the law and that high school personnel encourage undocumented students to take advantage of this opportunity. When the Immigrant Workers Freedom Ride came through Oklahoma, Cox was one of the co-chairs for the rally and reception held to support this group that is promoting immigrant workers' rights.

Conclusion

Catholics in the Crossroads have made a noteworthy historic transition, one that radically affects how they relate to other religious groups and to the public at large. While during the period of French and Spanish colonization Crossroads Catholics enjoyed majority status as the only legally recognized religion in the region, their influence on public life was virtually unchallenged by other Christian groups. Since the sale of the Louisiana Purchase to the emerging United States in 1803, Crossroads Catholics have had to negotiate their impact on public discourse from a minority position as Southern culture developed in tandem with the religious and social values of an ever-growing evangelical Protestant majority.

In general, and particularly in recent years, Crossroads Catholics have negotiated this minority status by forming coalitions with either mainline Protestants or evangelical Protestants, depending on the issue. Both statistical and interview data indicate that Crossroads Catholics are most likely to collaborate with mainline Protestants to oppose capital punishment and with evangelical Protestants to oppose abortion. However, the interview data also reveal a diversity of perspectives among Crossroads Catholics on public life issues such as birth control, same-sex unions, school vouchers, and universal health care.

This diversity in building coalition groups and in individual perspectives presents the complexity of Crossroads Catholicism as it has developed from the "Catholicisms" of Hispanic, Cajun, Irish, German, and Vietnamese cultural perspectives. On the one hand, Crossroads Catholicism has been shaped by the prevailing evangelical Protestant family-values conservatism, as noted by the historian Randall M. Miller. Yet at the same time, a controversial "show down" style has been demonstrated by some Crossroads Catholics who have taken strong stands against the dominant Southern culture.

For example, the anti-slavery voices of German Catholics in Texas and the anti-segregation voices of Archbishops Ritter and Rummel have been joined more recently by Sister Helen Prejean, who has become one of the leading national crusaders against the death penalty. Working from her home in a New Orleans housing project, Prejean was part of a small delegation that presented 2.5 million signatures from people around the world to United Nations Secretary General Kofi Annan in December 2000. Yet another contemporary Catholic leader who exhibits this controversial Crossroads style is Frank Keating, the former governor of Oklahoma. Keating was appointed by the U.S. Catholic bishops to the independent board charged with investigating the Church's child sexual abuse scandal. Keating left the board with "no apology" after charging that some bishops "act like La Cosa Nostra" in condoning criminal behavior and covering up information.

In addition to forming coalitions with Protestants and providing controversial individual leaders, Crossroads Catholics are also affecting public life through strong organizations within the Catholic Church, including regional groups, state-level Catholic Conferences, and the U.S. Conference of Catholic Bishops. These organizations enable Crossroads Catholic leaders to lobby effectively on behalf of the growing majority of Hispanic Catholics, new immigrant citizens, and residents without citizen status in the Crossroads region.

Similar to their social-justice work through these internal organizations, Crossroads Catholics are also leaders in faith-based community organizing, particularly in Latino communities in Texas. For example, Timothy Matovina notes that "in Texas half of the member congregations in faith-based community organizations are Hispanic Catholic parishes." The Communities Organized for Public Service (COPS) in San Antonio is the most well known of the predominately Latino faith-based community organizations, and six of the seven presidents of COPS have been Latino women who view their political work as an extension of their faith. These organizations provide opportunities for "congregations and their members to engage meaningfully in public discourse and decision-making processes that affect their lives."[17]

Thus through coalitions with Protestants, influential individual leaders, the strong internal organization of the U.S. Catholic Church, and faith-based community organizing, Crossroads Catholics are negotiating their regional citizenship and their religious identity to affect public life in the Southern Crossroads region—often in ways that transcend their numerical representation in the states of the mid-South.

Endnotes

1. Penrose St. Amant, "Louisiana," in Samuel S. Hill, *Religion in the Southern States: A Historical Study* (Macon: Mercer University Press, 1983), 124.

2. Howard Miller, "Texas," in Samuel S. Hill, *Religion in the Southern States: A Historical Study* (Macon: Mercer University Press, 1983), 313-14; J.W. Schmitz and G. Carie, "Texas, Catholic Church In," in Bernard L. Marthaler, *New Catholic Encyclopedia*, Vol. 13 (Detroit: Gale Group, Inc., 2003), 845.

3. J.F. Murphy, W.C. Garthoeffner, and J.D. White, "Oklahoma, Catholic Church in," in Berard L. Marthaler, *New Catholic Encyclopedia, Vol. 10* (Detroit: Gale Group, Inc., 2003), 574. For more information concerning Native Americans in the Crossroads region, see the chapter by Cheryl Kirk-Duggan in this book.

4. Raymond H. Schmandt, "An Overview of Institutional Establishments in the Antebellum Southern Church," in Randall M. Miller and Jon L. Wakelyn, *Catholics in the Old South: Essays on Church and Culture* (Macon: Mercer University Press, 1999), 57.

5. Jon L. Wakelyn, "Catholic Elites in the Slaveholding South," in Randall M. Miller and Jon L. Wakelyn, *Catholics in the Old South: Essays on Church and Culture* (Macon: Mercer University Press, 1999), 233. The term "creole" is

from Spanish *criollo*, a term designating those of Spanish (and, in the case of the spelling "creole," French) descent born in the New World.

6. Richard M. Pope, "Missouri," in Samuel S. Hill, *Religion in the Southern States: A Historical Study* (Macon: Mercer University Press, 1983), 201.

7. Cited in Dennis Clark, "The South's Irish Catholics: A Case of Cultural Confinement," in Randall M. Miller and Jon L. Wakelyn, *Catholics in the Old South: Essays on Church and Culture* (Macon: Mercer University Press, 1999), 202.

8. Miller, "Texas," 314-316.

9. George E. Pozzetta, "Nativism," in Samuel S. Hill, *Encyclopedia of Religion in the South* (Macon: Mercer University Press, 1984), 530.

10. Randall M. Miller, "A Church in Cultural Captivity: Some Speculations on Catholic Identity in the Old South," in Randall M. Miller and Jon L. Wakelyn, *Catholics in the Old South: Essays on Church and Culture* (Macon: Mercer University Press, 1999), 36-37.

11. Miller, "Texas," 324.

12. Gaines M. Foster, "Segregation," in Samuel S. Hill, *Encyclopedia of Religion in the South* (Macon: Mercer University Press, 1984), 683.

13. Randall M. Miller, "Roman Catholicism," in Charles Reagon Wilson and William Ferris, *Encyclopedia of Southern Culture*, (Chapel Hill: University of North Carolina Press, 1989), 1308.

14. Murphy, Garthoeffner, and White, "Oklahoma," 574-575.

15. Miller, "Roman Catholicism," 1309.

16. Information attributed to the individuals named throughout this section was gathered through telephone interviews conducted by the author during August and September 2003. I am deeply grateful to these persons for sharing their expertise and time with me. In addition to the persons named in the text, I am indebted to Heather Wecsler at *The News Star* (Monroe, La.) and Nancy Jeffery at the *Arkansas Democrat Gazette*.

17. Matovina, Timothy, "Latino Catholics and American Public Life," in Andrew Walsh, *Can Charitable Choice Work?: Covering Religion's Impact on Urban Affairs and Social Services* (Hartford: The Leonard E. Greenberg Center for the Study of Religion in Public Life, 2001), 58, 61-62, 63.

CHAPTER FIVE

AFRICAN-AMERICAN AND NATIVE-AMERICAN RELIGIOUS FOLK: DOWN BUT NOT OUT

Cheryl Kirk-Duggan

The landscape of African-American and Native-American religious practice is vast, intriguing, and in flux. The African-American church experience, born out of oppression, evolved when people of faith declared that they would worship despite the strictures of slavery and oppression. This insistence on a protected space in which to praise God in ways congenial to African-American culture continues amid the anxieties that beset people of color in the modern period. In African-American and Native-American religion, distinctive worship forms have emerged from African and native communal senses of life, with many gods, and a close connection with creation.

After being kidnapped and transported in the bowels of degradation, many Africans survived in slavery and their descendents eventually nurtured a distinctive kind of Christianity informed by their African roots. Native Americans, who settled the continent thousands of years before the arrival of Europeans, were soon proselytized by Christian missionaries. Many eventually adopted European religious practices; others continued to practice their indigenous ways of life, even while being slaughtered or forced to leave the lands they held sacred to live on reservations.

In response to such oppression, both groups developed religious traditions and practices that assert their humanity, often in the face of overwhelming hostility and violence. Both African-American and Native-American people of faith interpret religion through the lens of the oppression they have experienced; both recognize that such oppression is rooted in greed and cruelty.

In the Southern Crossroads, the overwhelming majority of both African Americans and Native Americans identify with evangelical forms of Protestantism, but they do so in ways and with meanings that are often strikingly distinct from the forms professed by white co-religionists. The formal theology of most black Protestants is virtually indistinguishable from that of white evangelicals, but its application is often startlingly different, especially in the realm of public life. And, in recent years, many Native Americans have reconnected with traditional belief systems, even while maintaining membership in a variety of Christian denominations. It is also important to remember that increasing numbers of African Americans are religiously unaffiliated, have turned to Islam, or have adopted other non-Christian forms of spirituality.

The African-American Presence

In the region overall, African-American Protestants make up a significant and sometimes pivotal minority, as seen in Table 5.1. They are the third largest religious group, behind white Catholics and white evangelicals. However, except in Louisiana and Arkansas, their presence is proportionally smaller than in the states of the Old Confederacy east of the Mississippi. And, especially in Texas, they may well be losing stature as Latinos and other immigrants shift the region's demography away from a simple polarization between whites and African Americans.

Nevertheless, African-American presence is one of the defining features of the Crossroads region. One reason is that African Americans and their churches occupy a distinct turf where they are strong influences on community life—a belt of mostly rural counties that runs in a broad swath across east Texas, into northern Louisiana and southern Arkansas, and then up along the Mississippi River in eastern Arkansas. This zone of African-American demographic predominance forms the western end of used to be called the "Black Belt," a chain of counties with high African-American population concentrations that crosses the Mississippi and stretches east through parts of Mississippi, Alabama, Georgia, the Carolinas, and into southern Virginia. In East Texas, African-American Protestants make up between 25 and 35 percent of all religious adherents. In lowland Arkansas and northern Louisiana, they total up 30 to 50 percent of the adherents in many counties. In Arkansas counties along the Mississippi, like Crittenden, Phillips, and Lee, the percentage of adherents who are African American reaches 60 percent.

This African-American belt contains few cities of substantial size, perhaps only Shreveport, Louisiana. Nonetheless, most of the region's major cities are home to very significant numbers of African Americans. In St. Louis, for exam-

Table 5.1   Historically African-American Protestants in the Southern
            Crossroads in 2000 (NARA)

State	African American	% of Total Adherents	% of Population
Arkansas	403,686	20.6	15.1
Louisiana	875,258	24.5	19.6
Missouri	377,486	11.3	6.7
Oklahoma	250,102	10.4	7.2
Texas	1,869,303	13.6	9.0

ple, 46 percent of adherents are African Americans; in Kansas City they total 24 percent. Tulsa (16.3 percent) and Oklahoma City (18.3 percent) also have sizable number of African-American adherents in a state where African Americans are only about 7 percent of the population. In Louisiana, Orleans parish (New Orleans) is an island of African-American Protestants strength in a part of the state dominated by Catholics. Forty percent of adherents in Orleans Parish are African-American Protestants, and only 36 percent are Catholics. Catholics, however, are a comfortable majority of the metropolitan population. (It's also worth noting that African Americans make up a significant share of Louisiana's Catholic population, and that of the adjoining coastal counties of east Texas. About 100,000 of Louisiana's 1.4 million Catholics are African Americans.)

In urban Texas, the African-American demographics vary considerably. Harris county, Texas, the core of the Houston metropolitan area, has a population of 3.4 million, about 600,000 of whom are African-American Protestants (18 percent of adherents). The proportion of African-American adherents in neighboring Galveston county is even higher, at 25 percent. In Dallas county, 22 percent of adherents are African-American Protestants, and in neighboring Tarrant county (Fort Worth), the rate is 14 percent. By contrast, only 7.5 percent of adherents are African-American Protestants in Bexar county (San Antonio) in south Texas, well south of the African-American belt.

Secondly, African-American Protestants practice a brand of publicly oriented, highly mobilized religion that has had a transformed public life in the region since the 1950s. Some of these changes, the fruits of the Civil Rights movement, have moved the region along the lines that black Protestants intended. But the African-American style of church-based politics, if not its content, has also profoundly influenced conservative white Protestants, who since the 1970s have adopted black Protestant techniques of mobilizing congregants to seize control of public life in most of the Crossroads states.

Native Americans

Tracking the religious affiliations of Native Americans is more difficult. Neither the American Religious Identification Survey (ARIS) nor the North American Religion Atlas (NARA) provides data for Indians. The 2000 Census reported that .8 percent of the national population was Native American. Five of the region's states report levels of Native American population below the national average. The dramatic exception in the region is Oklahoma, where Indians make up almost 8 percent of the population (third largest proportionally, behind Alaska with 16 percent and New Mexico with 9.5 percent). The total Indian population of Oklahoma was 275,230, second only to California.

Moreover, Oklahoma is home to more than two dozen organized Indian groups, most of which operate independent tribal governments, although they no longer govern territory. The best known of these groups are the descendents of the "Five Civilized Nations" forcibly relocated from the Southeast in the late 1830s (the Cherokee, Chickasaw, Choctaw, Creek, and Seminole). But many other tribal groups of Plains Indians and those relocated from what is now the Midwest, and even, like the Delaware, from the East Coast, make Oklahoma their home. The size of these groups ranges from a few hundred, like the Kaw, to the Cherokee Nation, who may total as many as 175,000 people in several states.

With statehood in 1906, the state's Indian reservations were dissolved, although federally recognized tribal governments were eventually reestablished. As a result, Indians now live as a small minority in most of Oklahoma, although there are some counties with large concentrations of Indian population. The 2000 Census, for example, records that in Cherokee county, in the northeastern corner of the state, 32 percent of the population is Native American, in Delaware county, the proportion is 22.7 percent.

Black and Native Religious Ethos: An Overview

African-American and Native-American religion in the Crossroads is evident in substantive, vital faith communities. The tension, confusion, and oppression that birthed these communities and the current chaos within the community life of minority groups is also apparent. The interaction of these various forces has produced many different shades of religious life. To employ a culinary metaphor, there are many stews within the Native-American and African-American religious experience, each with its distinct flavors, which cannot be reduced to a single recipe.

When brought west as human chattel, kidnapped African immigrants did not arrive *tabula rasa*, they had their own worldviews and cultural legacies. Many Africans arrived knowing and/or practicing Christianity or Islam; others brought with them indigenous religions. Slaveholders forced Christianity of a sort on slaves to make them obedient, subservient, and submissive. They manipulated scriptural texts to gain ideological and socio-psychological control over their human chattel. But by the early nineteenth century, many slaves were holding secret worship meetings in which they forged a distinctive African-American Christianity, which blossomed after Emancipation into independent black churches.

When Richard Allen, Absalom Jones, and James Varick were not allowed to approach the altar of St. George's church in Philadelphia, they formed the Free Africa Society, an incubator for a distinctive black American Protestantism. Three clusters of African-American denominationalism evolved after the Civil War, attracting the affiliation of an overwhelming majority of the black churches in the Crossroads and elsewhere.

Methodists organized first. The African Methodist Episcopal Church, or AME, founded in 1816, is the oldest existing African-American controlled organization in the United States, claiming 3.5 million members; the African Methodist Episcopal Zion Church (1821) claims 1.2 million members, and the Christian Methodist Episcopal Church (1870) reports 1 million members.

Larger, but much more loosely organized, are Baptist groups: the National Baptist Convention, U.S.A., Inc. (1895), is the largest traditional African-American Christian organization, with 8.2 million members; the National Baptist Convention of America (1915) has 3.5 million; the Progressive National Baptist Convention (1961) has 2.5 million; and the National Missionary Baptist Convention of America (1988) has 3.2 million members.

The Pentecostal cluster includes the Church of God in Christ (1897) with 5.5 million members, and numerous small denominations.

According to NARA, in 2001 these African-American denominations represented about 15 percent of all adherents in the Southern Crossroads. In addition, African Americans also hold membership in integrated mainline and megachurches, in Islam (e.g., the Nation of Islam, the American Muslim Mission), and in the Yoruba-based religions of Vodun and Santeria or Orisha.[2]

African-American religion as a distinctive derivative expression of West African diaspora emerged from five factors:

1. the African Americans' rejection of second-class citizenship in white churches;

2. the African cultural legacy retained despite the middle passage and dehumanizing persecution;

3. the harsh deformation of normative human relationships in slavery and its aftermath;

4. the brush or "hush" arbor, an "invisible church" that met clandestinely in the slave period; and

5. the spiritual leadership championed by independent black churches during slavery but especially after Emancipation.

In African-American religion, societal attempts to constrain freedom have produced a strong socio-political focus, along with a quest for black identity. With concerns ranging from civil rights and clergy preparation to political activism and social justice, black religion continues to be a critical force for black culture.[3]

African-American religion draws from a complex heritage of African religious cosmology, with tenets including:
- affirmation of a supreme being and other lesser divine beings;
- belief in the close relatedness of the sacred and the secular;
- a focus on community rather than the individual;
- respect and value for all life forms;
- ecstatic types of worship;
- acknowledgment and respect for women's leadership and authority;
- the transmission of culture orally with a focus on the communal production of the sacred.[4]

Within African-American churches that enfold this heritage in a Christian belief system, the keeper of tradition is often the black preacher.

To this day, few black ministers have seminary training, and often their belief systems are derived from their own Bible study coupled with popular tradition, which is often transmitted by notable white or black charismatic preachers either in written form or via television and radio. Some black preachers embrace a spontaneous preaching style, while others prepare their sermons laboriously, though they may or may not use a manuscript when delivering them.[5] Both the distinctive style and content of preaching and the music-making shape a distinctive black community of faith within a context of societal oppression. With a variety of musical styles and techniques, music-making helps congregants hold onto words of hope amid a struggle to survive, maintain identity, and access visibility.

The story of Native-American religious life in America is even more complex and multi-faceted. The case of the Cherokees, the largest group of Indians living in the Crossroads, is illustrative. Their collision with white missionaries in their original homelands in the Southeast began in the 1820s, and many Cherokees resisted Christianization for much of the nineteenth century. Scholars have tended to argue, however, that ancestral cultural practices that are still vigorously maintained are now rarely understood as being in conflict with Christianity. In Oklahoma, the vast majority of Native Americans are, like their white neighbors, evangelical Protestants. The complexity of the situation, where formal religion and cultural heritage are often held apart, is puzzling to outsiders. The Cherokee Nation's official Web site illustrates this complicated duality.

The CherokeeFIRST section of the Web site, for example, advertises a Cherokee National Youth Choir compact disc called "Jesus is Born Today," the literal translation of the Cherokee term for Christmas. The choir sings in Cherokee and the album is advertised as "in the spirit of the true meaning of the Cherokee Christmas holiday." But the songs are all Anglo Christmas carols like "Angels We Have Heard on High" and "Away in a Manger." Another section describes the work of Miss Cherokee 2002-03, a teen-ager named Kristen Smith-Snell. Her biography notes that she is 9/16 Cherokee and was chosen for her expertise in traditional skills like "basket making, pottery, marble game, stickball, bow-making, and blowguns." As Miss Cherokee she "has chosen to support the preservation of culture in today's youth as her message." But the first line of her biography also highlights the fact that Miss Cherokee is also "a member of the Bethel Baptist Mission and is very active in church-related activities."[6]

The Crossroads Region: Distinctive Black and Native Ethos

Regional identity in the Crossroads is a complex matter. On one hand, identity and culture are diverse, multi-layered and blurry around the edges. Not only do many African Americans have a mixture of African, Caucasian, and Native-American ancestry; European-American families also sometimes have mixed ancestry, including native or perhaps African roots that have been hidden and intentionally forgotten. The varied cultural heritages of the Crossroads, in which no one form typifies all variations, is evident in the mixture of foods, music, and house forms found throughout the region. Religion is only one among many factors pointing to the diverse shapes of the region's cultural landscape.

Yet despite the evident and flourishing diversity in religion, conservative forms of Protestantism command the loyalty of the overwhelming majority of the region's African Americans, whites, and Native Americans. The distinctive features of this form of Protestantism (as in the Southeast) are its homogeneity, marked by the predominance of evangelical Christianity, with its four focal points of religious faith and praxis: the centrality of the Bible, belief in direct personal connection with God, individualistic morality, and informal worship. Even those who wish to resist this dominant religious ethos must still deal with it.

But, for African Americans, the one overriding and unavoidable problem of life in the South, no matter what mythic incarnation we are considering, has been race. Rooted in the need for forced chattel labor to maintain a Southern planter aristocracy, racism and its attendant stereotypes required a relentless denigration of African-American culture.[7] Though laws have changed and the color line legally abolished since the 1950s, the number of the poor of all races continues to increase and racism persists even as its forms have become more subtle and sophisticated (and thus hidden).

In the Civil Rights struggle of the mid-twentieth century, black clergy and seminary students, along with strong black women who had organized themselves to protest, provided socially transforming leadership. And the black church has played a central role in nurturing leaders who have sought not merely to react to the shadow side of Southern society, but to transform it. Given its appreciation for the liberation of all God's children, black religion has not become anti-white, even faced with the most virulent forms of racist degradation.[8] White church leaders in the South, on the other hand, tended either at best to preach a moderation designed to thwart immediate social change, or at worst to espouse open racism and support for segregation. Although black pressure and intentional organizing produced some interracial, ecumenical fellowship and activism, by and large no institution in Southern society remains so segregated as the church.

African-American church life in the Crossroads demonstrates the continuing validity of C. Eric Lincoln's thesis that the black church is the focal point of African-American life across the South. Indeed, various indicators suggest that Lincoln's analysis may be even more pertinent to the Crossroads than Southern states east of the Mississippi. In particular, African-American religious culture in the Crossroads, as for Crossroads culture in general, may well be more individualistic and more confrontational than in the Old South. It is perhaps no accident that James Cone, the "inventor" of black theology, regarded by many mainstream theologians and churches as an in-your-face, home-grown manifestation of liberation theology, is Arkansas-born, Arkansas-bred, and Arkansas-educated.

In the Southeast, where other non-ecclesiastical cultural and social institutions had more time to develop, there are significant alternatives to the church when African Americans seek to organize politically or socially. Though the black church certainly played a key role in the Civil Rights struggle in places like Georgia and Alabama, one could well argue that it did so precisely because, in those states, it was buttressed by well-developed African-American social and political organizations that enabled ministers such as Martin Luther King, Jr., to organize quickly. However, while African Americans now move rather easily in the upper echelons of social and political structures in Atlanta, Columbia, or Raleigh, the same cannot be said of Crossroads cities such as Little Rock, Dallas, or Shreveport.

In this region spatially dominated by farms and small towns, in which African-American social and political life has had less time (and economic support) to organize than in the Southeast, the church often remains the sole factor holding a community together. Indeed, in not a few small Crossroads African-American communities, a church may be the *sole* institution dominating the community's social and political life. In such a cultural context, the black church has often adopted the confrontational style of the region in combating social injustice.

This analysis is confirmed by John A. Kirk's ground-breaking study *Redifining the Color Line*, the first book-length study of the Civil Rights era in Little Rock to focus on the role of black activism. Kirk notes that, in contrast to the states of the Southeast, Arkansas of the first half of the twentieth century lacked the sectional or machine politics found in Alabama and Virginia, as well as the overt race-baiting found in states such as South Carolina. This led to a personality-driven politics of constantly shifting factions and alliances within the state's black and white communities. In such a political milieu, confrontational styles abounded because of the overriding need to make one's voice heard among many competing voices.[9]

Kirk notes the crucial importance of the black church in the cacophony of voices competing for attention in the Civil Rights struggle. As he indicates, a black visitor to the city in the first half of the century found its African-American cultural life so completely church-dominated that he dubbed the city "over-churched," by which he apparently meant overcautious.[10]

However, as the bellwether event of the forced desegration of Little Rock Central High School in the mid-1950s crisis developed, other strands of black ministerial leadership became apparent. Daisy Bates, a key organizer of black activists promoting the integration of the school in 1957, was actively abetted by ministers Z.Z. Driver and W.H. Bass. Also assisting in the integration process was Rev. Dunbar Ogden, who, with his son David, accompanied the nine students integrating Central High (the so-called "Little Rock Nine") in September 1957 as they braved crowds of taunting whites to enter the school.[11]

In the 1950s and 1960s, many African-American ministers played significant roles in helping to form short-lived but effective activist coalitions to press for such social changes as the integration of public facilities and lunch counters. Within the "internal factionalism" that characterized the political life of African Americans in Little Rock and the state as a whole, these agenda-driven *ad hoc* coalitions exerted important influence, though they did not outlive the period of political agitation. Such groups included an Arkansas chapter of the Student Nonviolent Coordinating Committee (SNCC), founded by Rev. William Bush with the assistance of students at Philander Smith College, an African-American Methodist college in the city, and the Council on Community Affairs (COCA), created by Maurice A. Jackson, a Philander Smith graduate, as well as Rev. Negail Riley and Rev. Rufus K. Young; Riley was pastor to Philander Smith's "chapel," Wesley Chapel Methodist Church.[12] With the assistance of Philander Smith students, both groups organized the first sit-ins at lunch counters in the state.

In the individualistic, personality-driven political and cultural context of the Crossroads, where factions tend to form and dissolve rapidly as alliances shift, black ministers have exerted a strong social and political influence, often acting as political kingmakers. In the 2000 presidential campaign, the governor of Arkansas, Mike Huckabee, a Southern Baptist minister, created a sensation when he complained on a New York radio talk show about the way in which black churches get out the vote in Arkansas, often busing entire congregations to the polls. Huckabee, with roots in the rural, small-town culture of southwest Arkansas, knows whereof he speaks. The African-American churches of the Crossroads are still formidable political forces to be reckoned with by anyone seeking political preferment in the region.

Native Americans

If African-American cultural and religious life is hindered by its dispersion and the reality that blacks are a small minority in most parts of the region, Native Americans live with an opposite reality. While groups of Indians are active in all of the Crossroads states, and native cultures exerted a strong influence on the historical development of every state in the region, Indian communal life is concentrated in Oklahoma.

The history of the early settlement of Indian Territory (I.T.) sharply illustrates how the tensions present among the Cherokees of the Southeast regarding the "white man's religion" were transported west, and continued to trouble the lives of Indians. In nineteenth-century Oklahoma there was an extended contest between the largely Protestant forms of Christianity encouraged by missionaries and native converts on the one hand and traditionalist supporters of indigenous forms of religion on the other.

Over the course of the nineteenth century evangelical forms of Christianity (and among some groups, Catholicism) took hold among Oklahoma's displaced tribes, but they never erased all remnants of the old ways. Indeed, many observers think an increasing number of Native Americans in the region are seeking re-connection with their pre-Christian roots. As Walter L. Williams notes, even as the lifestyles of native Americans of the Southeast and the Crossroads have tended to adapt to the majority culture, many Native Americans continue to assert their distinctive identity and, in fact, are actively seeking to revive native languages, mythologies, and spirituality.[13]

In Arkansas, for example, where many people with historic roots in the state claim to have some Native-American heritage, but where public presence of Native Americans has long ago disappeared, Indians of various tribal backgrounds have been meeting for several years on designated Sundays to worship on a mountain outside Little Rock. Their worship does not follow the rituals or belief system of any particular Native-American group, but draws on elements of many groups, as well as Christian elements. This is, in short, a pan-Indian movement of religious retrieval that is syncretistic by choice.

Native-Black-White Interactions in the Crossroads

The complex interplay of race and religion affects all expressions of both phenomena in the Crossroads. Because the blending of religion and racially charged myth in this region informs its collective conscience, slavery and the Civil War both appealed to a blend of biblical piety and social ideology to form a Southern civil religion. Religion in the Crossroads is steeped in a conservative, tradition-based milieu and has close ties to politics; both churches and politicians promote fundamentalist or evangelical Protestant values. These sociopolitical values tend to frame social and moral issues for individuals, as well as society as a whole. It might be argued that, within this context, just as the activism of black Christians has mitigated Southern racism and sought social transformation, in the same way, as African Americans continue to become more politically active in the region, a more progressive tone may develop in the Crossroads politics and culture. In addition, as demographic expansion and the migration of people to the Southern Crossroads from elsewhere occurs, the rural, small-town ethos of Crossroads culture may slowly be transformed and a more cosmopolitan culture developed. Issues of both social and religious significance in the region—including alcohol consumption and gambling—are being viewed in new ways as social transformation occurs.[14]

One final important consideration as one reflects on how race and religion matter in the Crossroads: black-white relations have been the predominant focus of discussion regarding race and racism in the Crossroads, yet the struggles of Latinos in Texas and native people in Oklahoma cannot be overlooked in any overview of race in the Crossroads. The experience of African-American and Native-American Southerners in particular is intertwined in important ways, and at the same time often exhibits tensions. As an example: while the concept of community is supremely important to both African Americans and Native Americans, their communities have been played off against one another.

During colonial times, European explorers and early settlers usually kept Native Americans and blacks separated, because they did not want them to unite and overthrow the white minority. For a while both Indians and Africans were enslaved. Using the divide-and-conquer approach, planters employed blacks to fight Indians, and Indians were paid to capture runaways and punish rebellious blacks. Native Americans also practiced slavery, and this practice exacerbated class and cultural tensions in Native-American cultures. Slavery shifted the earlier egalitarian native societies into economies based on class and cash, creating a landed elite mirroring that of white planters.[15] Non-slaveholding Native Americans were relegated to the bottom of their society, and often clung to native traditions and religion as a defense mechanism, accusing slaveholding Indians of selling out to the white man.

Once Indians were moved to Indian Territory and the reservations, class resentments and internal strife flared up. Pro-slavery Indian factions aligned with the Confederates. Indian leaders sympathizing with the plantation system were sometimes ambushed and murdered by their compatriots who opposed such sympathy. The Indians of I.T. passed their own emancipation legislation and officially made freed blacks equal citizens within tribal governments. Both natives and blacks were dispossessed of their land after the creation of Oklahoma as a state in 1907.

Despite this heritage of shared oppression, subsequently the two groups tended to segregate and have not made common cause. And as long as blacks remained powerless in the South and Southwest, there were no reasons for Indians to identify with them. When African-American and Native-American intermarriage occurred, the Indian spouse was often taunted and merged into the black community. Yet intermarriage between the two groups was not rare, and many African Americans remember with pride their Indian ancestry.

The Civil Rights movement did not effectively diminish the separation experienced between the groups. While civil rights legislation helped Indians as well as blacks, black activism encouraged Indians to rally on their own behalf, the alliances that developed were sporadic, and the two groups remain essentially separate today.[16] At the same time they both embrace religious practices and philosophies rooted in their native cultures that help them deal with systemic oppression. And, in significant respects, these practices and philosophies overlap, even as the two groups remain divided by history, culture, and oppressive structures that require the separation of the oppressed into distinct, and often mutually conflicting, groups.

The Impact of Religion on the Region's Public Life

Louisiana

As many have observed, there are two zones of religion and culture in Louisiana. Northern Louisiana is heavily Protestant with a pietistic strain and definite Puritan culture. Southern Louisiana is heavily Roman Catholic, with a strong French and Spanish inheritance. This division transcends and complicates the race line in Louisiana. The colonial Creole culture of the French and Spanish comprised and assimilated a number of other ethnic groups, adding to the cultural mix of south Louisiana; these included Africans, native peoples, Irish, and Germans. Adding to the complexity, the term "Creole" was applied early on to both white and black Louisianans of French-Spanish descent born in the colonies, whereas Cajuns or Acadians, representing a separate stream of immigration and of French culture (namely, that found in the maritime provinces of Canada) tend to be white.[17] All of these Catholic cultures of the southern part of the state celebrate family, food, dance, strong coffee (chicory), and music.

The Protestant zone in northern Louisiana is mainly peopled, black and white, by those whose ancestors came west from other Southern states. The U.S. Congress banned the slave trade in 1803, shortly after Louisiana became a state. From that point to the Civil War, slaves arriving at New Orleans slave markets largely came from Virginia and the Carolinas, where there was a surplus of slave population. Unlike slaves born in colonial Louisiana, the Virginia and Carolina slaves spoke English and were Protestant. The overwhelming majority of their descendents are Baptists, Methodists, and Pentecostals, and today they make up the majority of the state's African-American population.

The patterns of Southern Louisiana were fixed during the colonial period, but they have been refreshed in recent years. Creoles of color descend from Louisiana's first slaves who had common-law marriages with white planters. When these dissolved, the white planters often freed their children and mistresses and gave them money, land, livestock, and sometimes slaves. These free people of color identified themselves as Creoles. This community continues today to have a distinctive identity and is thriving culturally, as recent interest in its Zydeco music demonstrates. In the antebellum period, Haitian immigrants also established a significant community in New Orleans, with approximately 10,000 refugees from Saint-Domingue (present-day Haiti), including free people of color and slaves, arriving at New Orleans in 1809.[18] The city's Afro-Haitian population has been renewed by significant immigration from Haiti since the 1980s. Over the course of time, there has been as well quite a bit of interchange with other Caribbean islands, including Cuba, from which people of mixed racial descent also came to south Louisiana.

The rich tapestry of cultures in New Orleans includes practices of syncretism that have influenced the Catholicism of many African Americans. Traces of Voodoo, derived from West African religions, may also be found in the region's black Protestant churches. Voodoo adapts to Western Christianity such African practices as communication with ancestors and animistic deities, and appears to have reached south Louisiana largely from the Caribbean, especially Haiti.[19] Where these African carryovers persist, one may find a mix of gospel songs, Catholic rituals, incense, and candles, with a "Mother" or "Father" known for charismatic religious presence directing worship. The syncretistic liturgy that results may include being slain in the Spirit, speaking in unknown tongues, and communing with the spirits of dead relatives. Exemplfying this syncretism of African religion and Christianity in south Louisiana is Marie Laveau, a free woman of color who exercised profound influence among both black and white New Orleanians during the first part of the nineteenth century, and around whom a cult of veneration developed and remains alive today.

According to William Hicks, the African-American Baptist heritage in Louisiana dates to Joseph Willis' entry into the state in 1804. While white preachers dominated Baptist ministry statewide prior to the Civil War, after the war African-American constituents separated from the white church and formed black-led congregations. These grew as missions specifically targeted the black population in the antebellum period, and as a statewide Baptist Association and Baptist schools were established.[20] According to the Glenmary Research Center's 2001 survey of Churches & Church Membership, African-American Baptists in Louisiana numbered 386,062 adherents in 1990, about half of the total of the state's African-American Protestants.[21]

Black Baptist churches have strong commitments to social and political justice, and strong connections to organized politics. Ministers always make time available for socio-political announcements during Sunday services. Pastors and leaders encourage voter registration, often support membership in the NAACP, endorse black businesses, and encourage property ownership by blacks. For example, the Rev. C.E. McLain, senior pastor of Little Union Baptist Church in Shreveport, continues the legacy of his father, who also pastored the church, by promoting political causes and social reform. He notes that the church needs to deal with people's educational, social, and economic needs, as well as to gather people for worship. In Shreveport, such pulpit influence is still strong in the black community because most African-American congregants are older females accustomed to this style of church—a style that, in the view of many, needs to be intentionally transmitted to a generation of youth who are not sufficiently informed about black history, problems that fuel contemporary oppression, and the role the black church has played in combating oppression.[22]

In Louisiana, more than the other Crossroads states, this tradition of political engagement has translated into substantial political power. In the current legislature, nine of 39 state senators are African Americans and 21 of 105 members of the state house of representatives. One of Louisiana's seven U.S representatives, William Jefferson of New Orleans, is also African American. All are Democrats in a state where Democrats control both houses of the legislature and the governor's office.

Arkansas

In Arkansas, those engaged in religious work encountered frontier conditions until well after the 1860s. In a state with a small, scattered, rural population, missionaries targeted Native Americans until this population was forced out of the area on the Trail of Tears. The Cherokee influence on the state's culture in its formative years is indisputable but has not yet been significantly studied. In the territorial period of the 1820s, Cherokee Chief John Jolly, who arrived in what became Arkansas in 1818, was the wealthiest man (and perhaps most extensive slaveholder) in the state-to-be. In fact, the much-vaunted "pioneers" who settled the state and tamed its wilderness were, to a great extent, the Cherokee, who cleared much of the land north of the Arkansas River. As John P. Gill notes, many present-day towns in that half of the state are founded on the site of former Cherokee villages; the Cherokee established the first school in what became Arkansas, and the first steamboat to come up the Arkansas to Little Rock carried supplies for the Cherokee mission. The first sermon preached in Little Rock was delivered by a missionary to the Cherokee. Finally, the Cherokee alphabet developed by Sequoyah was developed near what became Russellville, Arkansas.[23]

African Americans, who numbered a quarter of Arkansas' population by the 1860s, were also the object of missionary concern. With mission work by Methodists, Baptists, Presbyterians, and Episcopalians, about 7 percent of slaves in Arkansas had formal affiliation with churches prior to the Civil War. The figure is perhaps misleading, however, since even non-church-affiliated slaves participated in the secret worship meetings of brush or "hush" arbors.

By the time of the Civil War, though there were dissenting antislavery voices, particularly in highlands that dominate the northern and western sections of Arkansas where the slave system did not thrive, a significant proportion of the state was proslavery and many clergy were slave owners. The sentiments of the eastern lowlands area of the state were plain as Civil War approached in the statement of Henry Massie Rector, elected governor in 1860: "God in his omnipotent wisdom, I believe, created the cotton plant, the African slave and the Mississippi Valley to clothe and feed the world, and the gallant race of men and women upon its soil to defend it and execute that decree."[24]

The Civil War resulted in denominational splits in mainline white churches, and the subsequent rise of independent black churches. Racial strife continued in Arkansas as in other Southern states for many years following the war. The nature of this strife is starkly apparent in two key events—the Elaine riots and the integration of Central High School.

What happened on September 30, 1919 in Elaine, a small Delta town with two stores and 969 inhabitants, is still subject to controversy. But insofar as the facts may be determined, it appears that on the evening of September 30 shots fired in the community incited a riot in which posses of white men killed a number of African Americans in cold blood. The question of who initiated the shooting is highly disputed. It is clear that the riot occurred against the backdrop of racial strife in which African-American sharecroppers were meeting in a black church with union organizers. Fear of union influence among black sharecroppers elicited hysteria among white landowners.

What ensued is remembered differently by the white and black communities. Some whites have maintained that African-American activists ambushed white officers; African Americans have reported that white officers provoked a gunfight with black activists. Whatever the originating circumstances, it is clear that whites reacted to the turbulence by immediately forming posses of Arkansans and Mississippians to suppress what appears to have been considered an uprising of black citizens. The number of casualties is also disputed: one report claims that 20 African Americans died; another says 869 were killed. The event spun so quickly out of control that federal troops in Little Rock were deployed to restore order in the town.[25]

Almost four decades later, in 1957, President Dwight Eisenhower again mobilized federal troops in Arkansas, this time to protect nine courageous African-American students who integrated Central High School in Little Rock amidst an atmosphere of violence, hateful speech, and anger. The desire of black Arkansans to escape from persistent racial oppression through education, and their determination to gain an education equivalent to that available to the majority culture, are indicated in the fact that Arkansas' three African-American denominational colleges were founded in the latter part of the nineteenth century: Philander Smith (1877, United Methodist); Arkansas Baptist College (1884); and Shorter College (1886, African Methodist Episcopal).

Race relations have always been complex, and it is worth noting in passing that Arkansas was one of the few places in the South where at least some very prominent white Baptists backed desegregation as a matter of conscience. Brooks Hays, who despite his outspoken support for integration was twice elected president of the Southern Baptist Convention during the very heart of the Central High crisis (1957-1958), fought long and hard to encourage mainstream churches in the state to promote racial moderation. As early as 1948, Hays voiced the opinion (as chair of the Social Service Commission—later the Christian Life Commission—of the SBC) that African Americans deserved suffrage and the right to serve on juries. When the *Brown vs. Topeka Board of Education* decision was handed down in 1954, Hays announced that the decision was in tune with Baptist principles.

As a U.S. Representative from the state, Hays signed the "Southern Manifesto" in 1956 calling on Congress to allow the Southern states to handle integration in their own way and according to their own timeline, a decision he later recanted. Because of his outspoken support for integration during the Central High crisis, Hays paid a certain price: he was not re-elected to Congress in 1958.[26]

African-American Protestants are now a bulwark of the state's Democratic Party, which controlled both houses of the state legislature in 2004. Three of 35 state senators are African American, as are 13 of 100 state representatives. All are Democrats except one, Kevin Penix, a state representative from Fort Smith, whose religious affiliation, Southern Baptist, also makes him an outlier.

The black church remains a key participant in public life, as was made clear during a lengthy controversy over a state judicial board's decision in 2002 to censure

Wendell Griffen, a justice of the Arkansas Court of Appeals, for public remarks Griffen made to the Arkansas Black Legislative Caucus after the University of Arkansas basketball coach Nolan Richardson was fired. Griffen told the black legislative caucus that an investigation of the university hiring policies was overdue. "Most of the academic departments within the University of Arkansas have never employed a black faculty member, let alone one who held tenure."

Griffen, who happens to be a black Baptist minister, was immediately backed by the National Baptist Convention in Arkansas and at the national level. In January 2003, the convention supported Griffen's appeal with a national resolution stating that it "believes that the issue of racial justice deserves honest and serious attention from public officials in all branches and levels of public life, and considers the effort to punish Rev. Griffen both unwarranted and harmful to racial justice and is determined to support Rev. Griffen in his legal challenge to the letter of admonishment." In November of 2003, the Arkansas Supreme Court struck down the admonition.

Texas

Texas has a Catholic heritage dating from the Spanish era. Franciscan friars showed an interest in the area from the end of the seventeenth century. But because of the area's isolation, Indian hostility, and the mistaken idea that the French were no longer going to occupy the lower Mississippi, the Spanish missions were deserted in 1693 and the early Roman Catholic presence in the region was sporadic and scattered.

In the early 1800s, colonists led by Stephen F. Austin settled near the Brazos River, helping establish a Catholic presence. Though Austin was a religious skeptic who exhibited anti-Catholic tendencies, he nonetheless forbade non-Catholic services and deplored Protestant evangelical preachers.

Protestantism came to Texas immediately prior to the establishment of the Republic of Texas, between 1820 and 1836, as settlers from the United States with Protestant roots poured into the area in anticipation of a challenge to Mexican hegemony. European immigration later in the nineteenth century added not only Catholics of various non-Spanish heritages, but also significant numbers of Lutherans and Jews to the state's religious mix.

Early settlers of Texas included a sizable number of slaveholders, such that the 1860 Census indicated the presence of some 150,000 slaves in the state. Most white Texans supported slavery and secession, so the North-South division that occurred in the Baptist and Methodist churches affected Texas as it did the rest of the South and its Crossroads extension. After the war, in Texas as elsewhere in the South, formerly integrated denominations—especially Baptists—became racially segregated, though attempts were made by white Baptist constituencies to reach out to black congregations.

As in neighboring Arkansas, denominational colleges with a focus on education for freed slaves developed after the Civil War. These include Wiley College in Marshall (Methodist); Huston-Tillotson in Austin (today sponsored by the United Church of Christ and the Methodists); Paul Quinn College in Waco (AME); Jarvis College in Hawkins (Christian Church); Bishop College in Marshall (Baptist); and Butler (Baptist) and Texas College (CME) in Tyler.

Today, African-American congregations, like many white congregations, are in a state of marked flux due to the rapid development of an increasing number of competing independent, nondenominational, and Bible churches, many of them megachurches providing an array of ministries and activities.

Megachurches with a Pentecostal or charismatic influence, like Lakewood Community Church in Houston and Bishop T.D. Jakes' Potter's House in Dallas, are altering the mix of black religion profoundly. Jakes' immense congregation—perhaps more than 20,000 members—is remarkably dynamic and extremely effective at mobilizing African Americans. Jakes began his ministry in 1980 outside the Baptist ambit, at Greater Emmanuel Temple of Faith in Montgomery, West Virginia, where 10 people attended his first service. Using dramatic evangelistic conferences as his key method Jakes' congregation grew, and by 1993 he was broadcasting services on Black Entertainment Television. He moved to Dallas with 50 families in 1995 and his Potter's House megachurch exploded. Jakes' summer 2004 conferences, oriented toward personal healing and success, were scheduled for Atlanta and expected to attract 100,000 African-American participants.

With almost 2 million African-American adherents, it isn't surprising that black churches strive to play a key role in Texas politics. But it is an uphill struggle in a state where the Republican Party and a very large and highly mobilized white evangelical population are closely allied. Houston and Dallas have very large and complex black communities, large enough to elect African Americans to seats in the U.S. House of Representatives. But black electoral clout is more modest than in Louisiana or perhaps even Arkansas. In 2004 nine African-American state senators served in a Senate with 32 members and 22 African Americans held seats in the 150-member Texas house of representatives. Only two of Texas' 34-member delegation to the U.S. House of Representatives are black, Sheila Jackson Lee of Houston and Eddie Bernice Johnson of Dallas. The limits on African-American political power are even clearer at the level of municipal government, where only four of 14 Dallas city-council members are African Americans and only three of 14 in very diverse Houston.

As Texas becomes more diverse, and especially as the number of Latino voters swells, it's likely that black electoral power will continue to diminish. The future rests on the uncertain question of whether church-based African-American politics can forge complex coalitions with Latino Protestants, Latino Catholics, and white evangelicals who are more loosely attached to their churches than their once-a-week-attending brethren, who now vote overwhelmingly for Republicans and mobilize for conservative social policies.

Oklahoma

Plains Indians inhabited Oklahoma prior to 1820. Between then and the early 1840s, a large number of Indians from the Southeast and Midwest were forced from their homelands to Indian Territory. The most prominent of these included the "Five Civilized Trives"—Cherokees, Choctaws, Chickasaws, Creeks, and Seminoles. These tribes arrived in I.T. over a 20-year period as Indians were marched westward on the Trail of Tears, a term used to signify the incredible hardships those relocated to I.T. endured, which included the deaths of many children and elderly who could not endure the rigors of the march.

Following this forced removal to I.T., the tribes formed five quasi-autonomous republics, each with a separate government and four with written constitutions. Many other tribes were located on adjacent parcels. White missionaries were active in each republic and in some cases had actually accompanied the tribes on the westward trek. Beginning with the Moravians and the Presbyterians, in 1801 and 1817, missionaries organized schools as they continued their efforts to Christianize the native people. The Methodists and Baptists also worked among the tribes, persisting in missionary attempts begun before the removal as early as 1817.

These early missionary attempts to eradicate native religious customs met with mixed success. The era of the most concerted, and probably most effective, missionary effort to Christianize the native people of the territory began in the 1880s, when Indian lands were opened for white settlement. The prelude to this event was the Civil War, during which many Indians supported the Confederate cause, in part due to the proximity of I.T. to the Southern states, though many chiefs strongly counseled neutrality. After the war, the federal government used the tangential support of the Confederacy by Indians as an excuse to dissolve the tribal republics, a preliminary to disavowing all treaties it had made with the numerous tribes in the territory. By 1890, 70 percent of the territory's population was white.

In the same period, as the development of railroads encouraged attempts to homestead more and more western land, and as lumbering, mining, and ranching interests in the West increased, white attempts to claim the land of I.T. became ever more determined. As a result, the federal government abolished all tribal governments when Oklahoma entered the Union in 1907 (these were later re-established, but not as territorial entities). For the next seven decades, the life of the state was focused on developing industry, mining mineral deposits, increasing agriculture, and establishing white order and social customs.

The success of this attempt to establish a social order congenial to white interests is evident in the rather homogeneous evangelical Protestant ethos that has come to dominate the religiosity of the state. According to NARA, Oklahoma is the least religiously diverse of the Crossroads states. In terms of membership, Baptists, white and black, have an outright majority, with Methodists adding another 14 percent.[27] The Holiness and Pentecostal presence is also significant, at about 10 percent, with special strength in eastern Oklahoma. A number of noted evangelical-minister stars typify the dominant religious ethos of the state; these include Billy James Hargis and Oral Roberts, both of whose ministries have strong influence beyond the state. In this mix, African-American Protestants make up 10.4 percent of adherents.

Blacks were among the earliest settlers in Oklahoma, since many descendants of slaves were members of the Five Civilized Tribes. As in other areas of the Crossroads, they have developed distinctive black churches that diverge from the white evangelical model in their political activism, even when they espouse similar theological tenets.

Another significant exception to the dominant religious milieu of evangelical Protestantism is the Native-American Church, dating from 1906. In the Native-American Church, amidst diversity of practices, including the Sun Dance and Ghost Dance, one constant is the ritual use of peyote, a hallucinogenic outlawed except for religious use in the Native-American Church.[28]

African-American Protestants and Native Americans together comprise about 15 percent of the state's population, so the impact of each group on state politics is modest. In the state senate only two of 48 senators are African American, as are two of 101 state representatives. It is even possible to argue that in Oklahoma there has been measurably conservative influence on the African-American community. Otherwise, it's difficult to understand the career of J.C. Watts, who represented Oklahoma for four terms in the U.S. House of Representative in the late 1980s and early 1990s as the only African-American Republican in Congress. Watts shot up to the number-four position in the House Republican leadership and was one of the remarkable figures of the Reagan Revolution. A black Baptist minister, like so many other Crossroads African-American politicians, Watts stood out because he belonged to the overwhelmingly white (and overwhelmingly influential in the Sooner State) Southern Baptist Convention.

Missouri

The first humans to live in what we now call Missouri were Native Americans, people who generally maintained a cosmology in which invisible spirits ruled the natural world, with a belief system that included fetishes to promote good or control evil, and medicine men or prophets who interpreted or channeled the sacred world for their co-religionists. Blacks arrived in Missouri first as slaves, and then, during the period of exodus from the old Confederacy following the Civil War, as free people. Because the state was on the fringes of the slaveocracy, slavery was never as extensive or deeply entrenched as in other areas of the Crossroads.

As in other Crossroads states, slavery divided denominations in Missouri, and following the Civil War many African-American Christians, who were largely Methodist and Baptist, formed separate congregations with black preachers. At the end of the War, members of the 62nd United States Colored Infantry, composed primarily of Missourians, moved to establish an educational institution in Missouri, which they named Lincoln Institute. They wanted this school to benefit freed African-Americans and to combine study and labor. Funds given by the 62nd and the 65th Colored Infantries were set aside for this cause, and the school was established in 1866 in Jefferson. Lincoln Institute became a state institution in 1879 and a land-grant institution in 1890.[29]

The state's African-American population is concentrated in two major cities, St. Louis and Kansas City. St. Louis in particular was a major destination for migrants from the Deep South in the mid-twentieth century. In St. Louis, many African Americans observe that movement from small towns and farms to the inner-city ghetto shattered church ties for many people, and secularism has reduced the traditional church-directed community life of many black Missourians. The angst and restlessness that resulted from such social and religious dislocation generated new forms of music, including jazz and blues, and also resulted in an environment of religious pluralism in which some urban blacks left behind their traditional evangelical Protestantism for such religious groups as the Church of Christ Scientist and the Unity School of Christianity.[30]

Nevertheless, the African-American Protestant influence in public life is still important, partly because Missouri is currently a swing state in American politics Even at only 6.7 percent of the state's population, a mobilized African-American electorate can win elections for Democrats. One African-American U.S. Representative serves in Congress, William Lacy Clay, Jr. of St. Louis, whose father held the seat before him. Three of Missouri's state senators are African American, as are 13 of its 53 state representatives. All of them are Democrats from the St. Louis and Kansas City areas.

Religion and Voting in the Southern Crossroads

The most striking illustration of the impact of race on religion and public life in the Southern Crossroads is the polarization of voting behavior and political values exhibited by white and black Protestants. Both groups are highly mobilized in comparison to members of other religious traditions. They share the same faith. Their faith informs their citizenship. But they vote very differently.

According to the 2001 American Religious Identification Survey (ARIS), white Methodists and Baptists and black Protestants in the Southern Crossroads are registered to vote at about the same, very high, level: 91 percent of white Methodists, 88 percent of black Baptists, and 85 percent of white Baptists. By comparison, only 72 percent of the region's Latino Protestants and 73 percent of white Pentecostals are registered.

Exit polls from presidential elections in 1992, 1996, and 2000, collected by John Green and his colleagues at the University of Akron's Bliss Center, show that differences between white and black Protestants begin with party affiliation. White Protestants, who mostly voted Democratic until the 1970s, now identify strongly with the Republican Party. About 54 percent of white evangelicals who attend church once a week or more (high-commitment evangelicals), as well as white mainline Protestants (mostly Methodists in this region) identify as Republicans. White evangelicals who attend church less than once a week (low-commitment), are less likely to identify as Republicans, at about 43 percent. Low-commitment white evangelicals are also more likely to be Independents or Democrats (19 and 39 percent, respectively). By contrast, 75 percent of black Protestants identify as members of the Democratic Party. One measure of the pervasive conservatism of the Southern Crossroads is that more blacks in the region identify themselves as Republicans than in any other region of the nation: 20 percent in the Crossroads and 13 percent nationally.

When asked to identify themselves as liberal, moderate, or conservative, once again Crossroads Protestants skewed by race. Sixty-nine percent of high-commitment white evangelicals described themselves as conservative, as did 60 percent of mainline whites. Even low-commitment whites expressed a strong preference for conservatism, with 60 percent of low-commitment evangelicals and 50 percent of low-commitment white mainline Protestants saying they are conservative. By contrast 37 percent of black Protestants described themselves as liberal, 22 percent as moderate, and 40 percent as conservative. The national figure for black conservatives is 35 percent.

On specific issues white and black Protestants in the Crossroads take polar positions, with white Protestants, especially those who attend church weekly, supporting conservative positions by the largest margins, and black Protestants supporting liberal positions by the widest margin of any major religious group. (The most liberal positions were, in fact, routinely taken by the very small "Non Christian" category.)

On a relatively low-voltage issue like national health insurance, 65 five percent of black Protestants support or take a moderate position. Only 53 percent of high-commitment white evangelicals so. On more controversial issues, the spread grows. Sixty-three percent of black Protestants think the government should do more to help minorities. Thirty-one percent of both high-commitment and low-commitment white evangelicals agree, as do 34 percent of high-commitment white mainline Protestants and 29 percent of low-commitment white mainline Protestants.

Sixty percent of black Protestants support more spending on welfare, as do 50 percent of low-commitment white evangelicals, 44 percent of high-commitment white evangelicals, and 36 percent of high-commitment white mainline Protestants.

On the hottest-button issues, abortion and gay rights, the social conservatism of many African-American Protestants is more evident. Forty-six percent of black Protestants describe themselves as pro-life, a figure comfortably higher than both low-commitment white evangelicals and mainliners (41 and 29 percent, respectively). High-commitment white evangelicals are 74 percent pro-life. Black Protestants are also slightly less likely to support the pro-choice position than low-commitment white evangelicals or any white mainline Protestants (39 percent for black Protestants, 42 percent for low-commitment white evangelicals, 40 percent for high-commitment white mainline Protestants, and 52 percent for low-commitment white mainline Protestants).

On gay rights, these surveys taken in the 1990s and in 2000 show that 54 percent of black Protestants describe themselves as pro-gay rights, in the same ballpark as the levels for low-commitment white evangelicals (52 percent) and white mainliners (59 percent for the low-commited and 49 percent for highly committed). Only 25 percent of high-commitment white evangelicals in the region say they favor gay rights, and 57 percent say they are anti-gay rights.

Black Protestants in the Southern Crossroads, as in the rest of the nation, also form a much more coherent voting bloc than do white Protestants, although one special feature of the Crossroads is that high-commitment white mainline Protestants vote more conservatively than they do in other regions. Overall, however, in recent elections white Protestants and Catholics have divided their votes, with those who attend worship once a week or more tending to vote Republican and those who attend services less often tending to vote Democratic. So far, there is no such division among black Protestant voters, which heightens their impact on elections.

One can therefore suggest that it might be possible to cobble together a response to the link between conservative white Protestants and the Republican Party by mobilizing low-commitment evangelicals, Catholics, Latino Protestants, and African-American Protestants. On the other hand, it might just be plausible that Republican activists could drain off enough socially conservative African Americans and Latino Protestants to lock down their regional majority. They might be especially likely to target those located in the new urban and suburban megachurches and stress wedge issues like abortion and gay rights.

Whither the Black Church in Public Life?

During the summer of 2003, I developed a survey instrument and interviewed ministers, religious leaders, and professors of religion throughout the Crossroads region to develop contemporary profiles of African-American religious experience and practice for the five states.

The following observations reflect my conversations with religious representatives of the region. They focus primarily on the black religious experience of the contemporary Crossroads, though they touch on the Native-American presence insofar as it intersects with the black experience.

Across the Crossroads, as the twenty-first century unfolds, African-American churches, especially in cities, tend to be thriving and remain relevant to the health of the black community. They continue to be fonts of religious strength and catalysts for socio-political and economic empowerment. They continue to play their traditional role of thwarting soul-sickness and combating the ills of systemic oppression and poverty.

In each state churches tend to run the gamut from small (50-100 members) particularly in rural areas, to large (300-500), especially in urban areas, though small congregations may be found in many urban areas as well. Megachurches with 1,000+ members are represented in a number of metropolitan areas throughout the region, including New Orleans, Shreveport, and Baton Rouge in Louisana; Little Rock in Arkansas; Houston, Dallas-Fort Worth, and Austin in Texas; Oklahoma City and Tulsa in Oklahoma; and St. Louis and Kansas City in Missouri.

The megachurch phenomenon is particularly powerful in Texas. As in the white community, among black urban Texans (and elsewhere in the Crossroads) such churches exert great attraction due to the high-profile personality of their pastors, their location in strategic areas of cities, and the style of worship and preaching they employ, which has a strong entertainment bent. Also attractive to many are the social outreach of mega congregations, their wealth (and the gospel of prosperity many of them preach), and the ability of such churches to connect to people through media. The ability to meet congregants' emotional needs, including the needs of an emerging young-adult middle-class population that, after a hiatus in church affiliation, is returning to religious life, is also a factor contributing to the appeal of such churches.

Throughout the Crossroads region, my survey indicates that black churches of all sizes continue to play a significant role in social organizing and social outreach. African-American religious communities in the Crossroads have a long heritage in this regard, having actively engaged in the 1960s Civil Rights movement through nonviolent protest, marches, and boycotts, sometimes affiliating themselves with the Southern Christian Leadership Conference (SCLC), the

National Association for the Advancement of Colored People (NAACP), the Student Non-Violent Coordinating Committee (SNCC), the Urban League, or Operation PUSH, and often providing facilities in which freedom fighters were welcome to gather.

Texas has a more mixed heritage than the other Crossroads states. My sources report various interpretations of the level of participation of the African-American religious community in the 1960s Civil Rights movement, with some respondents indicating significant church involvement through voter registration drives, bus boycotts, and community education. Others point to the turning away of Dr. Martin Luther King, Jr. by some black Texans as a prime example of the limited political participation of its churches in the Civil Rights movement.

In Oklahoma the African-American religious community assisted the Civil Rights movement through its support for students during sit-ins, marches, and demonstrations. The Rev. W. K. Jackson took an active role in the struggle by leading his congregants, along with other members of other churches and community activists, in marches and sit-ins on behalf of garbage collectors striking for better salaries. In Missouri, as elsewhere in the Crossroads, there was strong support for the NAACP, agitation for school desegregation, election of black legislators, and appeals for hiring of minority contractors.

Today, throughout the Crossroads, black churches continue this heritage of political activism at many levels, including local grassroots community organizing. Issues that engage churches' attention in various parts of the region include environmental pollution, education, and healthcare. Many churches play engaged roles in elections, allowing candidates time during worship to make a pitch to the audience. In addition to promoting voter registration, many church communities rally against police brutality and racial discrimination, as well as advocate for employment for black youth. Programs sponsored by black churches include food distribution, summer employment opportunities for teens, hospice care, housing and clothing assistance, tutorial assistance for youths, prison ministry, assistance in organizing and supporting community-development corporations, support for historically black colleges and universities, and substance abuse treatment.

In the words of the Rev. Zan Holmes, a renowned United Methodist pastor in Texas who is now retired, the African-American religious community is often "priest to people, prophet in terms of community and political activism, and plays the role of care giver and nurturer." As the survey I administered in 2003 suggests, through its community outreach and ministries to transform society, the black church—whether in rural communities or cities—remains a cultural cornerstone of the black community, with a commitment to social, economic, and political empowerment of the larger community.

Church Matters: Considerations about Membership, Leadership, and Gender Roles in Contemporary Crossroads Black Churches

My survey indicates that the traditional drawing cards for membership in black churches remain strong in the Crossroads: family ties, friends, the teaching and preaching ministry of the church, and the status and reputation of the church are all factors contributing to the decision of black folks to join churches. In some instances outreach ministries and available programming may prove influential. Television and radio ministries also attract some congregants. Where these ministries are particularly influential, people appear willing even to drive considerable distances to hear charismatic preachers: for instance, some respondents reported that it is not uncommon for churchgoers to drive two and a half hours to Dallas from as far away as Oklahoma to hear Bishop T. D. Jakes.

Depending on the particular area and its economy and demographics, the composition of congregations varies. Some Crossroads churches have trouble holding young adults or teens (especially where employment for youth is limited). Others have a strong representation of senior citizens, singles, divorced, young adult, children, and youth. Regarding gay, lesbian, bisexual, or transgendered peoples, most denominations across the region have a "don't ask, don't tell" philosophy, while others are either intentionally exclusive of homosexuals based on their understanding of scripture, denominational policy or doctrine. In other cases they maintain an open-door policy to welcome gay, lesbian, bisexual, and transgendered members.

Crossroads churches report struggles with a number of educational issues centered around confronting and dispelling myths. A number of respondents indicate the presence of tensions regarding church: for some, by virtue of being a black leader, one is automatically trustworthy; others are suspicious about the integrity of black leadership. There are myths and tensions regarding the nature of what it means to be human, particularly around issues of sexuality, where homophobia may be a troubling factor. For some respondents, the African-American religious community is too inwardly focused and is in danger of losing its traditional role as an agent of community transformation; some attribute this shift to a cult of the pastor that thrives in many churches, where the congregation is entirely controlled by the preacher. There is suspicion in some congregations that Christians, particularly pastors, cannot maintain their integrity and serve in public office.

In some of the region's prosperous and rapidly growing urban centers, those polled reported a sense of unease that the church is losing touch with its roots. This unease was expressed as follows: the church has historically been a place where everyone is somebody; now it seems that there is more concern about socio-economic climbing—that the individual becomes qualitatively different simply because he/she is prospering. This was particularly noted vis-à-vis congregations that preach a gospel of prosperity. Some respondents noted that this focus on outward prosperity as a sign of inward grace removes the church from its traditional focus on black social empowerment, which is not the same thing as accumulating wealth.

Other respondents said that African-American religious communities are often mistakenly viewed as monolithic and one-dimensional, whereas the African-American religious experience runs the gamut. As several respondents indicated, many who stereotype black religionists would be surprised by the number of African Americans who pursue religious experience and affirmation in non-African-American settings, including, notably, neo-Pentecostal churches.

The leadership of Crossroads churches of almost all varieties is overwhelmingly male. There are indicators that female pastors comprise only 1 to 5 percent of pastors of black churches in the region. Husband/wife ministry teams appear to represent under 3 percent of Crossroads black church leadership and are found primarily in Pentecostal and nondenominational community church settings, often with television ministries. By contrast, many congregations reported female lay participation running as high as 85 percent.

Public Policy and Critical Issues: Crossroads Churches Confronting the Twenty-First Century

In addition to combating traditional racism and creating a safe place in the storm for African-American and Native-American humanity to assert itself against oppressive social structures, the black and native churches of the Crossroads will, if my survey results are an accurate indicator, continue to confront important social issues in the twenty-first century. Some of these issues will involve working through unresolved tensions that may erupt into open battles in some congregations, particularly as demographic changes occur, as a transition occurs to a new generation of church leaders, and as the educational level of many congregations rises.

In the view of some of my respondents, the traditional focus of many congregations on important health-care issues needs to be broadened. There is still suspicion (perhaps well-founded) of majority-culture doctors and health-care institutions; this often results in avoidance of needed medical intervention and requires education initiatives to encourage African Americans and Native Americans to seek (and demand) adequate health care. In addition, not only do many members of both minority groups have an inordinate amount of illnesses made worse by stress, including high blood pressure, diabetes, heart disease, auto-immune diseases such as lupus, and cancer, but more needs to be done in black and Native-American churches regarding understanding and communicating about sexuality and homosexuality. A healthy understanding of sexuality is critical, given the inordinate numbers of minorities contracting HIV/AIDS, notably heterosexual women and, more recently, senior citizens. From a religious perspective, the "don't ask, don't tell" policy is extremely problematic and exacerbates the health challenges now being faced by minority communities.

Obviously, to deal with this issue will require congregations to initiate discussion on matters traditionally considered taboo in African-American and Native-American churches (e.g., what does the Bible really say [and mean] about being homosexual; can the church welcome homosexuals without requiring them to deny their sexuality; and can a homosexual be a minister?). Facing these questions honestly will bring the church into a minefield of political and scriptural debates. Not facing the questions may further the spread of HIV/AIDS among both minorities and may eventually alienate younger congregants who are used to open discussion of such issues in American culture.

Another challenge for many Crossroads black churches is in inter-religious dialogue. Many Crossroads churches tend to remain locked into doctrinal stances that inhibit cross-church dialogue and cooperation and, as has previously been noted, some respondents in my survey found that this tendency often results in an inward focus that thwarts social transformation. For instance, though Native Americans and Latinos have good reason to make common cause with African Americans where these other minority groups are significantly represented in the Crossroads, there is usually little attempt among African-American churches to interact. Theologically, there is a clear need throughout the region to develop understandings and interpretation of biblical teachings about ministry whose focus is broader than the walls of the church itself.

As Andrew Manis's essay in this volume demonstrates, the Crossroads region has long experienced inter-religious competition and strife, which have in the contemporary period translated themselves into church-vs.-culture stances in which churches that previously refused to collaborate (e.g., Restorationists and evangelical Protestants) are increasingly willing to make common cause against perceived enemies of "Christian civilization." The black churches of the Crossroads are finding themselves drawn into this phenomenon.

Both conservatives and liberals are courting the black churches of the nation on the issue of gay marriage. African-American culture and churches have not adopted a uniform stance towards this issue. In the confrontational mode of the region, black church may stand against black church regarding gay-rights issues, as happened in the Civil Rights movement when churches in Texas refused to support Dr. King.

As the preceding analysis suggests, the educational role of the black church in the Crossroads is key, and deserves further consideration. In Arkansas, a state whose racial history is marked by the watershed of the Central High School event, and which sent a native son to the White House as the twentieth century ended, an HBO documentary "Banging in Little Rock" examines the heightened visibility and economic impact of gangs statewide. The documentary suggests that gangs flourish in an environment in which there is a lack of hope on the part of many young people. More than ever, it seems that churches and their social-educational outreach are needed, and it is important that churches not succumb to a business model in which dollars and cents count more than the mission of the black church, as historically understood.

As noted previously, in some affluent urban areas of the Crossroads—some cities of Texas are a prime example—"success thinking" has come to dominate some congregations. Yet for the vast majority of African Americans in the region (and at a national level as well), poverty remains a harsh reality. When high-profile African Americans who have "made it" are held up as examples to the black community, class and economic separations within the black community are exacerbated. The church cannot fulfill its function in such a social context if it abandons its historic focus on education, justice, and social equity, as well as community and economic development.

For Native Americans, both native religious traditions and churches integrating elements of native spirituality have created cultural cohesion and given sustenance to those struggling for justice. Native Americans in the Crossroads are increasingly making common cause with Native Americans throughout the nation to challenge the hegemony of the dominant culture and retrieve native culture and religious roots. Some native groups in Oklahoma have recently filed claims to recover land ceded over in the Ouachita Mountains area of Arkansas in the nineteenth century. The Pan-Indian movement noted above began in Oklahoma in the late nineteenth century as an attempt to protect the rights of native peoples across the nation. As JoAllyn Archambault notes, though this movement did not initially achieve all of its political aims, it provided the groundwork for the National Congress of American Indians (dating from 1944), which, along with the American Indian Movement (AIM, founded in 1968), were influential in promoting civil rights of Indians in the latter half of the twentieth century.[31]

In the view of Vine Deloria, Jr., the ability of Native Americans to assert their distinctive identities and demand equal treatment under American law has often demanded that they either resist the missionizing impulse of Christian churches or that they adapt Christianity to native culture and native needs. Deloria notes that those native people who have most successfully preserved their identity have also been those most resistant to missionization. He also notes that Pan-Indian attempts to retrieve native spirituality have energized movements for political resistance and political transformation and continue to do so: as Deloria argues,

"it seems beyond dispute that within tribal religions is a powerful spiritual energy that cannot be confined to a small group in the modern world."[32] Deloria
points to the powerful resurgence of native spirituality and forms of worship
among native people across the continent, the tendency of this resurgence to draw
on cross-tribal traditions, and the willingness of many churched Indians to syn-
cretize native spirituality with Christian beliefs and practices. He also predicts
that the Native-American Church will eventually replace traditional forms of
Christianity among Native Americans, though, as he indicates, in its evangelical
Protestant incarnations Christianity retains a strong base among the native people
of eastern Oklahoma.[33]

The enduring and transformative appeal of native spirituality in the Crossroads
is evident even in the non-Indian state of Arkansas. In the center of the state's
capital city, in historic Mount Holly Cemetery near the state capitol building,
John Ross's first wife Quatie Ross, who died on the Trail of Tears near Little
Rock in 1839, is commemorated by a memorial marker. Legend has it that Quatie
Ross died after giving up her cloak to warm a shivering child. That Quatie Ross
is not forgotten is evident in memorial offerings that are left regularly on her
grave by visitors; on repeated visits to the grave I have found rocks, feathers, and
other memorial objects. A Mount Holly board member and tour guide, Mary
Worthen, reports finding crystals the size of a fist, a red glass heart, a bracelet,
petrified wood, and coins at the memorial site in early April 2004.[34]

These memorial offerings suggest that Quatie Ross is not merely remembered
but cherished by those who refuse to forget what her people endured on their trek
through Arkansas in the 1830s. As the twenty-first century begins, such important
strands of Crossroads religion remain vital. They also face significant challenges
if they are to transmit their heritage to a new century.

Endnotes

1. Data from the North American Religion Atlas (NARA). NARA includes population estimates of African-American Protestants down to the state and county level. These estimates were commissioned by the Religion by Region project to compensate for one of the major drawbacks of the decennial Glenmary
   studies of adherents, members, and congregations claimed by American religious groups. Most African-American denominations have chosen not to participate in the Glenmary studies. The NARA estimates, specially prepared for
   this project by demographers at the Polis Center, do not include members or
   congregations. They are based on national populations claimed by African-
   American Protestants and undoubtedly fall on the high side.

2. Milmon F. Harrison, "African American Religions," in *Contemporary
   American Religion* (NY: MacMillan, 2000), 6.

3. C. Eric Lincoln, "Black Religion," *Encyclopedia of Religion in the South* (Macon: Mercer UP, 1984), 111-112.

4. Milmon F. Harrison, African American Religions" in W.C. Roof, *Contemporary American Religion* (NY: MacMillan, 2000), 5.

5. Bruce A. Rosenberg, "Black Preachers," in Charles Reagan Wilson and William Ferris, *Encyclopedia of Southern Culture* (Chapel Hill: University of North Carolina Press, 1989), 184-185.

6. www.cherokee.org/services/CherokeeFIRST/

7. Winthrop Jordan, "Racial Attitudes," in C. Reagan Wilson and W. Ferris, *Encyclopedia of Southern Culture* (Chapel Hill: University of North Carolina Press, 1989), 1118-1119.

8. James Sessions, "Civil Rights and Religion," in C. Reagan Wilson and W. Ferris, *Encyclopedia of Southern Culture* (Chapel Hill: University of North Carolina Press, 1989), 1282-1283.

9. John A. Kirk, *Redifining the Color Line: Black Activism in Little Rock, Arkansas 1940-1970* (Gainesville: Univ. Press of FL, 2002), 6, 164.

10. As cited with no other attribution, 13.

11. Ibid., 117, 129.

12. Ibid., 142-156.

13. Walter L. Williams, "Indians since 1840," *Encyclopedia of Southern Culture*, 413.

14. Todd A. Baker, "African Methodist Episcopal Churches: Religion and Social Class," in C. Reagan Wilson and W. Ferris, *Encyclopedia of Southern Culture* (Chapel Hill: University of North Carolina Press, 1989), 1297-1300. Already, many Southern towns on river fronts have gambling river boats. Gambling, as a get-rich-quick scheme, has become problematic where those who tend to gamble have the most to lose.

15. There is evidence that, among the Cherokees, the adoption of slavery created serious internecine struggles between slave-holding families like the Vanns and Rosses, and other Cherokees.

16. Walter L. Williams, "Indians and Blacks," in C. Reagan Wilson and W. Ferris, *Encyclopedia of Southern Culture* (Chapel Hill: University of North Carolina Press, 1989), 167-68.

17. The term "creole" is from the Spanish *criollo,* which meant, in the colonial period, anyone of Spanish descent born outside Spain in the new world, and adapted by the French, hence the term "creole." Originally pertaining to anyone of French descent born in the new world, the term "creole" was applied

to both white and black people in the Gulf Coast area of French descent. In recent years, some African Americans in some parts of the Gulf Coast have claimed the term applies exclusively to those of African descent. In south Louisiana, such exclusive use has been fiercely resisted by white Creoles, who say that the term has always applied to both black and white people of French descent in south Louisiana—excluding the Cajuns, who came at a later date and from a different source than the Creoles. White Creoles are urban and came to south Louisiana at a period prior to the Acadian (Cajun) migration. In *Hé,La-Bas*, by Reida Fuselier and Jolene Adam (1994), Adam states that the term "creole" is used by French Louisianans who claim African or Caribbean origin in addition to their French or Spanish origin, as well as by Louisianans who claim a European origin only.

18. See http://ccct.louisiana.edu/index.html.

19. Pemrose St. Amant, "Louisiana" in C. Reagan Wilson and W. Ferris, *Encyclopedia of Southern Culture* (Chapel Hill: University of North Carolina Press, 1989), 413; http://www.xula.edu/History.html.

20. http://docSouth.unc.edu/church/hicks/summary.html.

21. See http://www.adherents.com/Na/Na_67.html#385.

22. The *Shreveport Times*, http://www.nwlouisiana.com/html/1E5CA7F4-C6C2-4D0C-B864-35081451263C.shtml, posted June 1, 2003; http://www.oaoa.com/religionpage/religinpager132.htm

23. John P. Gill, *The Crossroads of Arkansas* (Little Rock: Butler Center for AR Studies, 2001), 20-1.

24. As cited, ibid., 24.

25. See Philip Dray, *At the Hands of Persons Unknown : The Lynching of Black America* (NY: Random House, 2002); C. Calvin Smith "Rumors & Reactions: Reconsidering the Elaine Race Riots of 1919—A Conference," *Arkansas Review: A Journal of Delta Studies*, 32/2 (August, 2001) at http://www.clt.astate.edu/arkreview/contents-32-2.html; and Grif Stockley, *Blood in Their Eyes: The Elaine Race Massacres of 1919* (Fayetteville: University of Arkansas Press, 2001).

26. See Terry D. Goddard, "Southern Social Justice: Brooks Hays and the Little Rock School Crisis," *Baptist History and Heritage* (Spring 2003), at www.findarticles.com.

27. James K. Zink, "Oklahoma," in C. Reagan Wilson and W. Ferris, *Encyclopedia of Southern Culture* (Chapel Hill: University of North Carolina Press, 1989), 553-569.

28. See Omer C. Stewart, *Peyote Religion: A History* (Norman: University of Oklahoma Press, 1993).

29. http://www.lincolnu.edu/~lupres/history.htm.

30. Richard M. Pope, "Missouri," in C. Reagan Wilson and W. Ferris, *Encyclopedia of Southern Culture* (Chapel Hill: University of North Carolina Press, 1989), 495-496.

31. JoAllyn Archambault, "Pan-Indian Organizations," in F.E. Hoxie, *Encyclopedia of North American Indians* (Boston: Houghton Mifflin Company, 1996), online at college.hmco.com.

32. Vine Deloria, Jr., *Custer Died for Your Sins*, 2nd edn. (Norman: University of Oklahoma Press, 1988), xi; see also 102, 106, 108.

33. Ibid., 112-115.

34. Leslie Newell Peacock, "Dig Deep and Help the Ladies Keep It Up—Sales Just Can't Do It," *Arkansas Times* (9 April 2004), 12.

CONCLUSION

SHOWDOWNS

William Lindsey and Mark Silk

Contemporary American religious politics was birthed in the Southern Crossroads when more than 10,000 people turned up at Reunion Arena in Dallas on August 21 and 23, 1980 for the Religious Roundtable's National Affairs Briefing. "You'll walk away with know-how to inform and mobilize your church and community," declared a circular. "Get 'em saved; get 'em baptized; get 'em registered."

In attendance were leading conservative religious leaders like Jerry Falwell and Pat Robertson, and prominent Republican politicians, most notably the GOP presidential candidate Ronald Reagan, who gave the after-dinner speech on the second day of the assemblage. Although Reagan followed the party line that this was not a partisan exercise, the disclaimers were not to be taken seriously. The event was designed to transform hitherto politically passive white evangelicals into active Republicans.

To a remarkable degree, it succeeded. A quarter century later, white evangelicals have moved decisively into the Republican camp and become the source of the party's activist core. Parachurch organizations and evangelical churches themselves have emerged as important agents of political mobilization for the GOP—comparable across the Bible Belt to the role organized labor has played for the Democratic party in the industrial heartland since the 1930s. Religion, evangelical style, has become a fixture of national political rhetoric and electioneering in a way absent and unanticipated only a generation ago. And in this new religio-political landscape, the Crossroads is center stage.

According to exit polling from recent presidential elections summed up in the Akron/Pew survey, the Crossroads is the most politically conservative region of the country—at 49.7 percent, more than five points higher than the country as a whole, and significantly higher than the next most conservative regions, the

Mountain West (47.4 percent) and the South (46 percent). This is due, in part, to the high proportion of America's most conservative class of voters—white evangelical Protestants who attend church at least once a week. But the neighboring Southern region also has a lot of frequent-attending (high-commitment) white evangelicals. What makes the Crossroads different is that here the evangelicals' views and values exert a greater gravitational pull on the rest of the population (including the non-religious).

Nationally, 66 percent of high-commitment white evangelicals report that they are politically conservative. In the Crossroads, it's 69 percent. (By comparison, the figure in the South is 60 percent.) Moreover, members of nine of the 10 other religious groups tracked in the Crossroads register as more conservative than the national average for their groups; only the region's low-commitment Catholics have a smaller proportion of conservatives than the nationwide sample.

Three large groups in the region are significantly more conservative than the national average. Fifty-one and a half percent of high-commitment Catholics in the Crossroads call themselves conservative, in comparison to the national average of 46 percent. Of the region's black Protestants, 40.6 percent say they are conservative, compared with a national rate of 35 percent. The most dramatic regional effect, however, occurs among high-commitment white mainline Protestants. In the nation at large, 51.5 percent call themselves conservative; in the Southern Crossroads the figure is 60 percent. Indeed, one of the salient regional characteristics is a far stronger alliance of high-commitment evangelical and mainline Protestants than exists elsewhere. (In the South, by contrast, 52.4 percent of high-commitment mainliners say they are conservative, just slightly above the national average.)

How does Crossroads conservatism manifest itself? On economic issues, the pull to the right is marginal, as it is on the environment. For example, 27 percent of all Crossroads voters oppose more environmental protection measures as against 26 percent in the national sample; an outright majority are pro-protection. (High-commitment white evangelicals are somewhat more likely to oppose tougher environmental enforcement, as are black Protestants.)

But on welfare spending the difference with the rest of the country is clear, and so is the distinctive Crossroads alliance of high-commitment white evangelicals and mainliners. Forty percent of the evangelicals and 39 percent of mainline Protestants in the Crossroads support less welfare spending. Elsewhere in the country the proportion of high-commitment mainliners against welfare is significantly lower: 33.3 percent nationwide and, notably, 31.5 percent in the South and 29 percent in the Mountain West. White Crossroads Catholics are even more conservative on this issue: 43 percent of those who attend Mass weekly and 36 percent who do so less frequently oppose more welfare spending. (The national averages for white Catholics are 30 and 32 percent respectively.) Another area where the high-commitment white mainliners stand with their evangelical peers in the Crossroads is national health insurance: 51.5 percent oppose it, as compared with 47 percent of frequently attending Crossroads evangelicals and 40 percent of high-commitment mainliners nationwide. In the South, national health care is opposed by only 34 percent of high-commitment mainliners.

Overall, no region of the country is as strongly opposed to legalized abortion as the Crossroads, with 49.9 percent of all voters saying they are pro-life, a figure slightly larger than in the South, the Mountain West, and the Midwest. (The national sample of voters shows 43.3 percent of voters taking pro-life positions.) In the Crossroads, 76.6 percent of high-commitment evangelicals are pro-life, just marginally above the national average. Low-commitment evangelicals, low-commitment Catholics, Latino Christians, and "other" Christians are all a few percentage points more pro-life in the Crossroads than their national averages. For black Protestants, high-commitment Catholics, non-Christians, and seculars the differentials are 4.3, 4, 12, and 10.6 percent respectively.

The Crossroads is also the most anti-gay-rights region of the country. Virtually every religious category in the Crossroads is more anti-gay than the national average, and many rank highest among the regions. Forty percent of high-commitment mainline Protestants in the Crossroads are anti-gay rights, as opposed to 33 percent in the South. Among low-commitment mainliners, 27 percent are against gay rights, as compared to some regions of the country where the percentage is in the single digits. Nationwide, 50.6 percent of high-commitment evangelicals oppose gay rights, but in the Crossroads it's 57 percent. In the aggregate, gay rights are opposed by 35.1 percent of Crossroads voters; that's 6.4 percentage points above the national average.

It should, then, come as no surprise that of the 12 states whose sodomy laws were struck down by the U.S. Supreme Court's 2003 *Lawrence v. Texas* decision, three of the four with laws prohibiting only *homosexual* sodomy were in the Crossroads— Missouri, Oklahoma, and Texas (the other was the neighboring state of Kansas). In the wake of *Lawrence*, the number of co-sponsors of the constitutional amendment to define marriage as "between a man and a woman" jumped to 75 members of Congress, of whom 14 came from Crossroads states. Texas led all states with eight co-sponsors, while only Arkansas—whose sodomy law had been tossed out by its own Supreme Court in 2002—failed to provide a single co-sponsor.

Looking more closely at particular religious groupings, it is possible to discern how political conservatism has gathered strength in the Crossroads. Holiness and Pentecostal folk, who historically tended to stand aloof from politics, are joining in with gusto. If theological differences continue to separate them from other evangelicals, those evangelicals—many of whom belong to churches that have fallen under the influence of charismatic worship style—show little reluctance to make common cause with them against the forces of liberalism. The Pentecostal impact on politics can also be seen in the growing movement of many Latinos from Catholicism into Pentecostal churches.

A telling indication of this trend in the Crossroads can be found in Arkansas' weekly Latino newspaper, *El Latino*, whose *Quien Es Quien?* of Hispanic Arkansas now lists comparable numbers of Pentecostal ministers and Catholic priests. Latino Protestants are much more likely to vote Republican than Latino Catholics—a tendency that shows signs of being on the increase: In voting for members of Congress in 2000 and 2002, Latino Catholics went from casting 30 percent of their votes for GOP candidates to 28 percent, while Latino Protestants went from 48 percent to 56 percent.[1] It is to be expected that the more acculturated into American society they become, the more Latino Pentecostals in the Crossroads will trend Republican.

As for Crossroads Catholics, their readiness to adapt to the dominant cultural values of the region has resulted in significantly greater conservatism in the aggregate. Yet there are many Catholicisms in the Crossroads, with important sub-regional and ethnic variations. For example, in Arkansas, which has a strong public-school tradition, Catholics tend to oppose school vouchers, whereas in Louisiana, with its plethora of Catholic schools and large Catholic population, support for vouchers is high and is being spun by diocesan spokespersons as a social-justice issue. And while Latino Catholics, supporting the teaching of the church hierarchy, may be part of the regional consensus on abortion and same-sex marriage, they remain (again like the hierarchy) well to the left on issues of social welfare and economic policy. In a region where half the Catholics are Latino, this bivalence is important to bear in mind.

African-American Protestants are also subject to the prevailing conservative winds. Many are divided over the question of including openly gay and lesbian individuals within the faith community and have adopted a "don't ask, don't tell" or avowedly exclusionary stance. Moreover, black churchgoers in the Crossroads are increasingly targeted by political initiatives designed to move them away from their traditional alliance with the Democratic Party; these initiatives often seek to use issues like same-sex marriage as a means of gaining greater entrée to the African-American faith community. At a time of decreased social welfare spending, the "faith-based" policies of George W. Bush's administration have been attractive to many black churches, which have long seen themselves as providers of social welfare services to the communities they serve. What the political consequences of receiving such funds will be remains to be seen, but indications are that the black pastors of large megachurches like T.D. Jakes' Potter's House will not be inclined to alienate politicians who keep public funds flowing into their ministries.

How Crossroads conservatism plays out on the religious stage can best be seen in the current cultural struggle over homosexuality.[2] In denominations divided on the issue, Crossroads churches have disproportionately supported the anti-gay side. The United Methodist Church, for example, has for several years seen a debate between "Reconciling" conferences and congregations—those that accept gays and lesbians as full participants in the life of the church—and "Transforming" conferences and congregations—those that offer support for homosexuals who want to leave their gay lifestyles and believe that transformation to a straight lifestyle is possible. In 1997, when at least 18 Methodist conferences addressed this issue, the Northwest Texas conference was one of the few to call for the "healing and transformation" of gays. The following year, Northwest Texas decided simultaneously to become a Transforming and a "Confessing" conference. (The Confessing movement, while similar to the Transforming movement in its position on homosexuality, is a broader movement, which, like Good News, aims to "enable the United Methodist Church to retrieve its classical doctrinal identity."[3]) Subsequently, 45 of the Methodists' 66 conferences chose not to vote to maintain the church's official position against homosexuality ("the practice of homosexuality is incompatible with Christian teaching"), but five of the 12 conferences in the Crossroads—Missouri West, North Arkansas, and Central, North, and Northwest Texas—voted to support it.

In June 2003, Arkansas Methodists passed resolutions calling on Methodist seminaries to remain faithful to traditional doctrinal standards and for the denomination to maintain its current stance on human sexuality and marriage. Later that month, after the *Lawrence* decision, the Reverend William Hinson of Houston, president of the Confessing movement, claimed that the "vast majority of United Methodist people agree that Jesus got it right, that marriage is between a man and a woman." Conceding that the Supreme Court was correct on the privacy issue, he nevertheless insisted that the church "should be a guide for the culture and not a reflector of the culture."[4]

Though less divided than the Methodists on homosexuality, Crossroads Baptists have been wounded on this battlefield as well. In March 1998 the Baptist General Convention of Texas voted to reject financial contributions from University Baptist Church in Austin and asked the church to cease publishing materials noting an affiliation with the state convention. Three years earlier the congregation had been removed from the Austin Baptist Association after ordaining a self-professed homosexual as a deacon. "You may not all agree with the way our church ministers with gays and lesbians and their families," Pastor Larry Bethune told the Convention's Executive Board. "In fact, we don't all agree at University Baptist Church but we are creating one of the few safe places for your Baptist homosexual children to work out their salvation with fear and trembling."

In 1998, the church renounced its affiliation with the more liberal Cooperative Baptist Fellowship after the Fellowship approved a new policy against hiring gays or funding organizations that "condone, advocate, or affirm homosexual practice"—a policy Fellowship officials characterized as "welcoming but not affirming" of gays. Stan Hastey, director of the Washington, D.C.-based Alliance of Baptists, explained the new policy as a "made in Texas" phenomenon. "The Texas influence dominates Cooperative Baptist Fellowship life, and has from the beginning," Hastey said, adding that talks of merger between the Alliance and the Fellowship broke off years earlier because Texas leaders of the Fellowship felt "we were too far left of center on women's issues and really off the charts when it came to homosexuality."[5]

Along the same lines, in 2003 the Missouri Baptist Convention withdrew funding from William Jewell College because the school had allowed the student senate to consider adding sexual orientation to the list of protections in the Student's Bill of Rights and permitted a theater student to produce portions of "The Vagina Monologues" at her senior recital. Together with its 154-year relationship with Missouri Baptists, the college lost 3 percent ($900,000) of its operating budget.

On another front, 2,000 conservative Episcopalians from around the country showed up at Christ Church in the town of Plano north of Dallas in October 2003 to mobilize opposition to the Episcopal Church USA for confirming Gene Robinson's appointment as bishop of New Hampshire. But while Plano had become a national center of opposition to the full acceptance of homosexuality in the Episcopal church, Crossroads Episcopalian leaders were themselves at odds on the question: The Texas and Louisiana bishops voted against Robinson's confirmation and the bishops of Arkansas, Oklahoma, and Missouri voted to confirm him.

In Dallas itself, a number of Episcopalians celebrated Robinson's election, revealing Texas to be a culture war in microcosm, and not for the first time. Back in the 1980s the Lone Star State not only generated much of the fundamentalist energy that captured the Southern Baptist Convention (SBC), but also created some of the sharpest opposition to that fundamentalism. Key churches in urban parts of Texas have either totally or partially removed themselves from the Convention, and the moderate General Baptist Convention of Texas has succeeded in maintaining control of a fourth of the board of Texas's premier Baptist university, Baylor. Likewise, the attempt to create an alternative to seminaries controlled by the SBC is centered in Texas. The ferocity of this intra-ecclesial struggle has deep roots in the historical contentiousness of religionists in Texas and in the Crossroads generally.

As in ecclesial, so in secular politics. For all its prevailing conservatism, the Crossroads has not become the GOP stronghold that might have been predicted—

at least not yet. While Texas and Oklahoma now seem safely ensconced in the Republican "red zone," Louisiana, Arkansas, and Missouri remain battleground states in which Democrats retain fighting chances in both statewide and presidential elections.

Missouri will not soon forget the 2000 election, when John Ashcroft lost his bid for reelection to the Senate to his archrival Mel Carnahan a month after Carnahan died in a plane crash. In 2002, staunchly Catholic south Louisiana prevailed over the conservative Protestant northern part of the state in electing liberal Democrat (and Catholic) Kathleen Babineaux Blanco to the governor's seat in a hotly contested election in which national Republican money and interest groups were giving strong support to Bobby Jindal, the son of Indian immigrants. Even in Oklahoma, surprises can happen. Also in 2002, a strong turnout by Cherokee voters—evangelical Protestants, for the most part, but heavily courted by the Democrats—was widely credited with defeating one of the Christian Right's rising stars, Steve Largent, in his bid to become governor.

Among high-commitment white evangelicals, Democratic identity remains stronger in the Crossroads (31 percent) than in the South (27.6 percent), which helps explain why white Democratic politicians remain thicker on the ground. In Arkansas, for example, they outnumber Republicans 70 to 30 in the state house of representatives and 27 to 8 in the state senate. In the 2000 presidential election, Arkansas Gov. Mike Huckabee, a Southern Baptist minister, made national news by complaining that several counties had opened their polls on Sunday in order to make it easier for black churches to bus their members to the voting booths. What angered Huckabee, who endorses the involvement of churches in politics, was simply the fact that the arrangement seemed intended to benefit Democratic candidates. And then there was the months-long drama of Texas' Democratic legislators decamping to Oklahoma and New Mexico in an ultimately unsuccessful effort to prevent the GOP powers that be from redistricting. In the Crossroads, you don't go down without a fight.

It's a style of florid partisanship that became the norm in Washington in the 1990s. The impeachment of Bill Clinton was nothing less than a Crossroads morality play featuring a Restorationist Savonarola out of West Texas (the special prosecutor Kenneth Starr) in hot pursuit of the kind of Arkansas Baptist (Clinton) who knocks up your sister and still your momma's sweet on him. In the sequel, the reins of power passed to the Crossroads likes of John Ashcroft, Tom Delay, Dick Cheney, and above all George W. Bush.

Bush's denominational journey was a typical Crossroads pilgrim's progress: from his father's Connecticut Episcopalianism to his mother's New York Presbyterianism to his wife's Texas Methodism. The story of his personal conversion is a classic of evangelical rescue: the walk with the famous evangelist (Billy

Graham), the turning away from alcohol, the strengthening of his family life, the progress to the pinnacle of worldly success. Asked in a candidates' debate for the thinker or philosopher who had influenced him most, he answered in the spirit of Wesleyan sanctification, "Christ, because he changed my heart," and went on to explain, "When you turn your heart and your life over to Christ, when you accept Christ as the savior, it changes your heart. It changes your life. And that's what happened to me."

As his presidential administration opened, this made for the kind of social philosophy that animated evangelical reformers of the nineteenth century: Bring individuals to Christ, change their hearts, and society will change with them. Before the attacks of September 11, the only policy Bush seemed to have a personal stake in was his faith-based initiative, which aimed to make it possible for religious organizations to obtain public money to provide social services without hiding their spiritual light under a bushel.

While many of his supporters in the Religious Right looked askance at the government entanglements this seemed to invite, the president was unperturbed. Like his forebears in the perfectionist tradition, he seemed to believe that the state could only profit from the ministrations of the church, and that neither was a threat to the other. Male and female, black and white, Jew and Gentile, all could be one in the Bush White House. And politically, there were no qualms about seeking to mobilize them all by appealing to their several faith-based interests, be it abortion or school vouchers or the state of Israel.

After September 11, Bush harked back to another piece of the Crossroads past: the Christian Republicanism of J.R. Graves, complete with the conviction that the United States had been given a sacred trust to further the replacement of absolutist and clerical regimes with its own principles of government and religion. Of course, there also seemed to be something personal about Bush's determination to invade Iraq, especially since he was not above noting that Saddam Hussein had once tried to kill his father. Or maybe it was just typical Crossroads pugnacity. As he put it at a news conference on July 2, 2003, "There are some who feel like that, you know, the conditions are such that they can attack us there. My answer is bring them on."

Endnotes

1. John Green and Mark Silk, "The New Religion Gap," *Religion in the News* (Fall, 2003), 3.

2. The following account of Crossroads religion and homosexuality was provided by Andrew Manis.

3. United Methodist News Service (NMNS) Press Release, November 2, 1998; also see http://www.umaffirm.org/jcnono.html.

4. UMNS Report on Annual Conferences, Arkansas Conference, June 11-14, 2003, http://umns.umc.org/acreports/Arkansas.htm; UMNS Press Release, June 27, 2003.

5. American Baptist Press (ABP) Press Releases, March 4, 1998 and August 22, 2001.

APPENDIX

In order to provide the best possible empirical basis for understanding the place of religion in each of the regions of the United States, the Religion by Region project contracted to obtain data from three sources: the North American Religion Atlas (NARA); the 2001 American Religious Identification Survey (ARIS); and the 1992, 1996, and 2000 National Surveys of Religion and Politics (NSRP).

NARA For the Project, the Polis Center of Indiana University-Purdue University at Indianapolis created an interactive Web site that made it possible to map general demographic and religious data at the national, regional, state-by-state, and county-by-county level. The demographic data were taken from the 2000 Census. The primary source for the religious data (congregations, members, and adherents) was the 2000 Religious Congregations and Membership Survey (RCMC) compiled by the Glenmary Research Center. Because a number of religious groups did not participate in the 2000 RCMS—including most historically African-American Protestant denominations—this dataset was supplemented with data from other sources *for adherents only*. The latter included projections from 1990 RCMC reports, ARIS, and several custom estimates. For a fuller methodological account, go to *http://www.religionatlas.org*.

ARIS The American Religious Identification Survey (ARIS 2001), carried out under the auspices of the Graduate Center of the City University of New York by Barry A. Kosmin, Egon Mayer, and Ariela Keysar, replicates the methodology of the National Survey of Religious Identification (NSRI 1990). As in 1990 the ARIS sample is based on a series of national random digit dialing (RDD) surveys, utilizing ICR, International Communication Research Group in Media, Pennsylvania, national telephone omnibus services. In all, 50,284 U.S. households were successfully interviewed. Within a household, an adult respondent was chosen using the "last birthday method" of random selection. One of the distinguishing features of both ARIS 2001 and NSRI 1990 is that respondents were asked to describe themselves in terms of religion with an open-ended question: "What is your religion, if

171

any?[1]" ARIS 2001 enhanced the topics covered by adding questions concerning religious beliefs and membership as well as religious switching and religious identification of spouses/partners. The ARIS findings have a high level of statistical significance for most large religious groups and key geographical units, such as states. ARIS 2001 detailed methodology can be found in the report on the American Religious Identification Survey 2001 at *www.gc.cuny.edu/studies/aris-_index.htm.*

NSRP   The National Surveys of Religion and Politics were conducted in 1992, 1996, and 2000 at the Bliss Center at the University of Akron under the direction of John C. Green, supported by grants from the Pew Charitable Trusts.

Together, these three surveys include more than 14,000 cases. Eight items were asked in all three surveys (partisanship, ideology, abortion, gay rights, help for minorities, environmental protection, welfare spending, and national health insurance). The responses on these items were pooled for all three years to produce enough cases for an analysis by region. These data must be viewed with some caution because they represent opinion over an entire decade rather than at one point in time. A more detailed account of how these data were compiled may be obtained from the Bliss Institute.

Endnote

1. In the 1990 NSRI survey, the question wording was: "What is your religion?" In the 2001 ARIS survey, the phrase, "…if any" was added to the question. A subsequent validity check based on cross-samples of 3,000 respondents carried out by ICR in 2002 found no statistical difference between the pattern of responses according to the two wordings.

BIBLIOGRAPHY

Campbell, Randolph B. *Gone to Texas*. New York: Oxford, 2003.

Ehle, John. *Trail of Tears*. New York: Doubleday, 1988.

Glass, William R. *Strangers in Zion: Fundamentalists in The South, 1900-1950*. Macon, GA: Mercer University Press, 2001.

Goff, James R., Jr. *Fields White Unto Harvest: Charles F. Parham and the Missionary Origins of Pentecostalism*. Fayetteville: University of Arkansas Press, 1988.

Green, John Clifford, Mark J. Rozell, and Clyde Wilcox, eds. *The Christian Right in American Politics: Marching to the Millennium*. Washington, D.C.: Georgetown University Press, 2003.

Hankins, Barry. *Uneasy in Babylon: Southern Baptist Conservatives and American Culture*. Tuscaloosa: University of Alabama Press, 2002.

Hill, Samuel S., ed. *Encyclopedia of Religion in the South*. Macon, GA: Mercer University Press, 1984.

Hill, Samuel S., ed. *Religion in the Southern States: A Historical Study*. Macon, GA: Mercer University Press, 1983.

Hunter, James Davison. *Culture Wars: The Struggle to Define America*. New York: Basic Books, 1990.

Lind, Michael. *Made in Texas: George W. Bush and the Southern Takeover of American Politics*. New York: Basic Books, 2003.

Matovina, Timothy and Gary Riebe-Estrella, eds. *Horizons of the Sacred: Mexican Traditions in U.S. Catholicism*. Ithaca, NY: Cornell University Press, 2002.

Miller, Randall M., and Jon L. Wakelyn, eds. *Catholics in the Old South: Essays on Church and Culture*. Macon, GA: Mercer University Press, 1999.

Smith, Oran P. *The Rise of Baptist Republicanism*. New York: New York University Press, 1997.

Sweet, William Warren, ed. *Religion on the American Frontier, 1783-1840*. New York: Cooper Square, 1964.

Wilson, Charles Reagan and William Ferris, eds. *Encyclopedia of Southern Culture*. Chapel Hill: Univ. of NC Press, 1989.

INDEX

abortion: African Americans and, 149;
Catholics and, 114, 116, 118, 120, 122;
Christian Right and, 75; conservatives
and, 163; Dobson and, 98; *Good News
Magazine* and, 73;
Holiness/Pentecostal tradition and, 95;
Southern Crossroads and, 51, 64
Acadians (Cajuns), 104, 106, 138, 157n17
Adam, Jolene, 158n17
adaptation, religious, in Southern
Crossroads, 15–17, 28, 30
adherents, claimed by religious groups,
23, *24*
Africa: and Louisiana, 11–12; religions of,
130–32, 139
African American corridor, 39, *41*, 128
African Americans: Baptist, 38, 131,
139–40, 143; Catholic, 113, 129;
demographics of, 33, *34*, 128–29, *129*;
diversity among, 153; and Holiness
movement, 80, 84–85, 96–97, 101n5,
131, 139; and ideology, 162, 164;
issues with demographics of, 156n1;
Jakes and, 29; and Native Americans,
137–38; and political issues, 153–55;
and public life, 138–47; and regional
identity, 133–36; religious ethos of,
130–32; in Southern Crossroads,
127–59
African Methodist Episcopal Church
(AME), 131, 142, 144
African Methodist Episcopal Zion Church,
131

agriculture, in Southern Crossroads, 33
Ahlstrom, Sydney, 82
Albach, Susan Hogan, 115
alcohol: Baptists and, 39, 74; Catholics
and, 110–11; Church of the Nazarene
and, 83; Pentecostals and, 82
Alldredge, E. P., 66
Allen, Richard, 131
Alliance of Baptists, 166
Allison, Lenora, 100
America, Graves on, 58
American Baptist Association, 59
American Baptist Churches, USA, in
Oklahoma, 46
American Indian Movement (AIM), 155
American Muslim Mission, 131
American Religious Identification Survey
(ARIS), 23, 35, 113, 171–72
Americans United for the Separation of
Church and State, 69, 74–75
Ammerman, Nancy, 64
Amnesty International, 122
Anabaptist groups, demographics of, *35*
Angelus Temple, 89
Annan, Kofi, 123
Anthony, J. J., 11
anti-Catholic sentiment, 109
anti-German sentiment, 58, 65
Apache people, 104
Archambault, JoAllyn, 155
Arkansas: African Americans in, *129*,
140–43; Baptists in, 42, 59, 74;
Catholics in, 107, 117–18; character of,

11, 13–14; demographics of, 41–43; Native Americans in, 140–43; population of, 33, 41; racial composition of, *34*; settlement of, 58. *See also* Southern Crossroads

Arkansas Baptist College, 85, 142

Arkansas Baptist Convention, 59

Arkansas Post, 104

Arkansas River, 107–8

Ashcroft, John, 16, 60, 79, 99–100, 167

Asian Catholics, 113

Assemblies of God, 16, 31, 80; in Arkansas, 42; Ashcroft and, 99–100; and cultural mainstream, 92–93; formation of, 86–87; in Missouri, 45; and settlement, 60; in Texas, 48

Atoka, OK, 105

Austin, Stephen F., 108, 143

Austin, TX, *49–51*, 116

Azusa Street revival, 84–85

Bachelor, Wilson, 11

Bakker, Jim and Tammy Faye, 79

baptism in Holy Spirit, 80, 83–84, 86

Baptist Bible College, 60

Baptist Bible Fellowship, 38, 62

Baptist Bible Institute, 60

Baptist corridor, 38, *39*

Baptist Faith and Message (BF&M), 74–75

Baptist General Association of Texas, 59

Baptist General Convention of Texas (BGCT), 47, 59, 75, 166

Baptist Missionary Association, 59

Baptists: adherents claimed by, in Southern Crossroads versus United States, *24*; African-American, 131, 139–40, 143, 147; in Arkansas, 42, 59; and Catholics, 120; and conservatism, 62; demographics of, 34, *35*; dominance of, 36–38; and gay rights, 165–66; and Holiness movement, 85; in Louisiana, 43, 60; and Native

Americans, 145–46; in Oklahoma, 46; and party preference, 50; and Pentecostals, 17; self-identification as, in Southern Crossroads versus United States, *25*; and settlement, 16, 59–60; in Texas, 47, *49*, 67–68, *69*, 143. *See also* Southern Baptists

Barrow, Clyde, 20

Bass, W. H., 135

Bates, Daisy, 135

Baton Rouge, LA, 44

battleground states, in Southern Crossroads, 167

Baylor University, 166

Belgian Catholics, 109

Bell, Eudorus N., 87

Benedictines, 107

Bertrand, Alvin, 64

Bethel Bible College, 84

Bethune, Larry, 165

Bexar County, TX, 129

biblicism, 57, 133. *See also* fundamentalism

birth control, Catholics and, 116

Black Belt. *See* African American corridor

Black Entertainment Television, 144

Blanco, Kathleen Babineaux, 17, 167

Bliss Institute, 49, 113, 172

Bloom, Harold, 67

Blumhofer, Edith, 86, 89

Bogard, Ben, 59, 63

Breazeale, Kathlyn, 19, 103–25

Broadman Press, 66–67

Brown, Dee, 10

Brown v. Board of Education, 64, 142

brush arbor. *See* hush arbor

Buddhists, demographics of, 36

burned-over district, 27–33

Bush, George H. W., 30

Bush, George W., 30, 55, 73, 113–14, 164, 167–68

Bush, William, 135

Butler College, 144

Caddo people, 104
Cain, Bernest, 70
Cajuns (Acadians), 104, 106, 138, 157n17
Calvary Temple Assembly of God, 93
Campbell, Alexander, 57–60
camp meetings, 82
Cane River area, 11
Caribbean Catholics, 104, 111, 139
Carnahan, Mel, 75, 167
Carroll, B. H., 59
Carthage, MO, 112
Catholic Charities, 121
Catholic corridor, 38–39, 40
Catholic Renewal Movement, 94
Catholics: adherents claimed by, in
    Southern Crossroads versus United
    States, 24; African-American, 129; in
    Arkansas, 42–43, 117–18; and charis-
    matic movement, 31, 94; demographics
    of, 34, 35, 113; diversity of, 119; evan-
    gelicals and, 31; Graves on, 58; history
    in Southern Crossroads, 103–9; and
    ideology, 162, 164; Latino, 35, 112–13;
    in Louisiana, 11, 43–44, 104, 119–20;
    in Missouri, 15, 44–45, 120–21; Native
    American, 136; in Oklahoma, 46,
    121–22; and party preference, 50; self-
    identification as, in Southern
    Crossroads versus United States, 25; in
    Southern Crossroads, 17, 103–25; in
    St. Louis, 15, 45–46, 107, 111; in
    Texas, 13, 47–48, 49; voting behaviors
    of, 17
Central Oklahoma Turning Point, 122
Chafer, Lewis Sperry, 63–64
Chafetz, Janet Saltzman, 40
Charismatics: adherents claimed by, in
    Southern Crossroads versus United
    States, 24; beliefs of, 31; in Louisiana,
    44; in Missouri, 45; movement of, 94;
    in Oklahoma, 46–47; self-identification
    as, in Southern Crossroads versus
    United States, 25; in Texas, 48

Cheney, Richard, 167
Cherokee County, OK, 130
Cherokee National Youth Choir, 133
Cherokee people, 105, 130, 132–33,
    140–41, 145; and political participa-
    tion, 167; and slavery, 157n15
Chickasaw people, 105, 130, 145
Choctaw people, 105, 130, 145
Christ Church Episcopal, Plano, TX, 30
Christian, John T., 60
Christian Church. See Disciples of Christ
Christian Coalition, 68–69, 97
Christian Holiness Partnership, 83
Christian Methodist Episcopal Church,
    131
Christian Right, 29–30, 161; Bush and,
    168; and culture war, 68; influence of,
    68
Church of Christ, 60; and political partici-
    pation, 65; as Restorationist, 65
Church of Christ (Holiness) U.S.A., 85
Church of Christ Scientist, 147
Church of God, 31
Church of God (Cleveland, TN), 94; in
    Arkansas, 42; in Louisiana, 44; in
    Missouri, 45; in Oklahoma, 46; in
    Texas, 48
Church of God in Christ, 80, 85–86;
    demographics of, 101n5
Church of the Nazarene, 33, 80–81;
    Dobson and, 98; formation of, 83; in
    Texas, 48
City of Faith, 91
Civil Rights movement: Native Americans
    and, 138; Texas and, 151; women and,
    134
Civil War: and Arkansas, 14; Catholics
    and, 109–10; Native Americans and,
    105, 138, 145
Clay, William Lacy, Jr., 147
Clinton, Hillary, 71
Clinton, William J., 13, 20, 30, 65, 71–72,
    167

Code Noir, 109–10
Coffelt, Charlotte, 69
Coleman, Adele, 12
Comanche people, 104–5
Communities Organized for Public
    Service (COPS), 124
Community of the Mother Co-
    Redemptrix, 112
competition, religious, in Southern
    Crossroads, 57
concealed weapons, Catholics and, 120
Cone, James, 134
Confessing movement, 73, 165
Confessional/Reformed/non-UCC
    Congregational churches, demograph-
    ics of, *35*
Conger, Kimberly H., 68
conservatism: in South, 61–62; in Southern
    Crossroads, 29–30, 49, 161–68
controversialism. *See* showdown mentality
conversionism, 28, 30–31, 52, 80
Cook, Alison, 12–13
Cooperative Baptist Fellowship, 75, 166
Copeland, Kenneth, 29
Coronado, Francisco Vazquez de, 105
Cotton, Emma, 86
Council on Community Affairs (COCA),
    135
Coushatta riots, 12
Cox, Shirley, 121
Creek people, 105, 130, 145
Creoles, 11–12, 139; term, 138, 157n17
Criswell, W. A., 67
Cross, Whitney, 27
Cuba, 139
culture wars: issues in, 68–76; Southern
    Crossroads and, 9, 20, 29–30, 55–77,
    161–68; Texas and, 166
Currie, David, 74
Czechs, in Texas, 13

Dallas, TX, 47, *49–51*; African Americans
    in, 129, 144; Catholics in, 115–16

Dallas Theological Seminary, 63–64
Daly, Richard, 115–17
Darwinism: Christian Right and, 69–70;
    evangelical Protestants and, 62–63
Davis, Jefferson, 59
death penalty: Catholics and, 117–20,
    122–23; in Southern Crossroads, 34
Defense of Marriage Act, 69
Delaware County, OK, 81, 130
Delaware people, 130
DeLay, Tom, 55, 69, 167
Deloria, Vine, Jr., 155–56
Democratic Party: African Americans and,
    140, 142, 148; Catholics and, 116;
    Holiness/Pentecostal tradition and, 96;
    Southern Crossroads and, 50, 167
desegregation, 110–11, 135, 141–42
De Soto, Hernando, 103, 105
de Tonti, Henri, 104
Disciples of Christ, 36, 60; in Arkansas,
    59; demographics of, *35*; as
    Restorationist, 65; in Texas, 48
divorce, in Southern Crossroads, 31, 34
Dobson, James, 79, 98–99
Dodd, David O., 11
Dollar, Creflo, 29
Douay, Anastase, 104
Douglas, Mack R., 67
Driver, Z. Z., 135
dualism, Ashcroft and, 99–100

Eagle, James P., 59
Eastern religions: adherents claimed by, in
    Southern Crossroads versus United
    States, *24*; demographics of, *35*; self-
    identification as, in Southern
    Crossroads versus United States, *25*; in
    Texas, 48
Ebaugh, Helen Rose, 40
education: African Americans and, 152,
    154–55; Catholics and, 118; in
    Southern Crossroads, 33
Edwards, W. Ross, 67

Eisenhower, Dwight D., 142
Elaine riots, 141
Eliot, T. S., 9
Elliott, Ralph, 66–67
El Paso, TX, 104
Engle v. Vitale, 64
environment, Holiness/Pentecostal tradition and, 95
Episcopalians: in Arkansas, 42; and charismatic movement, 94; demographics of, *35*, 36; and gay rights, 166; in Missouri, 45–46; in Oklahoma, 46; and settlement, 16, 57, 60; in Texas, 47–48
establishment: in Texas, 108. *See also* quasi-establishment
ethical issues. *See* political issues
Evangelical Free Church, 46
evangelicalism, 31
evangelical Protestants: African Americans and, 128; characteristics of, 133; Native American, 132, 136, 145–46, 156; in Oklahoma, 46; and political participation, 65; in Texas, 47. *See also* Baptists
Evening Light Saints, 84
evolution: Christian Right and, 69–70; evangelical Protestants and, 62–63

faith based community organizing, Catholics and, 124
Falwell, Jerry, 38, 60, 97, 161
family issues, 19–20; Catholics and, 119; Holiness/Pentecostal tradition and, 95–96
Family Life America and God (FLAG), 72
Faubus, Orval, 13, 20
Fayetteville, AR, 43
Fellowship Church.com, 29, 47
feuds: in Arkansas, 14; in Missouri, 15
Fillmore, Millard, 109
Findley, Fred H., 71
Finney, Charles G., 27, 30, 82

First Assemblies of God Church, 93
First Baptist Church, Fort Worth, TX, 62
First Pentecostal Church, North Little Rock, AR, 93
Five Civilized Nations, 130, 145
Fletcher, Jesse, 67–68
Flores, Patricio F., 112
Focus on the Family, 79, 98–99
Fort Smith, 10, 108
Fort Worth, TX, 47, *49–51*, 115–16
France, 9, 15, 103–4, 106
Franciscans, 104, 143
Free Africa Society, 131
French Catholics, 109
frontier mentality, in Southern Crossroads, 9, 28, 32
Fulbright, J. William, 13, 20
Full Gospel Temple, 90
fundamentalism: Baptists and, 64–68, 73–74; history of, 61; Independent Baptists and, 38; and modernism, 61–64
Fuselier, Reida, 158n17

Galveston, TX, *49–51*, 108; African Americans in, 129; Catholics in, 115; Holiness movement in, 84
gambling, 157n14
gay marriage, 20; African Americans and, 154; Christian Right and, 69; Holiness/Pentecostal tradition and, 95
gay rights: African Americans and, 149, 152; Catholics and, 114, 119; Christian Right and, 69, 75–76; conservatives and, 163, 165–66; *Good News Magazine* and, 73; Holiness/Pentecostal tradition and, 95–96; Southern Crossroads and, 30, 51
gender issues. *See* women
German Catholics, 13, 15, 104–10, 138
German-Roman Catholic Benevolent Society, 107

Ghost Dance, 146
Gibson, David, 116
Gill, John P., 141
Gilley, Mickey, 91
Glass, William R., 63
Glenmary Research Center, 41, 43, 171
glossolalia, 31, 80, 83–85, 88, 139
Good News Magazine, 72–73
Gore, Al, 75, 113
Graham, Billy, 167–68
Graves, Bill, 70
Graves, J. R., 55–58, 60, 168
Gray, Helen T., 120–21
Great West. *See* Southern Crossroads
Green, John C., 49, 68–69, 113, 172
Griffen, Wendell, 143
Gritz, Jack L., 67

Hackney, Sheldon, 61–62
Hague, Diane, 119
Haitians, 139
Hall, J. L., 88
Halter, Deborah, 117–19
Hankins, Barry, 62, 64
Harding College, 65
Hargis, Billy James, 146
Harris, Jane, 18–19, 79–102
Harris County, TX, 129
Harry Potter books, 74
Hasinai people, 104
Hastey, Stan, 166
Hayden, Samuel A., 59
Hays, Brooks, 142
healing: Church of the Nazarene and, 83;
    Holiness movement on, 31, 84;
    McPherson and, 89; Roberts and, 91
health care issues, African Americans and,
    153–54
health-wealth gospel. *See* prosperity
    gospel
Hearn, Lafcadio, 12
Heidinger, James III, 72–73
Herbert, David, 70

Herrod, Ron, 74
Hicks, William, 139
Hill, Samuel S., 67
Hindus, demographics of, 36; in Texas, 48
Hinson, William, 165
Hinton, Carla, 122
Hispanic Americans. *See* Latinos
historically African American Protestant
    churches: in Arkansas, 42; church mat-
    ters in, 152–53; demographics of, 23,
    25–35, *35*; future of, 150–51; and ide-
    ology, 162, 164; in Southern
    Crossroads, 127–59, *129*
historically African American Protestant
    corridor, 39, *41*, 128
HIV/AIDS, African Americans and, 154
Holiness movement: adherents claimed by,
    in Southern Crossroads versus United
    States, *24*; in Arkansas, 42; celebrities
    of, 88–92; and cultural mainstream,
    92–94; demographics of, *35*, *81*; histo-
    ry of, 33, 82–88; Native Americans
    and, 146; in Oklahoma, 46; and politi-
    cal participation, 163–64; self-identifi-
    cation as, in Southern Crossroads ver-
    sus United States, *25*; in Southern
    Crossroads, 16, 79–102; on Spirit,
    30–31; in Texas, 48
Holmes, Zan, 151
Holy Name of Jesus Church, 111
Holy Spirit: baptism in, 80, 83–84, 86;
    Holiness/Pentecostal traditions and,
    79–102; and Southern Crossroads reli-
    gion, 30–31
Holy Trinity Church, 106
Homeland Security Office, 120
homosexuality. *See* gay marriage; gay rights
Horne, J. W., 82
Housh, Nancy, 121–22
Houston, TX: African Americans in, 129,
    144; Catholics in, 115; demographics
    of, 40–41, 47, *49–51*; Holiness move-
    ment in, 84

Huckabee, Mike, 71–72, 136, 167
Hughes, Richard T., 64–65
hush arbor, 131, 141
Hussein, Saddam, 168
Huston-Tillotson College, 144
Hutchinson, Tim, 71–72

ideology: African Americans and, 148; in
     Southern Crossroads, 49, 162. *See also*
     conservatism
Immaculate Conception Church, 117
immigrants, Catholic, 104–9, 120
Immigrant Workers Freedom Ride, 122
incarcerations, in Southern Crossroads, 34
Independent Baptists, 37–38
Independents: Holiness/Pentecostal tradition
     and, 96; in Southern Crossroads, 50
Indian Territory (I.T.), 10, 136. *See also*
     Oklahoma
inerrantism, 67
Interfaith Alliance, 74
International Church of the Foursquare
     Gospel: establishment of, 88–90; in
     Louisiana, 44; in Oklahoma, 46; in
     Texas, 48
International Communion of the
     Charismatic Episcopal Church, 94
Iraq war, 168
Irish Catholics, 13, 104–7, 109–10, 138
Italian Catholics, 104–5, 108, 110

Jackson, Andrew, 106
Jackson, Jesse, 71
Jackson, Maurice A., 135
Jackson, W. K., 151
Jakes, T. D., 29, 79, 144, 152
James, Frank and Jesse, 15, 20
Jefferson, William, 140
Jesuits, 105
Jewish Federation, 120
Jews: adherents claimed by, in Southern
     Crossroads versus United States, *24*; in
     Arkansas, 43; Catholics and, 120–21;

demographics of, *35*, 36; in Louisiana,
     44; in Missouri, 45–46; in Oklahoma,
     46; self-identification as, in Southern
     Crossroads versus United States, *25*; in
     Texas, 48, 143
Jindal, Bobby, 17, 167
Johnson, Eddie Bernice, 144
Joliet, Louis, 103
Jolly, John, 140
Jones, Absalom, 131
Jones, C. P., 85
Jones, Jim, 116
justification, 30

Kansas City, MO, 45, 107, 121; African
     Americans in, 129, 147
Kaw people, 130
Keating, Frank, 14–15, 123
Keysar, Ariela, 23, 171
King, Larry, 36–37
King, Martin Luther, Jr., 134, 151
Kiowa people, 105
Kirk, John A., 135
Kirk-Duggan, Cheryl, 19, 127–59
Know-Nothing party, 109
Kosmin, Barry A., 23, 171

labor movement: Catholics and, 117; and
     Elaine riots, 141
Lakewood Church, Houston, TX, 29, 47,
     144
Land, Richard, 75
Landmark Belt, 58
landmarkism, 57–60, 63, 66, 72, 98
Lankford, Sarah, 82
Largent, Steve, 98–99, 167
La Salle, Robert Cavalier de, 104
Las Hermanas, 112
Latinos: in Arkansas, 117; Catholic, 35,
     112–13; Christian Right and, 69;
     demographics of, 18, 31, 33, *34*, 35;
     and ideology, 164; in Missouri, 121; in
     Oklahoma, 122; and party preference,

50; Pentecostal, 87–88; and presidential elections, 113–14; racism and, 137; in Texas, 13, 47, 115–16; voting behaviors of, 17
Laveau, Marie, 139
Lawless, Elaine J., 80
Lawrence v. Texas, 163
leadership, black churches and, 152–53
Lee, Ann, 27
Lee, Sheila Jackson, 144
Leonard, Bill, 16, 18, 20, 27–53, 113, 116
Le Propagateur, 106
Lewinsky, Monica, 71
Lewis, Jerry Lee, 91
liberalism, in Southern Crossroads, 49
Lincoln, C. Eric, 134
Lincoln Institute, 147
Lind, Michael, 55, 67
Lindsey, William, 9–22, 161–69
Little Rock, AR, 43
Little Rock Central High School, 135, 141–42
Loar, Daniel, 119
Long, Huey, 20
Long, Lewis, 70
Los Adaes, 10
Louisiana: African Americans in, 129, 138–40; Catholics in, 11, 43–44, 104, 119–20; character of, 11–12; demographics of, 43–44; Native Americans in, 138–40; population of, 33; public opinion, 43; racial composition of, 33, 34; settlement of, 60. See also Southern Crossroads
Louisiana Catholic Conference, 120
Louisiana College, 74
Louisiana Family Forum, 120
Louisiana Interchurch Conference, 120
Louisiana Purchase, 106
Lutheran Church, Missouri Synod, 46
Lutherans: demographics of, 35; and settlement, 60; in Texas, 143
Lynn, Barry, 75

mainline Protestants: adherents claimed by, in Southern Crossroads versus United States, 24; in Arkansas, 42; and charismatic movement, 31; demographics of, 35, 36; and ideology, 162; in Missouri, 45; and party preference, 50; and Restorationist groups, 17; self-identification as, in Southern Crossroads versus United States, 25; in Texas, 47–48
Manis, Andrew, 18, 20, 55–77, 98
Marquette, Jacques, 103
marriage: interracial, 138–39. See also gay marriage
Marsden, George, 61
Marty, Martin, 61
Mary Queen of Vietnam Parish, 112
Mason, Charles Harrison, 85–86
Mather, Cotton, 15
Matovina, Timothy, 124
Mayer, Egon, 23, 171
McLain, C. E., 140
McPherson, Aimee Semple, 88–90
McPherson, Harold Steward, 88–89
media ministries, 29, 52; African Americans and, 144, 152; McPherson and, 89; Roberts and, 90–91
megachurches: African Americans and, 150; definition of, 29; Pentecostal, 88, 92–93; in Texas, 47, 144, 150
Membré, Zenabe, 103–4
Mencken, H. L., 13
Methodists: African American, 139, 147; and gay rights, 165; and Native Americans, 145–46; and Pentecostals, 17, 82; and settlement, 16, 57, 59
Mexican Catholics, 111–12
Mexico, 58, 108
Miller, Randall M., 109, 112, 123
Miller, William, 27
minorities, aid to: African Americans and, 148–49; Catholics and, 114
Mississippi River, 9, 103

Missouri: African Americans in, *129*, 146–47; Catholics in, 120–21; character of, 15; demographics of, 44–46; elections in, 167; Native Americans in, 146–47; population of, 33, 44; racial composition of, 33, *34*; settlement of, 60. *See also* Southern Crossroads

Missouri Baptist Convention, 166

modernism, evangelical Protestants and, 61–64

Mohler, Albert, 37

Moral Majority, 30, 68, 97

Moran, Roger, 74–75

Moravians, 145

Mormons, 32–33; adherents claimed by, in Southern Crossroads versus United States, *24*; in Arkansas, 43; demographics of, *35*; self-identification as, in Southern Crossroads versus United States, *25*; in Texas, 48

Morrell, Z. N. "Wildcat," 59

Mountain West, conservatism in, 162

Mount Gale Missionary Baptist Church, 85

Mullins, Edgar Y., 66

multiculturalism: Catholics and, 104; Christian Right and, 69

Musgrave, Marilyn, 95

music: African American religions and, 132, 147; in Louisiana, 139

Muslims: adherents claimed by, in Southern Crossroads versus United States, *24*; African American, 128, 131; in Arkansas, 43; Catholics and, 120–21; demographics of, *35*, 36; in Louisiana, 44; in Missouri, 45; in Oklahoma, 46; self-identification as, in Southern Crossroads versus United States, *25*; in Texas, 48, *51*

Nader, Ralph, 113

National Association for the Advancement of Colored People (NAACP), 151

National Association for the Promotion of Holiness, 83

National Baptist Convention, USA, 38, 131

National Baptist Convention of America, 38, 131

National Camp Meeting Association for the Promotion of Holiness, 82

National Congress of American Indians, 155

national health insurance: African Americans and, 148; conservatives and, 163

National Missionary Baptist Convention of America, 131

National Surveys of Religion and Politics (NSRP), 49, 113, 172

Nation of Islam, 131

Native American Church, 146, 156

Native Americans: and African Americans, 137–38; Catholics and, 103, 105, 113, 136; demographics of, 130; in Oklahoma, 14; and political issues, 155–56; and public life, 138–47; and regional identity, 133, 136; religious ethos of, 132–33; in Southern Crossroads, 127–59

Network of Anglican Communion Dioceses and Parishes, 30

New Orleans, LA, 44, 104; African Americans in, 129; Battle of, 106; Catholics in, 106, 111

New Orleans Baptist Seminary, 60

new religious movements, in Southern Crossroads, 15–16, 32–33

New Religious Right. *See* Christian Right

Nolan, Bruce, 119

non-Christian religions: African Americans and, 128; in Arkansas, 43; demographics of, 36; in Southern Crossroads, 31. *See also* Eastern religions

Nones: adherents claimed by, in Southern Crossroads versus United States, *24*; African American, 128; demographics of, *35*; self-identification as, in Southern Crossroads versus United States, *25*; in Southern Crossroads, 31; in Texas, 47

Norris, J. Frank, 62, 66

North American Religion Atlas (NARA), 23, 34, *35*, 60, 112–13, 131, 171

Noyes, John Humphrey, 27

O'Connell, Diane, 71–72

O'Donnell, John F., 117

Ogden, David, 135

Ogden, Dunbar, 135

Oklahoma: African Americans in, *129*, 145–46; Catholics in, 105, 121–22; character of, 14–15; demographics of, 46–47; Native Americans in, 130, 145–46; population of, 33; racial composition of, *34*; settlement of, 60. *See also* Southern Crossroads

Oklahoma Christian Coalition (OCC), 70

Oklahoma City, OK, 14, 47, 129

Oklahoma Conference of Churches, 122

Oneness Pentecostals, 88

Operation PUSH, 151

Opperman, D. C. O., 86

Oral Roberts University, 91

Orisha, 131

Orthodox Christians, demographics of, *35*

Osage people, 103, 105

Osteen, Joel, 29

outreach ministries: Assemblies of God and, 100; Catholics and, 115–17, 119, 121

Oxford movement, 57

Ozman, Agnes N., 84

pacifism, 65

Padres, 112

Palmer, Phoebe, 82

Pan-Indian movement, 155–56

Parham, Charles Fox, 83–84, 86

Parker, Bonnie, 20

Parker, Isaac, 10

party preference: African Americans and, 148; Catholics and, 116; Holiness/Pentecostal tradition and, 96; in Southern Crossroads, 49–50

Patriot Act, 99–100, 120

Patterson, Pauge, 67

Paul Quinn College, 144

Pedobaptists, 60

Penix, Kevin, 142

Pennington, Edith Mae (Patterson), 90

Pentecostal Church of God, 48, 80

Pentecostals: adherents claimed by, in Southern Crossroads versus United States, *24*; African American, 131, 139; in Arkansas, 42; and cultural mainstream, 92–94; demographics of, *35*, *81*; history of, 16–17, 33, 79–80, 82–88; in Louisiana, 44; in Missouri, 45; Native American, 146; in Oklahoma, 46; and political participation, 163–64; self-identification as, in Southern Crossroads versus United States, *25*; in Southern Crossroads, 79–102; on Spirit, 30–31; in Texas, 48

Pentecostals of Alexandria, 88

Perez, Leander, 111

perfectionism, 27, 31, 33, 82–83

Perry County, MO, 103

Perryville, 107

peyote, 146

Philander Smith College, 135, 142

Pietist/Anabaptist groups, demographics of, *35*

Pine Bluff, 10

Plains people, 105, 130

Plano, TX, 20

Plant of Renown, Inc., 90

pluralism, evangelical Protestants and, 62, 64

Pohl, Keith, 73
Polish Catholics, 105, 109
political issues: African Americans and, 153–55; Catholics and, 112–22; in culture war, 68–76; Holiness/Pentecostal tradition and, 94–100; Native Americans and, 155–56; in Southern Crossroads, 49–51
political participation: African Americans and, 132, 135–36, 140, 144, 146–47; evangelical Protestants and, 65; Holiness/Pentecostal churches and, 163–64
Pope, Tim, 70
Portis, Charles, 10
Potawatomi people, 105
Potters' House, 29, 47, 144
poverty: African Americans and, 155; Catholics and, 118–19; in Southern Crossroads, 31
Prejean, Helen, 123
premillennialism, 63
Presbyterian Church (USA), 36; in Arkansas, 42; in Louisiana, 44; in Missouri, 45–46; in Oklahoma, 46; in Texas, 48
Presbyterian Church in America, in Arkansas, 42
Presbyterians: demographics of, 35, 36; in Louisiana, 44; and Native Americans, 145; and settlement, 59–60; in Southern Crossroads, 16; in Texas, 47
presidential elections: African Americans and, 148; Catholics and, 113–14
Pressler, Paul, 67
Prestonwood Baptist Church, Dallas, TX, 47
Progressive National Baptist Convention, 38, 131
Project 1000, 74
prosperity gospel, 29, 31; African Americans and, 153, 155

Protestants. See evangelical Protestants; historically African American Protestant churches; mainline Protestants; specific denominations
Pryor, David, 72
Pryor, Mark, 72
public life: African Americans and, 129, 138–47, 150–51; Native Americans and, 138–47; in Southern Crossroads, 18–20

Quapaw people, 103
quasi-establishment: Baptists as, 36; evangelical Protestants as, 56
Quinn, Joe, 72

racial diversity: Assemblies of God and, 100; in Southern Crossroads, 33, 34
racism, 133–34, 137, 141, 143; Catholics and, 111, 117
railroads, and Catholicism, 105, 108
rationalism, Graves on, 58
Reagan, Ronald, 12, 30, 65, 71, 161
Reconciling congregations, 165
Reconstruction, 12
Rector, Henry Massie, 141
Reed, Ralph, 69
Reese, Jim, 70
region, importance of, 5
religion, in Southern Crossroads, 9–22, 161–69
religious affiliation, in Southern Crossroads versus United States, 23, 24–25, 34–36
Religious Congregations and Membership Survey (RCMS), 23, 171; limitations of, 156n1
Religious Right. See Christian Right
Religious Roundtable, 29, 71, 161
Republican Party: African Americans and, 148; Christian Right and, 30, 161; and culture war, 68–69; Dobson and, 98; evangelical protestants and, 65;

Holiness/Pentecostal tradition and, 96; Independent Baptists and, 38; Latinos and, 164; in Southern Crossroads, 50; Southern Crossroads and, 166–67; Texas and, 55
restorationism, 16–17, 64–65
revivalism, 30–31, 57, 91
Rice, Patricia, 120
Richardson, Nolan, 143
Riley, Nancy, 70
Riley, Negail, 135
Ritter, Joseph E., 111
Robb, Ed, Jr., 72
Roberts, Oral, 14, 29, 79, 90–91, 93, 146
Roberts, Richard, 91
Robertson, Pat, 71, 79, 97, 161
Robinson, Gene, 20, 30, 166
Robison, James, 29, 71
Roe v. Wade, 64
Rogers, Adrian, 67
Rogers, AR, 43
Roosevelt, Teddy, 76
Roseberry, David, 30
Ross, John, 156
Ross, Quatie, 156
Rummel, Joseph Francis, 111
rural areas, in Southern Crossroads, 33

Salvation Army: in Arkansas, 42; in Louisiana, 44; in Oklahoma, 47; in Texas, 48
San Antonio, TX, *49–51*
sanctification, 30–31, 82–84, 86
San Marcos, TX, *49–51*
Santeria, 131
school prayer, Christian Right and, 70
schools: Catholic, 110, 119; Cherokee, 141
school vouchers, Catholics and, 114, 118–20
Schultze, Quentin, 92
Scofield, Cyrus I., 63
Seaborn, Miles, 75
Second Baptist Church, Houston, TX, 29

secularism, 32, 61. *See also* Nones
self-identification, with religious groups, 23, *25*, 34
Seminole people, 105, 130, 145
Semple, Robert, 88
Sequoyah, 141
settlement, of Southern Crossroads, 9–10, 16, 56–61
sex education, Christian Right and, 69
sexuality: African Americans and, 154; Catholics and, 116; conservatives and, 163; Holiness/Pentecostal tradition and, 95–96. *See also* gay marriage; gay rights
Seymour, William J., 84
Shawnee people, 103
Sheffield Family Life Center, 92, 100
Sherman, Bill, 122
Shorter College, 142
showdown mentality: African Americans and, 134–35; Ashcroft and, 99–100; Catholics and, 123; Graves and, 58; in nineteenth century, 56–61; in Southern Crossroads, 20, 32, 55–77, 161–69; in twentieth century, 61–68
Sikhs, in Texas, 48
Silent Migration, 14
Silk, Mark, 5–7, 161–69
Sisters of Mercy, 107, 109
Sixties, evangelical Protestants and, 64
slavery: in Arkansas, 141; Catholics and, 109–10; in Louisiana, 11, 139; in Missouri, 147; Native Americans and, 137–38, 157n15; in Texas, 12, 143
Smith, Joseph, 27
Smith, Nettie, 84
Smith, Oran P., 37, 62
Snell, Kristen Smith, 133
Sosna, Morton, 64
South: conservatism in, 61–62, 162; versus Southern Crossroads, 15
Southern Baptist Conservatives of Texas (SBCT), 75

Southern Baptists: in Arkansas, 43; demo-
    graphics of, 36–37, *37*; ideological
    struggle among, 64–68, 73–74; in
    Louisiana, 43; in Missouri, 45; in
    Oklahoma, 46–47; in Texas, 20, 47,
    67–68, *69*
Southern Baptist Theological Seminary
    (SBTS), 59, 66
Southern Christian Leadership Conference
    (SCLC), 150
Southern Crossroads: boundaries of, 9–11;
    cultural profile of, 33–34; definition of,
    6, 9; demographics of, 27–53; future
    of, 51–52; in nineteenth century,
    56–61; population of, 33; racial com-
    position of, 33, *34*; religion in, 9–22,
    161–69; religious affiliation in, versus
    United States, 23, *24–25*, 34–36; reli-
    gious characteristics of, 55–77; and
    Southern Baptist Convention takeover,
    65–68; subregional patterns in, 38–40;
    transition in, 31–32; in twentieth centu-
    ry, 61–68
Southern Manifesto, 142
Southwestern Seminary, 59
Spain, 10, 103–4, 106, 143
Spanish Catholics, 104
Springdale, AR, 43
Springfield, MO, 16, 60
Starr, Kenneth, 65, 167
St. Genevieve, 104
St. Joseph, MO, 107
St. Louis, MO: African Americans in,
    128–29, 147; Catholics in, 15, 45–46,
    107, 111; demographics of, 45–46;
    establishment of, 104
St. Louis Cathedral, New Orleans, LA,
    106
St. Mary's Academy, 107
Stowe, Harriet Beecher, 11
St. Patrick's Church, 106Stone, Barton, 57
Student Nonviolent Coordinating
    Committee (SNCC), 135, 151

Subiaco Abbey, 107
Sun Dance, 146
Swaggart, Donny, 92
Swaggart, Jimmy, 20, 29, 79–80, 91–92
Swiss Catholics, 107, 109
syncretistic religions, 136, 139, 156

Talent, Jim, 98–99
Tarrant County, TX, 129
television: and secularism, 61. *See also*
    media ministries
temperance, Baptists and, 39
Temporary Assistance for Needy Families
    (TANF), 119
Ten Commandments, Christian Right and,
    70
Texas: African Americans in, 129, *129*,
    143–45, 151; Baptists in, 47, *49*,
    67–68, *69*, 143; and Bush, 55;
    Catholics in, 108–9, 115–17, 143;
    character of, 12–13; and culture
    war, 166; demographics of, 47–48,
    49–51; and evolution, 63; megachurch-
    es in, 47, 144, 150; Native Americans
    in, 143–45; population of, 33,
    47; racial composition of, 33, *34*;
    Republic of, 10, 58, 106, 108–9; settle-
    ment of, 58–59. *See also* Southern
    Crossroads
Texas Catholic Conference, 115–16
Texas Christian Coalition (TCC), 68–69
Texas College, 144
tobacco, Church of the Nazarene and, 83
Tomlinson, A. J., 94–95
tongues, speaking in. *See* glossolalia
Toobin, Jeffrey, 99
Trail of Tears, 140, 145
Transforming congregations, 165
Trask, Thomas E., 95, 97
Tull, James E., 57–58
Tulsa, OK, 47, 129
Twain, Mark, 13
Twitchell, Marshall Harvey, 12

United Church of Christ: demographics of, 35; in Missouri, 45–46

United Methodists: in Arkansas, 42–43; and culture war, 72–73; demographics of, 35, 36; in Louisiana, 44; in Missouri, 45–46; in Oklahoma, 46–47; in Texas, 48, 50

United Pentecostal Church, 31, 80, 88

Unity School of Christianity, 147

University Baptist Church, 165

Upchurch, Cackie, 117–18

urban areas: in Arkansas, 43; in Louisiana, 44; in Missouri, 45–46; in Oklahoma, 47; in Southern Crossroads, 33, 64; in Texas, 47–48, 49–51

Urban League, 151

Ursulines, 104, 109, 119

Vara, Richard, 115–16

Varick, James, 131

Victory Christian Center, 90

Vietnamese Catholics, 104, 111–12, 117

Vineland, NJ, 82

Vineyard churches, in Louisiana, 44

violence: in Arkansas, 11; in Louisiana, 12; in Oklahoma, 10–11

vodun (voodoo), 131, 139

voluntarism, 57

voter registration: Holiness/Pentecostal tradition and, 95; in Southern Crossroads, 49–50

voting behaviors: African Americans and, 147–49; of Latinos, 17; Native Americans and, 147–49

Wacker, Grant, 84, 95

Wakelyn, John, 109

Walwoord, John, 64

war, Catholics and, 118

Watts, J. C., 146

wealth-health gospel. See prosperity gospel

Weber, Lawrence, 120

welfare spending: African Americans and, 149; Catholics and, 114; conservatives and, 162–63

Wesley, John, 57, 82–83, 86

Wesleyan Holiness groups, 30, 57; in Arkansas, 42; demographics of, 81; history of, 82–88; in Oklahoma, 46

West, and Southern Crossroads, 16

Western Missouri Coalition to Abolish the Death Penalty, 120

Westlake, George, 92

White, K. Owen, 67

Whitsitt, William, 59

Wiley College, 144

William Jewell College, 166

Williams, Tennessee, 15

Williams, Walter L., 136

Willis, Joseph, 139

Wilson, John, 11

women: African American religions and, 132, 152–53; Assemblies of God and, 87, 100; Baptists and, 75; Catholics and, 109, 118, 124; Church of God in Christ and, 86; and Civil Rights movement, 134; Foursquare Gospel and, 88–90; Southern Crossroads and, 19–20

Woodell, Tony, 72

Woodworth-Etter, Maria, 86

worship style: of African American religion, 132; of Church of God in Christ, 85; of Pentecostals, 93

Worthen, Mary, 156

xenoglossia, 84

Yoruba, 131

Young, Edwin, Jr., 29

Young, Rufus K., 135

Zink, James K., 14

Zydeco, 139

CONTRIBUTORS

Kathlyn Breazeale is assistant professor of religion at Pacific Lutheran University in Tacoma Washington. A specialist in feminist and womanist theologies, she holds a doctorate from the Claremont Graduate School. She is the author of articles on the theology of marriage and ecofeminist theology.

Jane Harris is associate professor and area chair for the humanities at Hendrix College in Conway, Arkansas. A specialist in American religious history and women's studies, she holds a bachelor's degree from Meredith College, an M.Div. from Southeastern Baptist Theological Seminary in North Carolina, and a Ph.D. from the University of North Carolina. She is the author of "America's Evangelical Women: More Than Wives and Mothers—Reformers, Ministers, and Leaders," in the *Encyclopedia of Women and Religion in North America* to be published in 2005. She is also directing an oral history project on Arkansas Methodism based at Hendrix.

Cheryl Kirk-Duggan is professor of theology at Shaw University Divinity School in Raleigh, North Carolina. She holds an undergraduate degree from Southwest Louisiana State University, graduate degrees from the University of Texas and the Austin Presbyterian Theological School, and a Ph.D. from Baylor University. Her publications include *Refiner's Fire: A Religious Engagement With Violence,* (Augsburg/Fortress, 2000) and *Misbegotten Anguish: A Theology and Ethics of Violence* (Chalice Press, 2001).

Bill Leonard is dean of the divinity school and professor of church history at Wake Forest University Divinity School in Winston-Salem, North Carolina. An ordained Baptist minister, he holds a B.A. from Texas Wesleyan College, an M.Div. from Southwestern Baptist Theological Seminary, and a Ph.D. from Boston University. He has written or edited 14 books, including *Christianity in Appalachia: Profiles in Regional Pluralism*, (University of Tennessee Press, 1999), and *The Encyclopedia of Religious Controversies* (Greenwood Press 1997). He is currently writing a new history of the Baptists for Judson Press.

William Lindsey is dean of instruction at Philander Smith College in Little Rock Arkansas. He holds a B.A. from Loyola University in New Orleans, an M.A. from Tulane University, and an M.A. and Ph.D. from the University of St. Michael's College, Toronto. His publications include *Shailer Mathews's Lives of Jesus: The Search for a Theological Foundation for the Social Gospel* (State University of New York Press, 1997) and *Singing in a Strange Land: Praying and Acting with the Poor* (Sheed & Ward Press, 1991). He also authored the textbook *Morality and Ethics* used in the adult ministry program of Loyola University (LIMEX).

Andrew Manis is assistant professor of history at Macon State College in Macon, Georgia. He holds a bachelor's degree from Samford University and a doctorate in American religious history from the Southern Baptist Theological Seminary in Louisville. He is the author of, among other books, *Southern Civil Religions in Conflict: Civil Rights and the Culture Wars* (Mercer University Press, 2002) and *A Fire You Can't Put Out: The Civil Rights Life of Birmingham's Reverend Fred Shuttlesworth* (University of Alabama Press, 1999).

Mark Silk, coeditor of the volume, is associate professor of religion in public life and founding director of the Leonard E. Greenberg Center for the Study of Religion in Public Life at Trinity College in Hartford, Connecticut. A former newspaper reporter and member of the editorial board at the *Atlanta Journal-Constitution*, he is the author of *Spiritual Politics: Religion and Politics in America Since World War II* (Simon and Schuster, 1988) and *Unsecular Media: Making News of Religion in America* (University of Illinois Press, 1995). He is editor of *Religion in the News,* a magazine published by the Greenberg Center that examines how journalists handle religious subject matter.